Lady Killer

JOËLLE JONES
MICHELLE MADSEN

DARK HORSE BOOKS

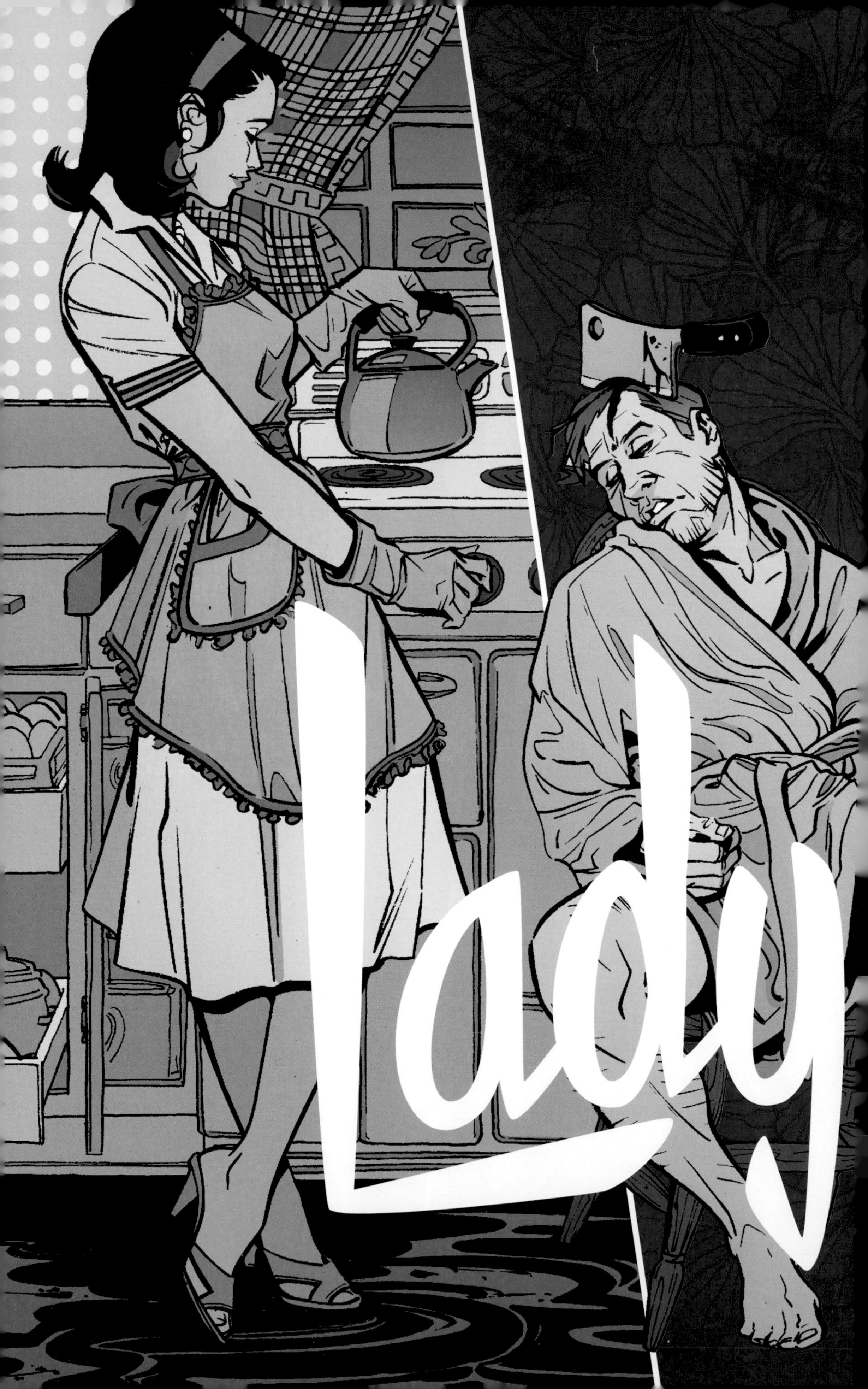
Lady

STORY AND ART BY
JOËLLE JONES

COLORS BY
MICHELLE MADSEN

LETTERS BY
CRANK!

COLORS ON CHAPTER 1
TITLE PAGE BY
LAURA ALLRED

Killer™

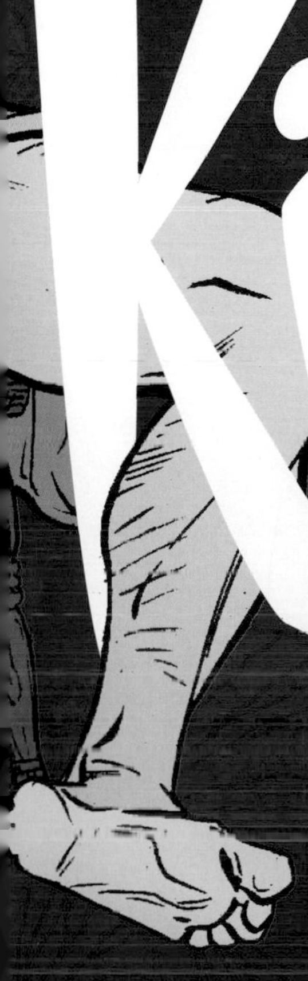

PUBLISHER **MIKE RICHARDSON**

EDITORS **SCOTT ALLIE** & **SHANTEL LaROCQUE**

ASSISTANT EDITORS **KATII O'BRIEN**

DESIGNERS **JIMMY PRESLER** & **ETHAN KIMBERLING**

DIGITAL ART TECHNICIAN **CHRISTIANNE GOUDREAU**

SPECIAL THANKS TO **JAMIE S. RICH**

Published by Dark Horse Books
A division of Dark Horse Comics, Inc.
10956 SE Main Street
Milwaukie, OR 97222

First edition: October 2017
ISBN 978-1-50670-029-8

1 3 5 7 9 10 8 6 4 2
Printed in China

Advertising Sales: (503) 905-2237
International Licensing: (503) 905-2377
Comic Shop Locator Service: comicshoplocator.com

DarkHorse.com
Facebook.com/DarkHorseComics
Twitter.com/DarkHorseComics

This volume collects *Lady Killer 2* #1–#5.

Executive Vice President NEIL HANKERSON Chief Financial Officer TOM WEDDLE Vice President of Publishing RANDY STRADLEY Vice President of Marketing MATT PARKINSONVice President of Product Development DAVID SCROGGY Vice President of Information Technology DALE LAFOUNTAIN Vice President of Production and Scheduling CARA NIECEVice President of Media Licensing NICK MCWHORTER Vice President of Book Trade and Digital Sales MARK BERNARDI General Counsel KEN LIZZI Editor in Chief DAVE MARSHALL Editorial Director DAVEY ESTRADA Executive Senior Editor SCOTT ALLIE Senior Books Editor CHRIS WARNER Director of Specialty Projects CARY GRAZZINI Art Director LIA RIBACCHI Director of Print Purchasing VANESSA TODD Director of Digital Art and Prepress MATT DRYER Director of Product Sales SARAH ROBERTSON Director of International Publishing and Licensing MICHAEL GOMBOS

Library of Congress Cataloging-in-Publication Data

Names: Jones, Joëlle, author, artist. | Allred, Laura, colourist. | Crank!
    (Letterer), letterer. | Madsen, Michelle (Illustrator), colourist.
Title: Lady Killer.
Description: First edition. | Milwaukie, OR : Dark Horse Books, 2015- |
    Volume 1: story by Joëlle Jones & Jamie S. Rich ; art by Joëlle Jones ;
    colors by Laura Allred ; letters by Crank!. | Volume 2: story and art by
    Joëlle Jones ; colors by Michelle Madsen ; letters by Crank! ; colors on
    Chapter 1 title page by Laura Allred. | Volume 1: "This volume collects
    Lady Killer #1-#5" | Volume 2: "This volume collects Lady Killer 2 #1-#5."
Identifiers: LCCN 2017012877| ISBN 9781616557577 (v. 1 : paperback) | ISBN
    9781506700298 (v. 2 : paperback)
Subjects: LCSH: Comic books, strips, etc. | BISAC: COMICS & GRAPHIC NOVELS /
    Crime & Mystery.
Classification: LCC PN6728.L229 J66 2015 | DDC 741.5/973--dc23
LC record available at https://lccn.loc.gov/2017012877

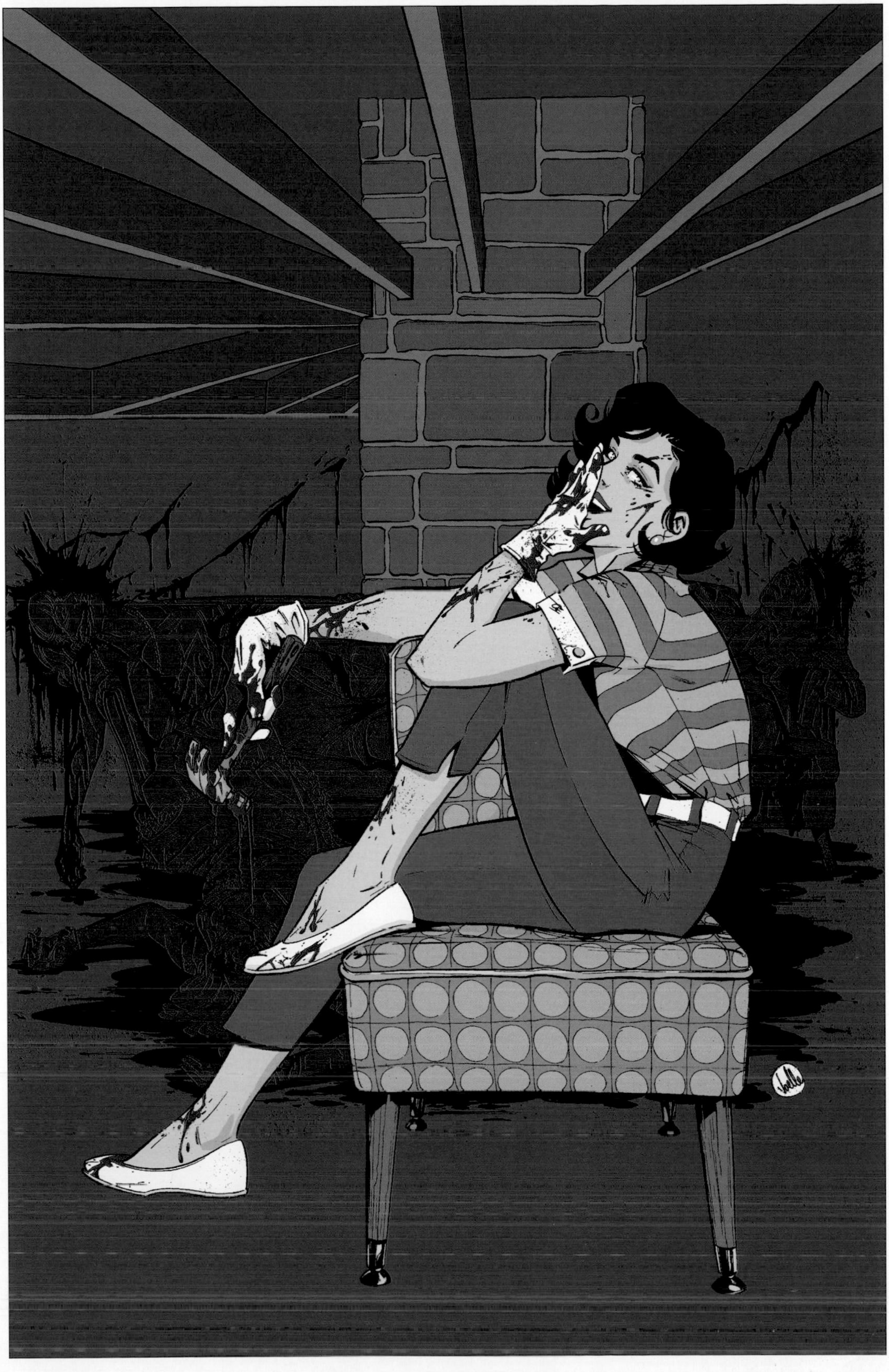

CHAPTER ONE

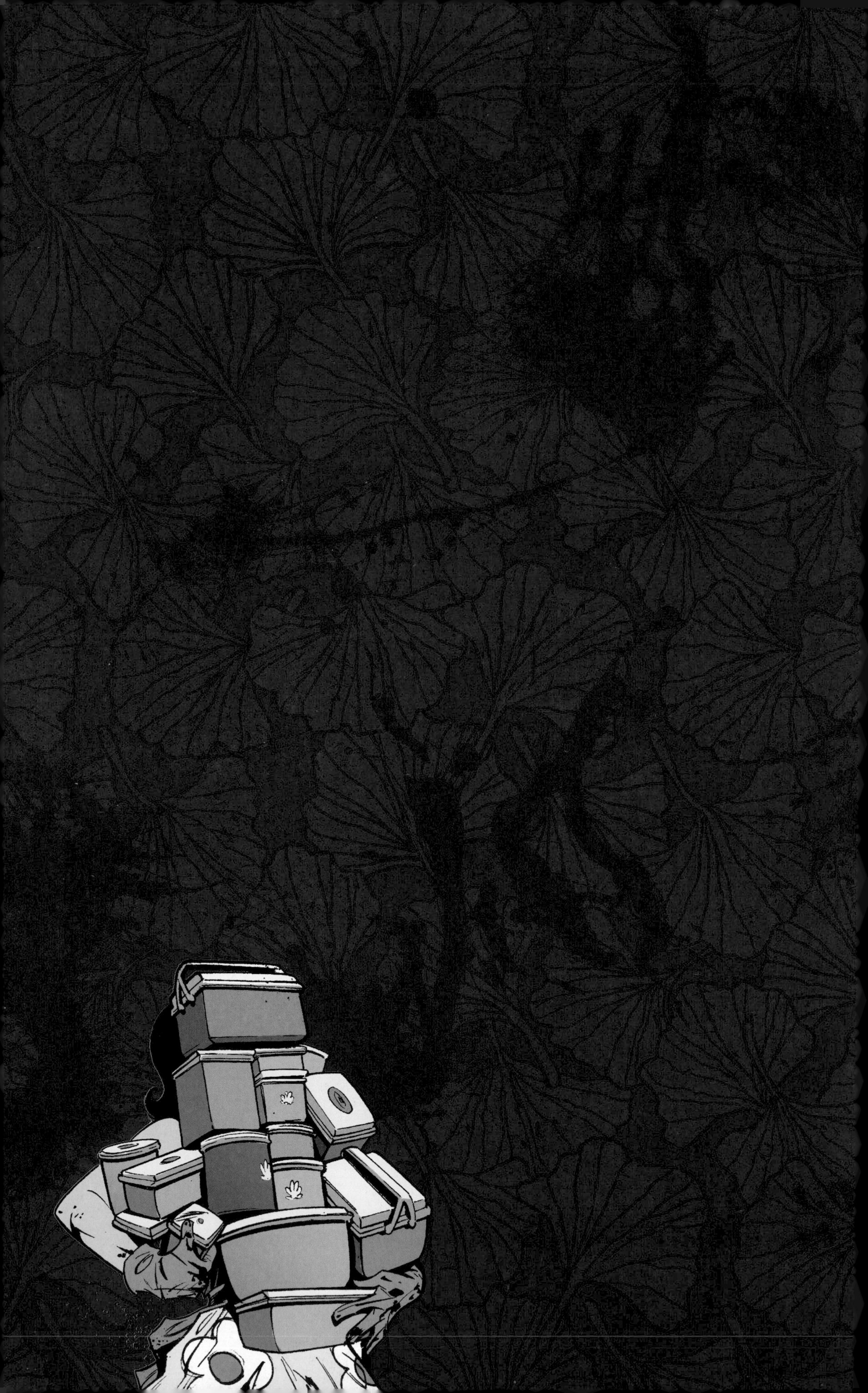

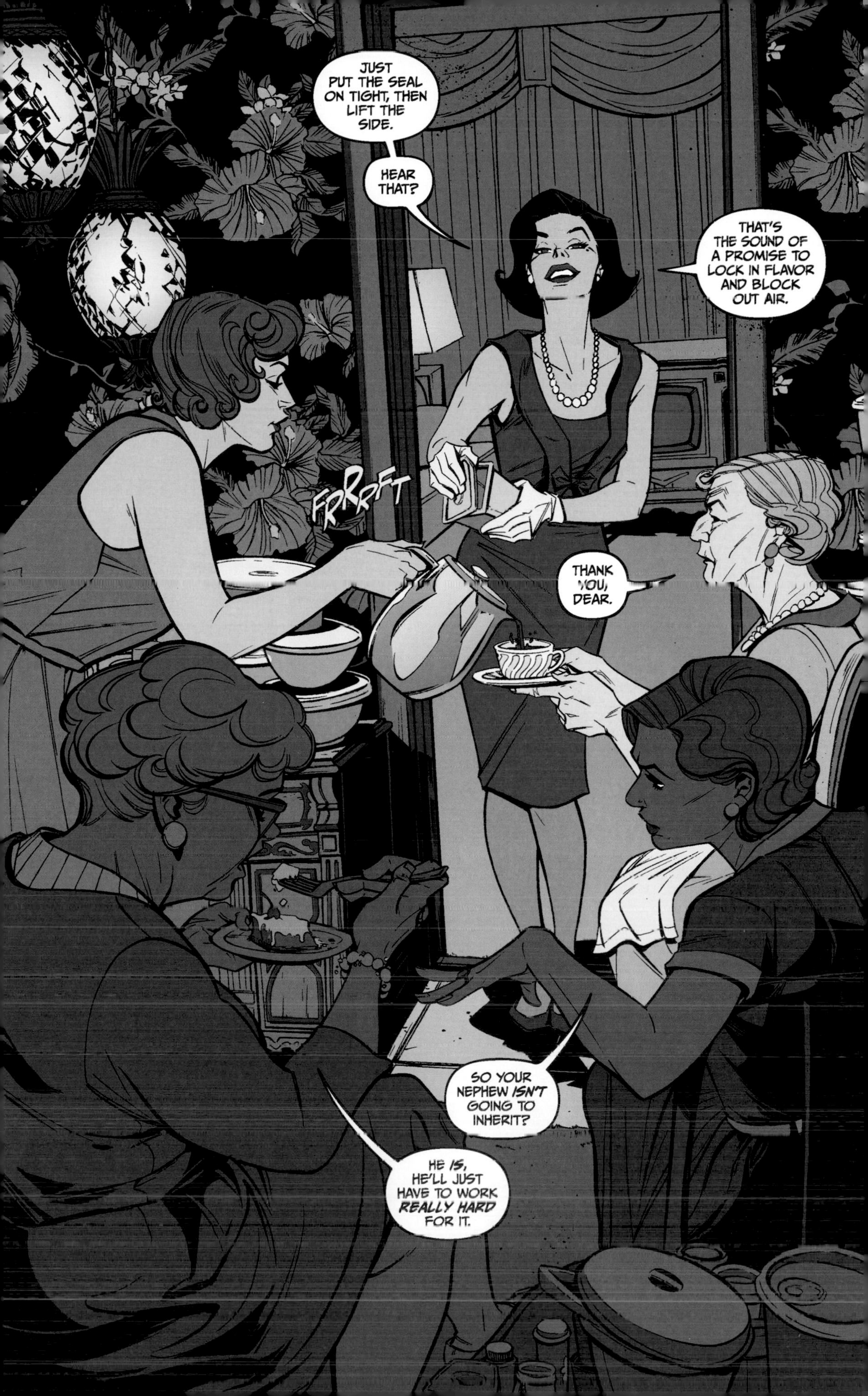
JUST PUT THE SEAL ON TIGHT, THEN LIFT THE SIDE.
HEAR THAT?
THAT'S THE SOUND OF A PROMISE TO LOCK IN FLAVOR AND BLOCK OUT AIR.
FRRRPFT
THANK YOU, DEAR.
SO YOUR NEPHEW ISN'T GOING TO INHERIT?
HE IS, HE'LL JUST HAVE TO WORK REALLY HARD FOR IT.

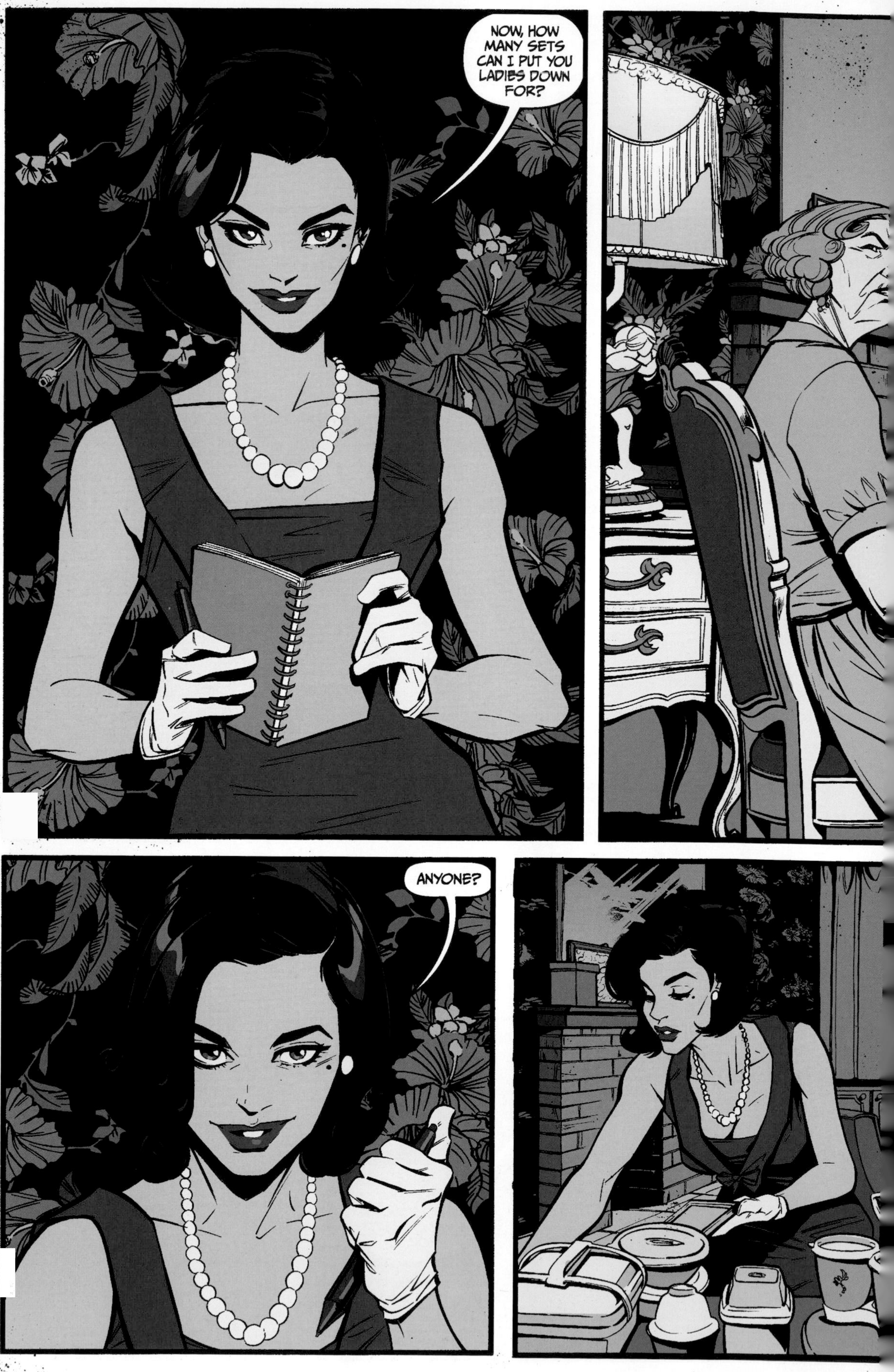
NOW, HOW MANY SETS CAN I PUT YOU LADIES DOWN FOR?
ANYONE?

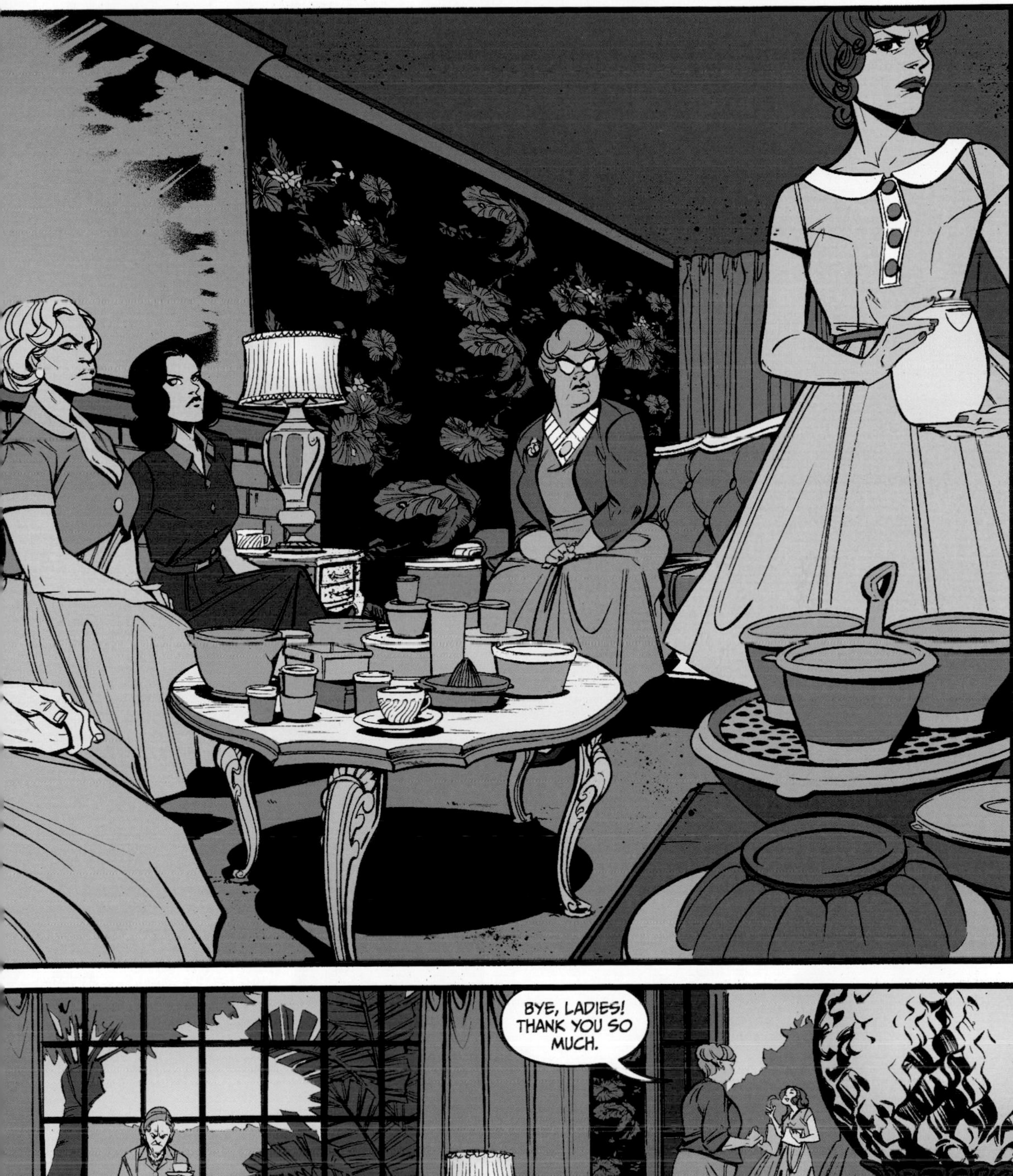

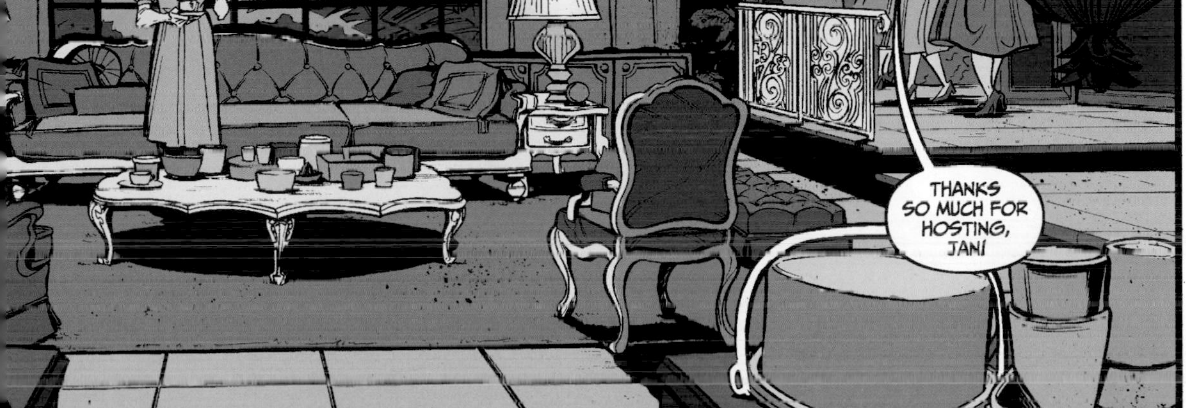
BYE, LADIES! THANK YOU SO MUCH.
THANKS SO MUCH FOR HOSTING, JAN!

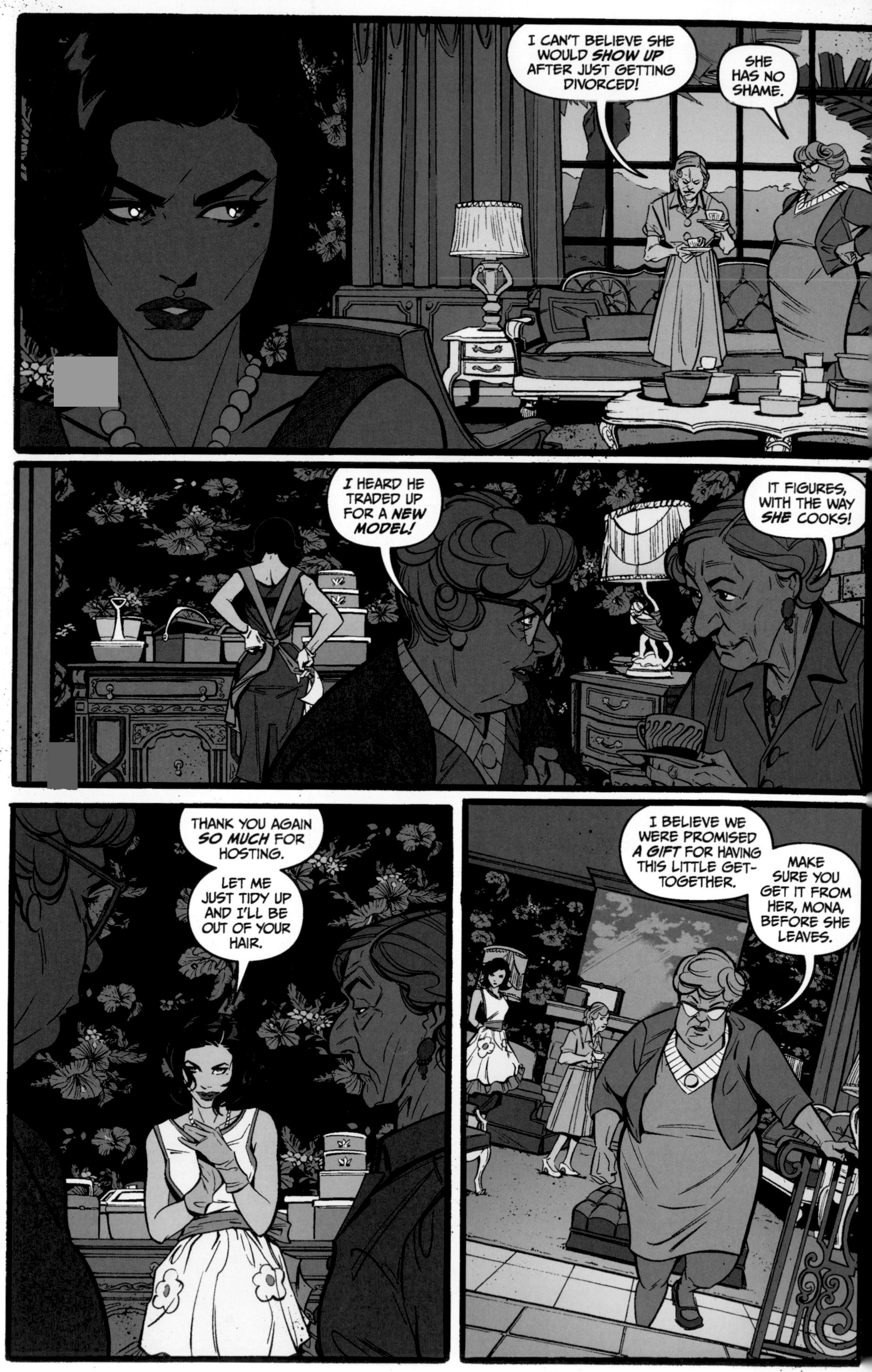

I CAN'T BELIEVE SHE WOULD SHOW UP AFTER JUST GETTING DIVORCED!
SHE HAS NO SHAME.
I HEARD HE TRADED UP FOR A NEW MODEL!
IT FIGURES, WITH THE WAY SHE COOKS!
THANK YOU AGAIN SO MUCH FOR HOSTING.
LET ME JUST TIDY UP AND I'LL BE OUT OF YOUR HAIR.
I BELIEVE WE WERE PROMISED A GIFT FOR HAVING THIS LITTLE GET-TOGETHER.
MAKE SURE YOU GET IT FROM HER, MONA, BEFORE SHE LEAVES.

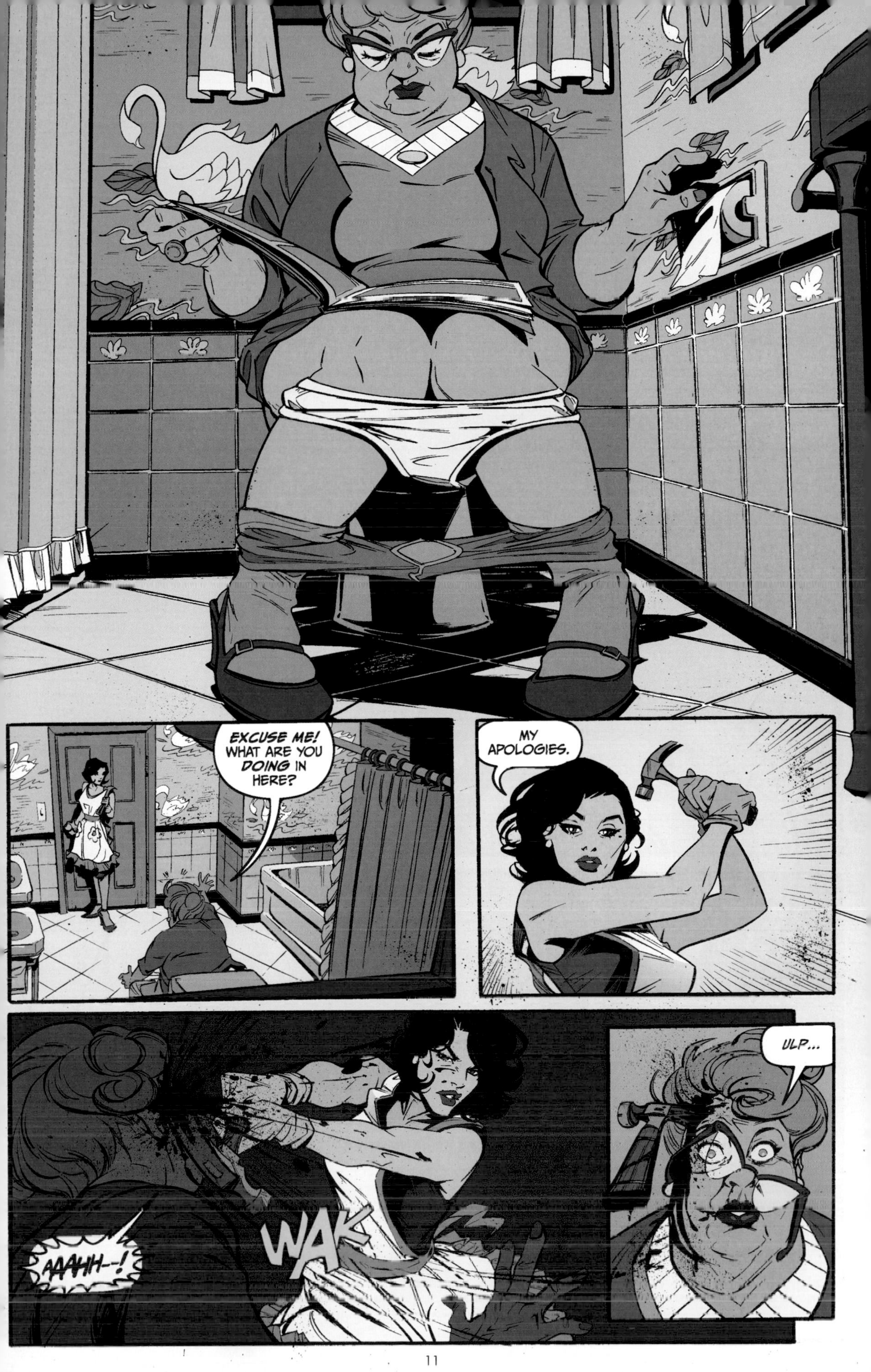
EXCUSE ME! WHAT ARE YOU DOING IN HERE?
MY APOLOGIES.
WAK
AAAHH--!
ULP...

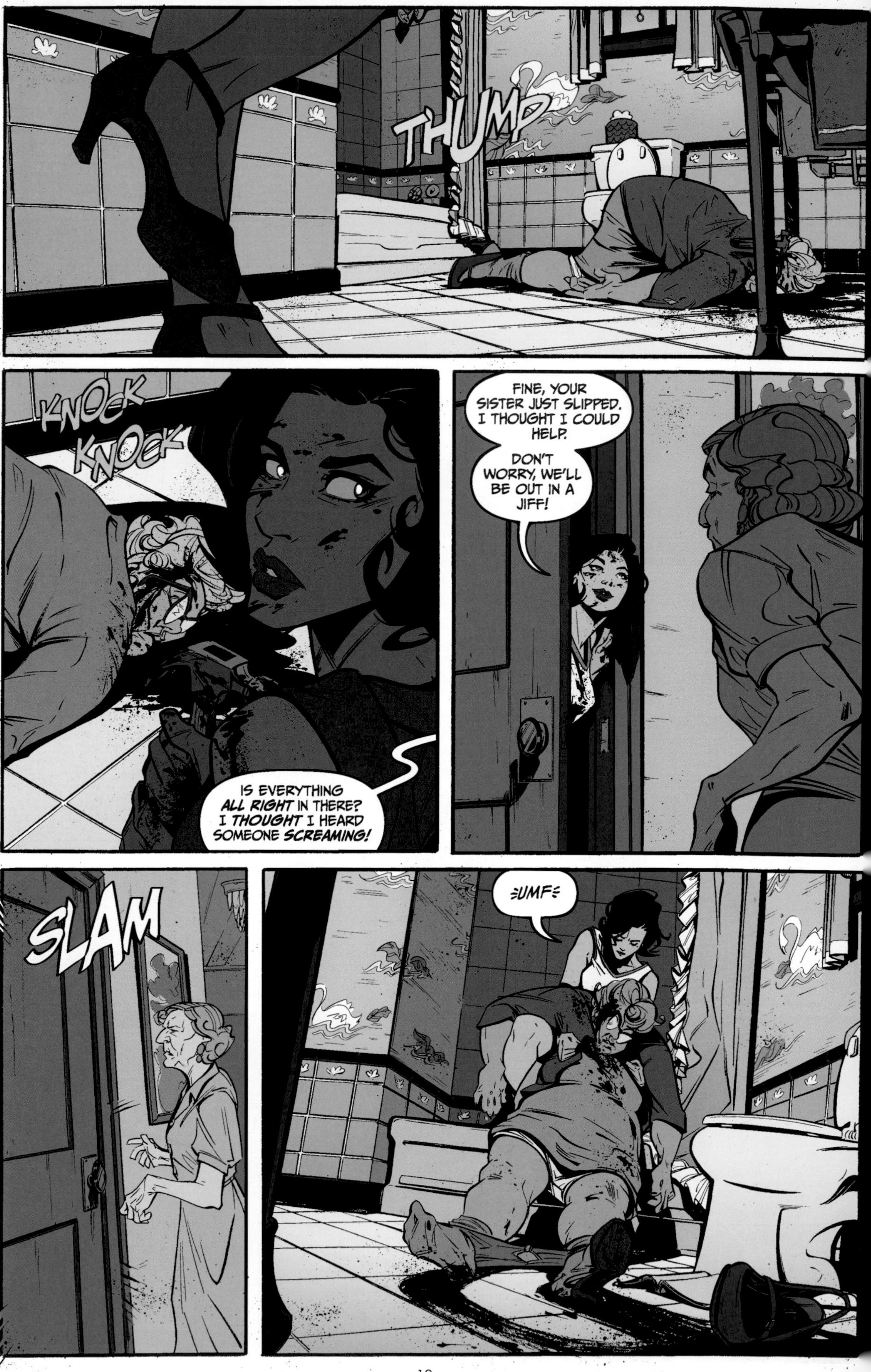
THUMP
KNOCK KNOCK
IS EVERYTHING ALL RIGHT IN THERE? I THOUGHT I HEARD SOMEONE SCREAMING!
FINE, YOUR SISTER JUST SLIPPED. I THOUGHT I COULD HELP.
DON'T WORRY, WE'LL BE OUT IN A JIFF!
SLAM
UMF

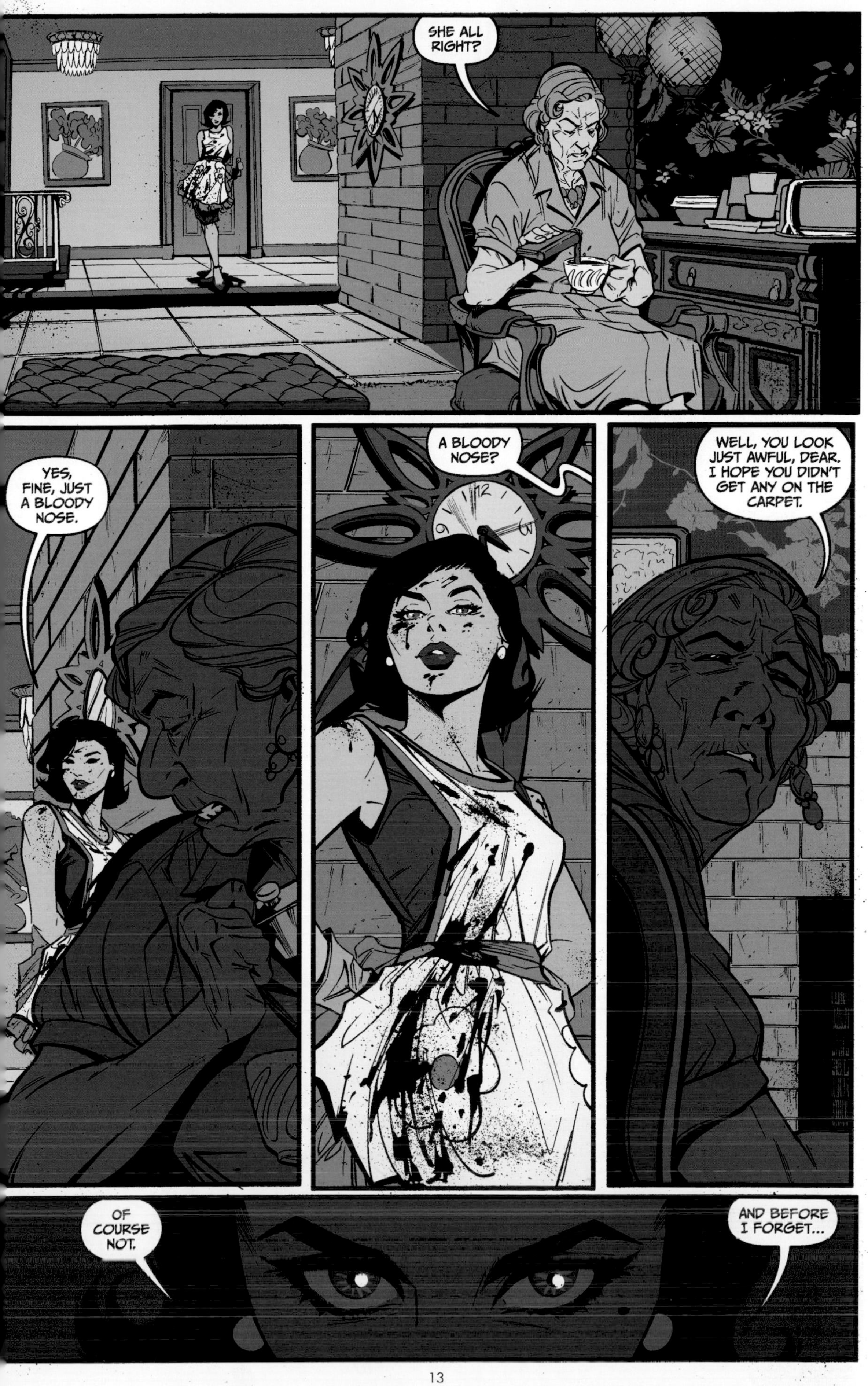
SHE ALL RIGHT?
YES, FINE, JUST A BLOODY NOSE.
A BLOODY NOSE?
WELL, YOU LOOK JUST AWFUL, DEAR. I HOPE YOU DIDN'T GET ANY ON THE CARPET.
OF COURSE NOT.
AND BEFORE I FORGET...

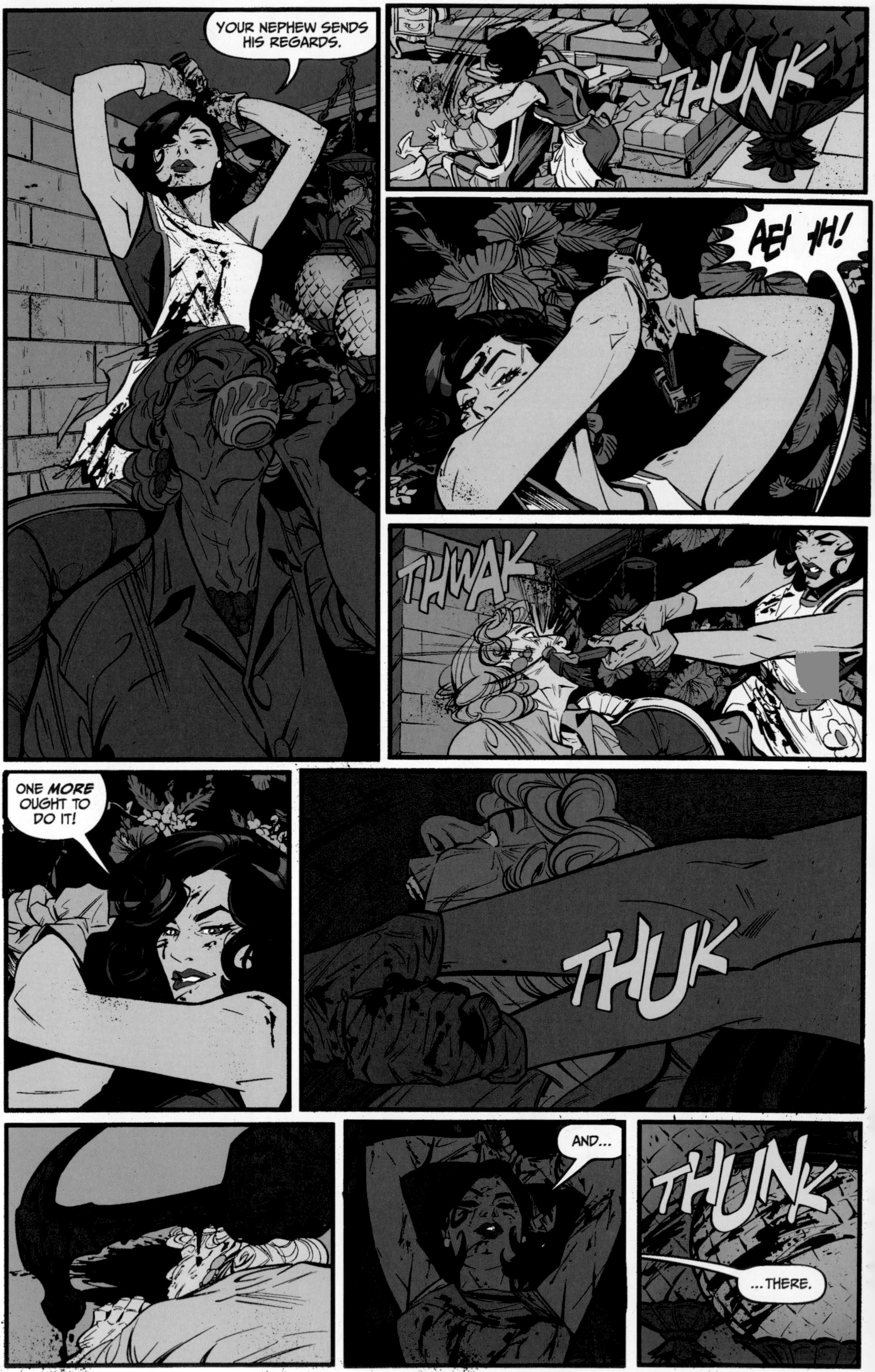

YOUR NEPHEW SENDS HIS REGARDS.
THUNK
AEI HH!
THWAK
ONE *MORE* OUGHT TO DO IT!
THUK
AND...
THUNK
...THERE.

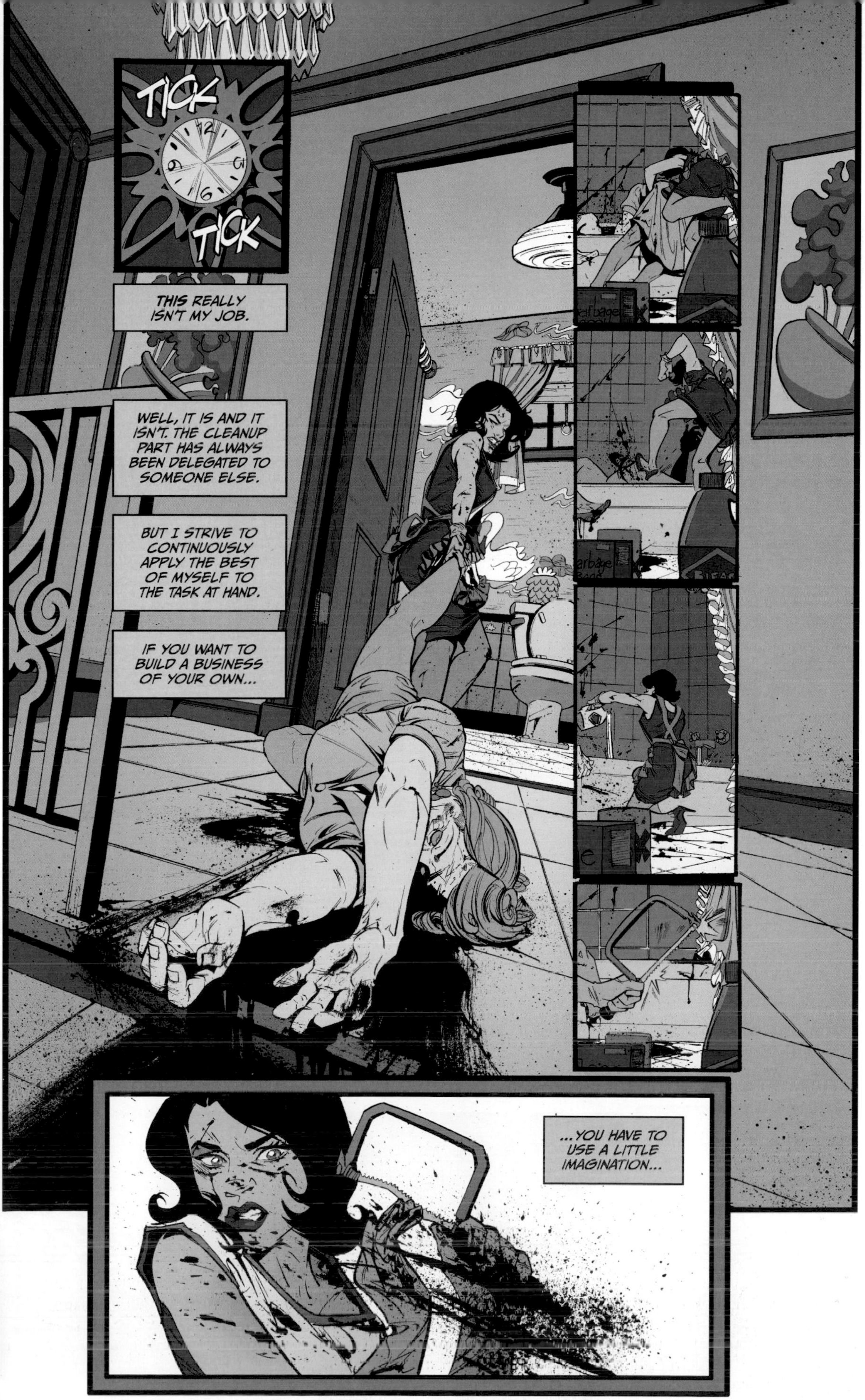
TICK
TICK
THIS REALLY ISN'T MY JOB.
WELL, IT IS AND IT ISN'T. THE CLEANUP PART HAS ALWAYS BEEN DELEGATED TO SOMEONE ELSE.
BUT I STRIVE TO CONTINUOUSLY APPLY THE BEST OF MYSELF TO THE TASK AT HAND.
IF YOU WANT TO BUILD A BUSINESS OF YOUR OWN...
...YOU HAVE TO USE A LITTLE IMAGINATION...

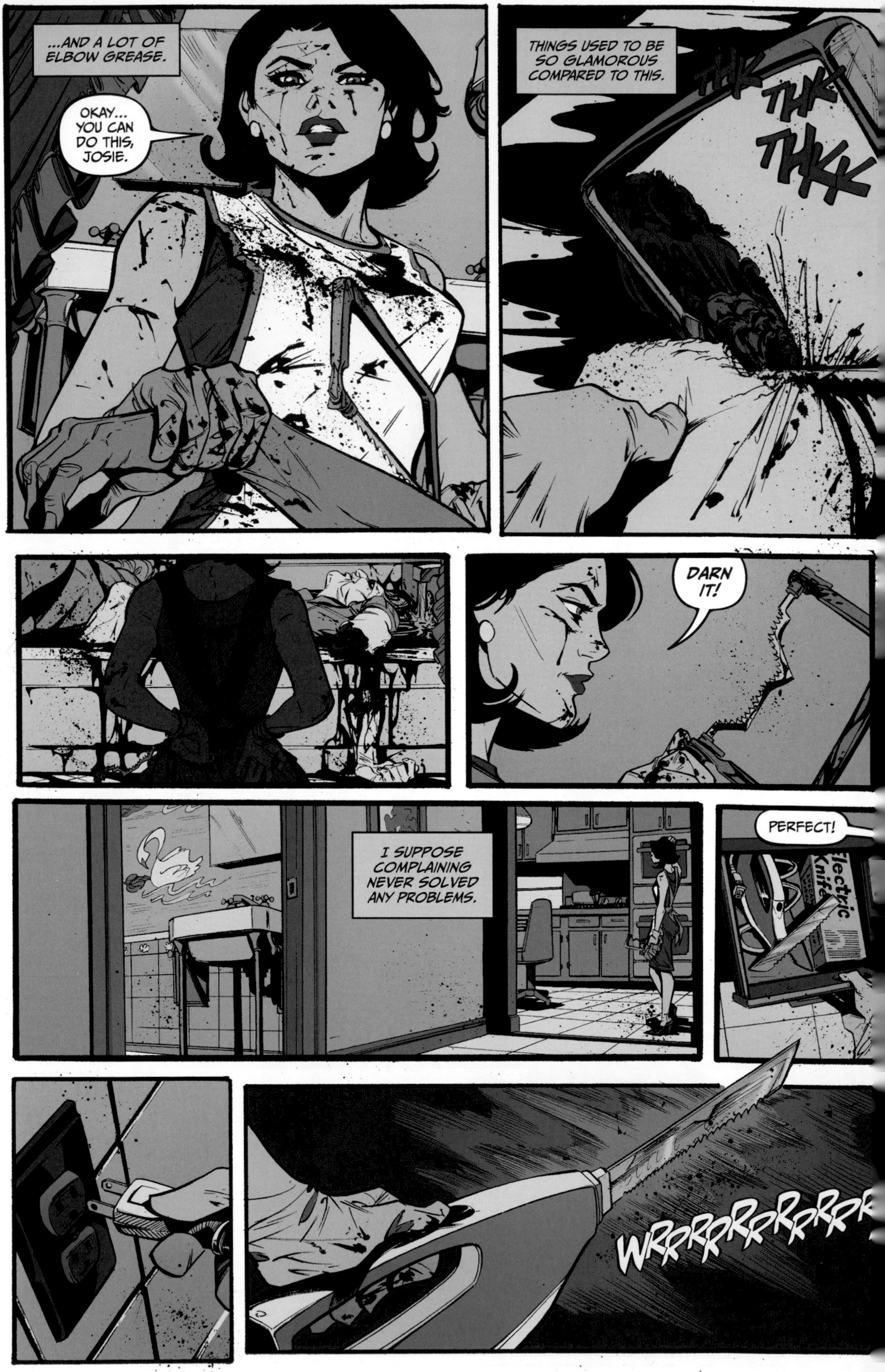
...AND A LOT OF ELBOW GREASE.
OKAY... YOU CAN DO THIS, JOSIE.
THINGS USED TO BE SO GLAMOROUS COMPARED TO THIS.
THK THK THKK
DARN IT!
I SUPPOSE COMPLAINING NEVER SOLVED ANY PROBLEMS.
PERFECT!
Electric Knife
WRRRRRRRRRRR

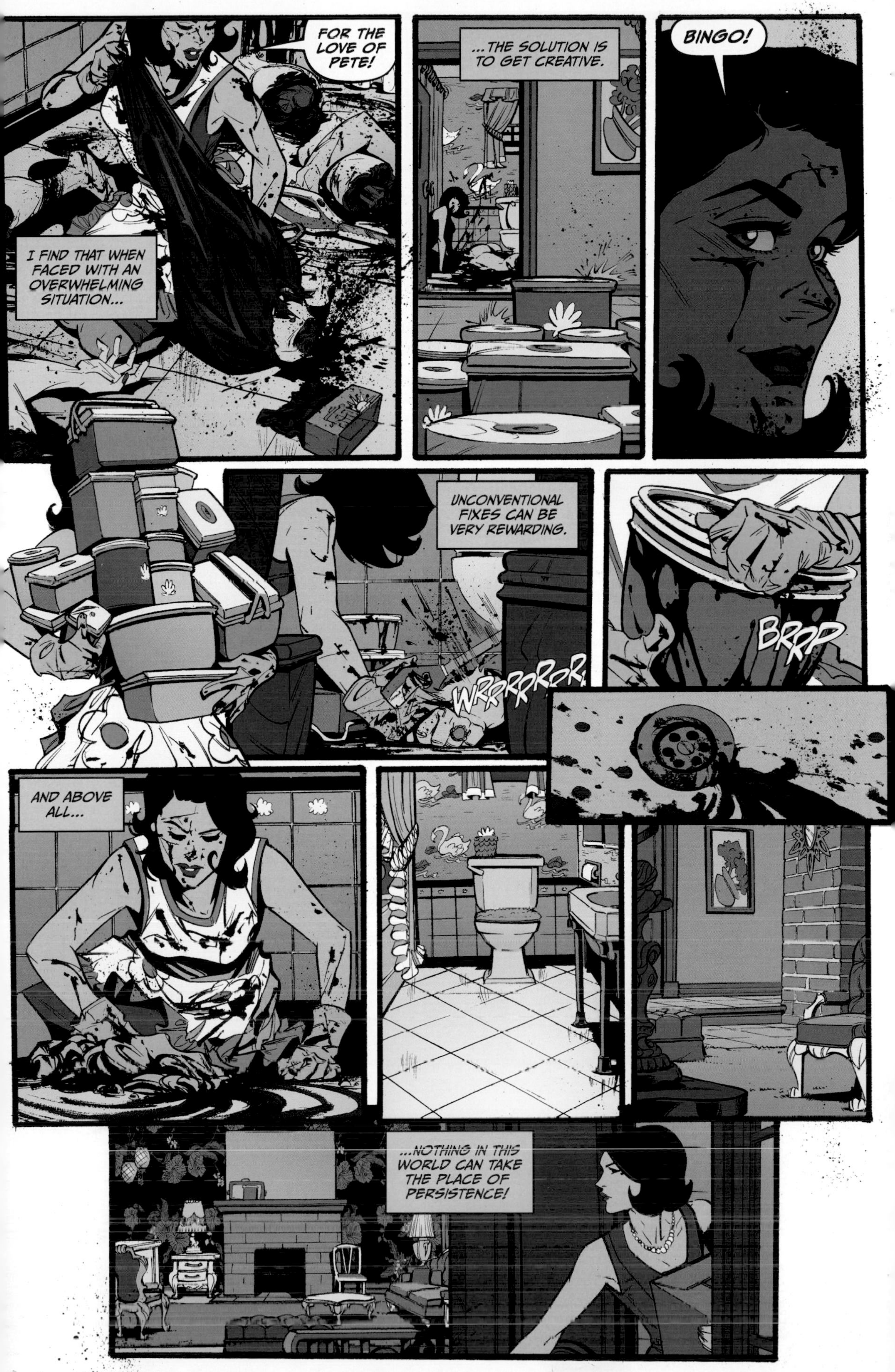
FOR THE LOVE OF PETE!
I FIND THAT WHEN FACED WITH AN OVERWHELMING SITUATION...
...THE SOLUTION IS TO GET CREATIVE.
BINGO!
UNCONVENTIONAL FIXES CAN BE VERY REWARDING.
WRRRRRRR
BRRP
AND ABOVE ALL...
...NOTHING IN THIS WORLD CAN TAKE THE PLACE OF PERSISTENCE!

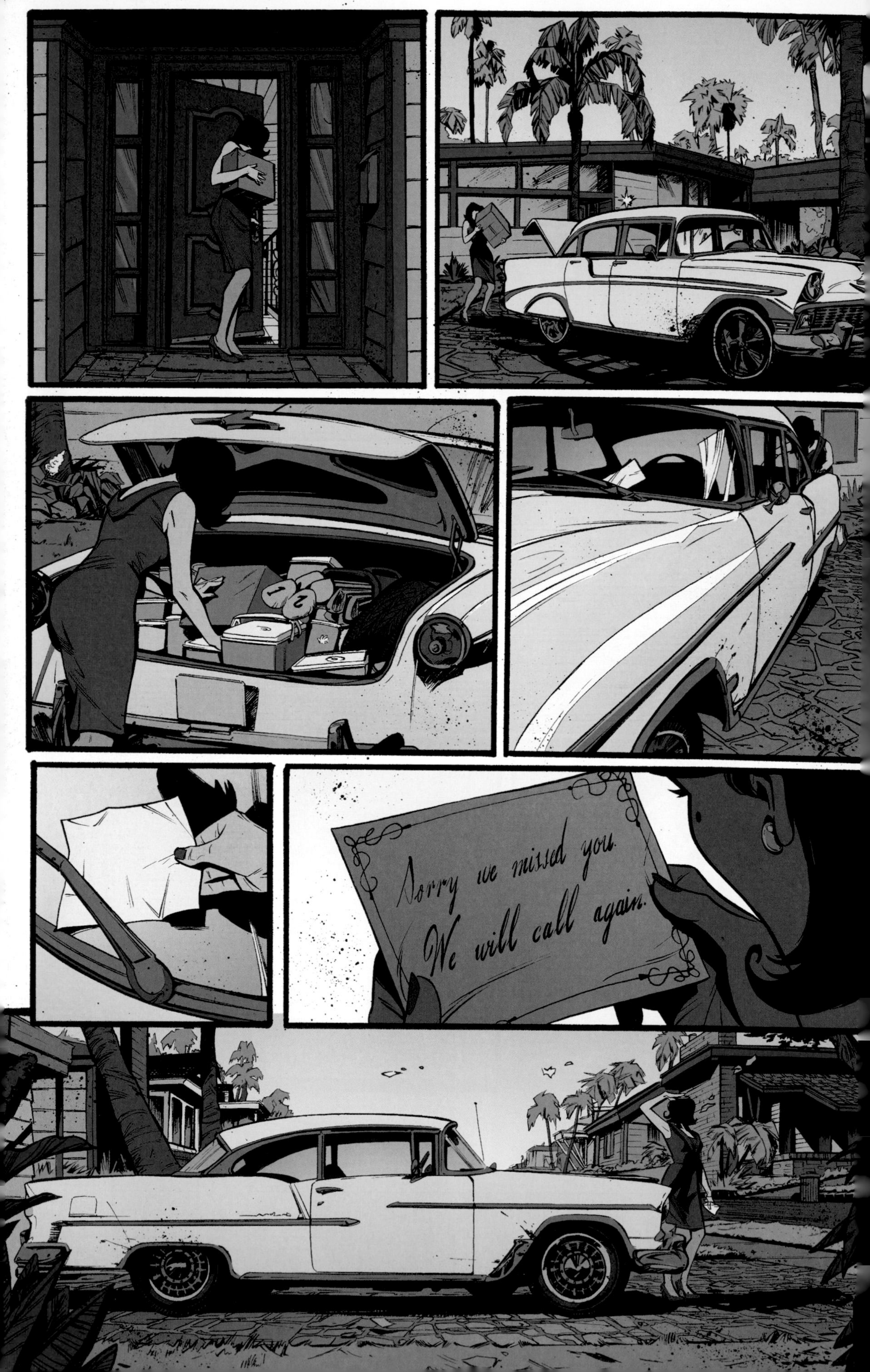
Sorry we missed you.
We will call again.

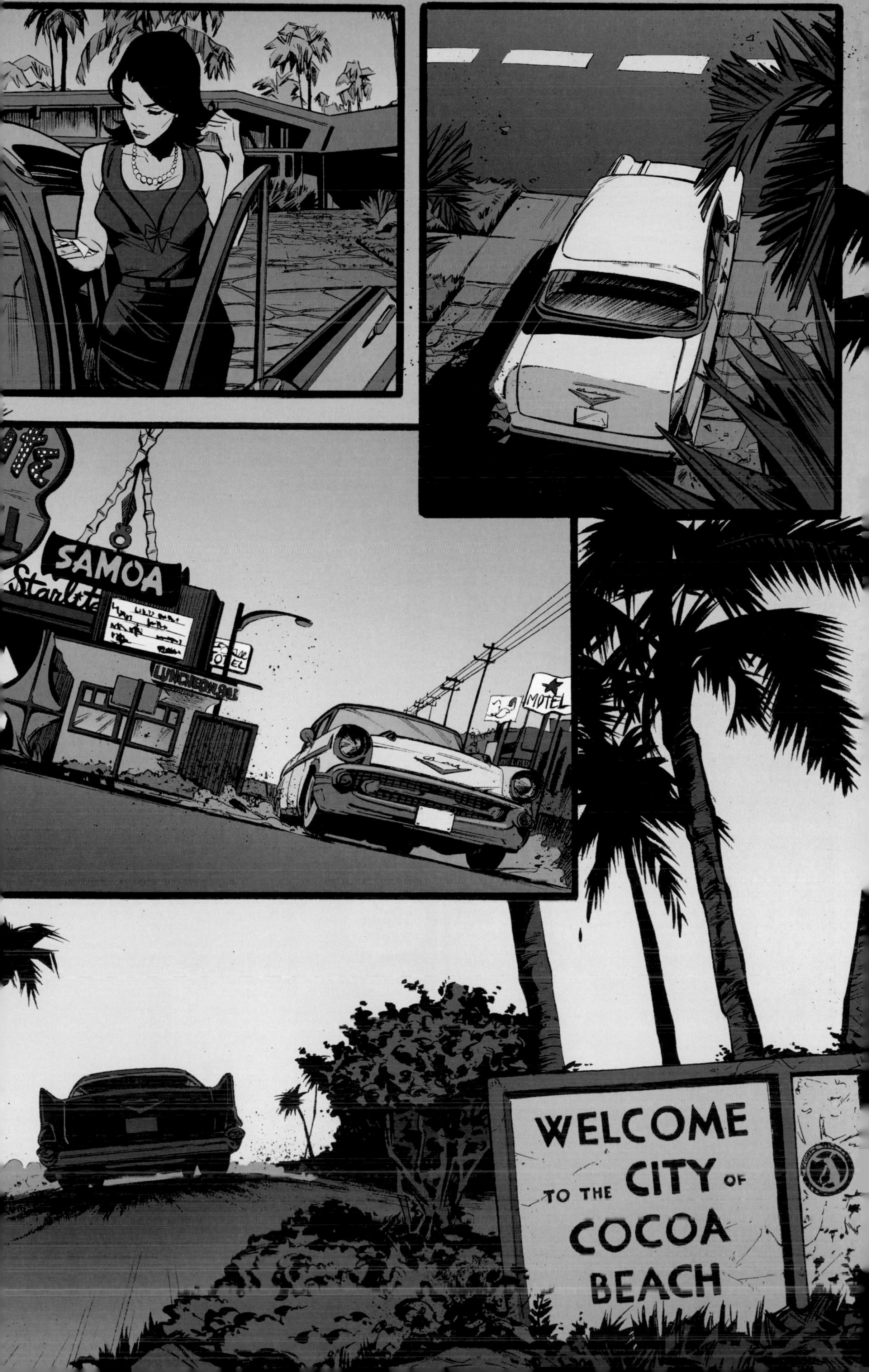
SAMOA
Starlite
LUNCHEON 99¢
MOTEL
WELCOME TO THE CITY OF COCOA BEACH

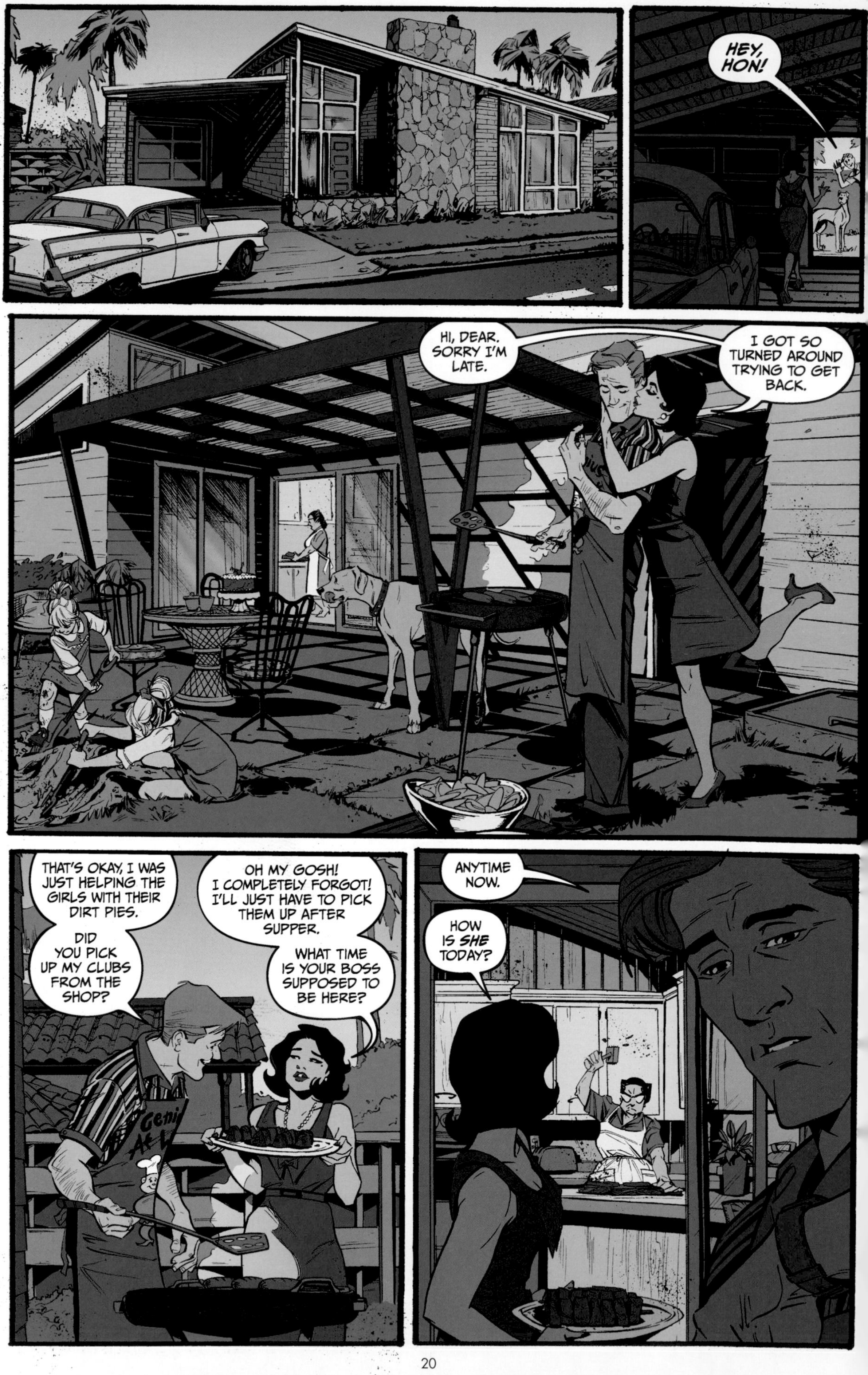
HEY, HON!
HI, DEAR. SORRY I'M LATE.
I GOT SO TURNED AROUND TRYING TO GET BACK.
THAT'S OKAY, I WAS JUST HELPING THE GIRLS WITH THEIR DIRT PIES.
DID YOU PICK UP MY CLUBS FROM THE SHOP?
OH MY GOSH! I COMPLETELY FORGOT! I'LL JUST HAVE TO PICK THEM UP AFTER SUPPER.
WHAT TIME IS YOUR BOSS SUPPOSED TO BE HERE?
ANYTIME NOW.
HOW IS SHE TODAY?

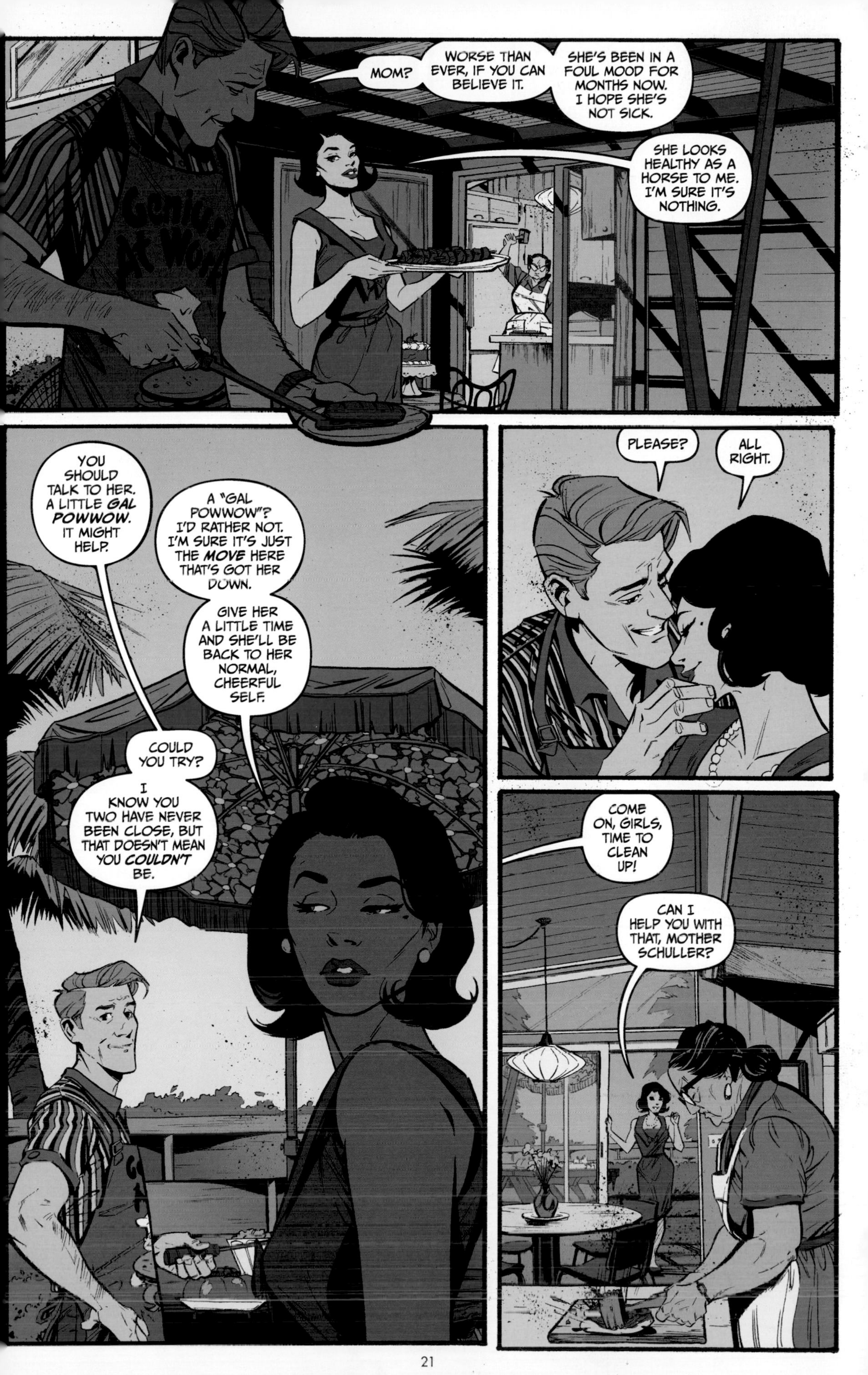
MOM?
WORSE THAN EVER, IF YOU CAN BELIEVE IT.
SHE'S BEEN IN A FOUL MOOD FOR MONTHS NOW. I HOPE SHE'S NOT SICK.
SHE LOOKS HEALTHY AS A HORSE TO ME. I'M SURE IT'S NOTHING.
YOU SHOULD TALK TO HER. A LITTLE *GAL POWWOW*. IT MIGHT HELP.
A "GAL POWWOW"? I'D RATHER NOT. I'M SURE IT'S JUST THE *MOVE* HERE THAT'S GOT HER DOWN.
GIVE HER A LITTLE TIME AND SHE'LL BE BACK TO HER NORMAL, CHEERFUL SELF.
COULD YOU TRY?
I KNOW YOU TWO HAVE NEVER BEEN CLOSE, BUT THAT DOESN'T MEAN YOU *COULDN'T* BE.
PLEASE?
ALL RIGHT.
COME ON, GIRLS, TIME TO CLEAN UP!
CAN I HELP YOU WITH THAT, MOTHER SCHULLER?

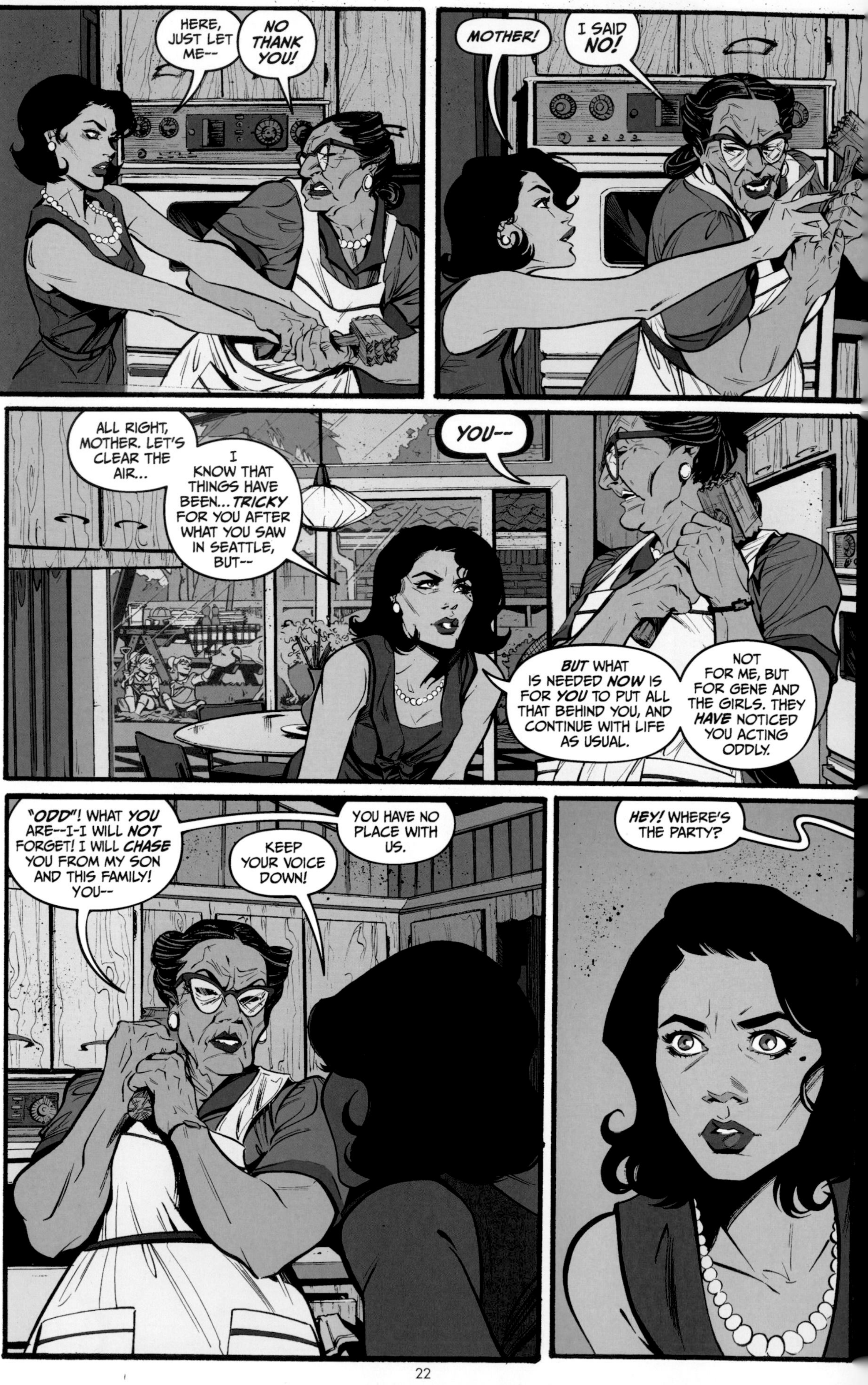
HERE, JUST LET ME--
NO THANK YOU!
MOTHER!
I SAID NO!
ALL RIGHT, MOTHER. LET'S CLEAR THE AIR...
I KNOW THAT THINGS HAVE BEEN... TRICKY FOR YOU AFTER WHAT YOU SAW IN SEATTLE, BUT--
YOU--
BUT WHAT IS NEEDED NOW IS FOR YOU TO PUT ALL THAT BEHIND YOU, AND CONTINUE WITH LIFE AS USUAL.
NOT FOR ME, BUT FOR GENE AND THE GIRLS. THEY HAVE NOTICED YOU ACTING ODDLY.
"ODD"! WHAT YOU ARE--I-I WILL NOT FORGET! I WILL CHASE YOU FROM MY SON AND THIS FAMILY! YOU--
KEEP YOUR VOICE DOWN!
YOU HAVE NO PLACE WITH US.
HEY! WHERE'S THE PARTY?

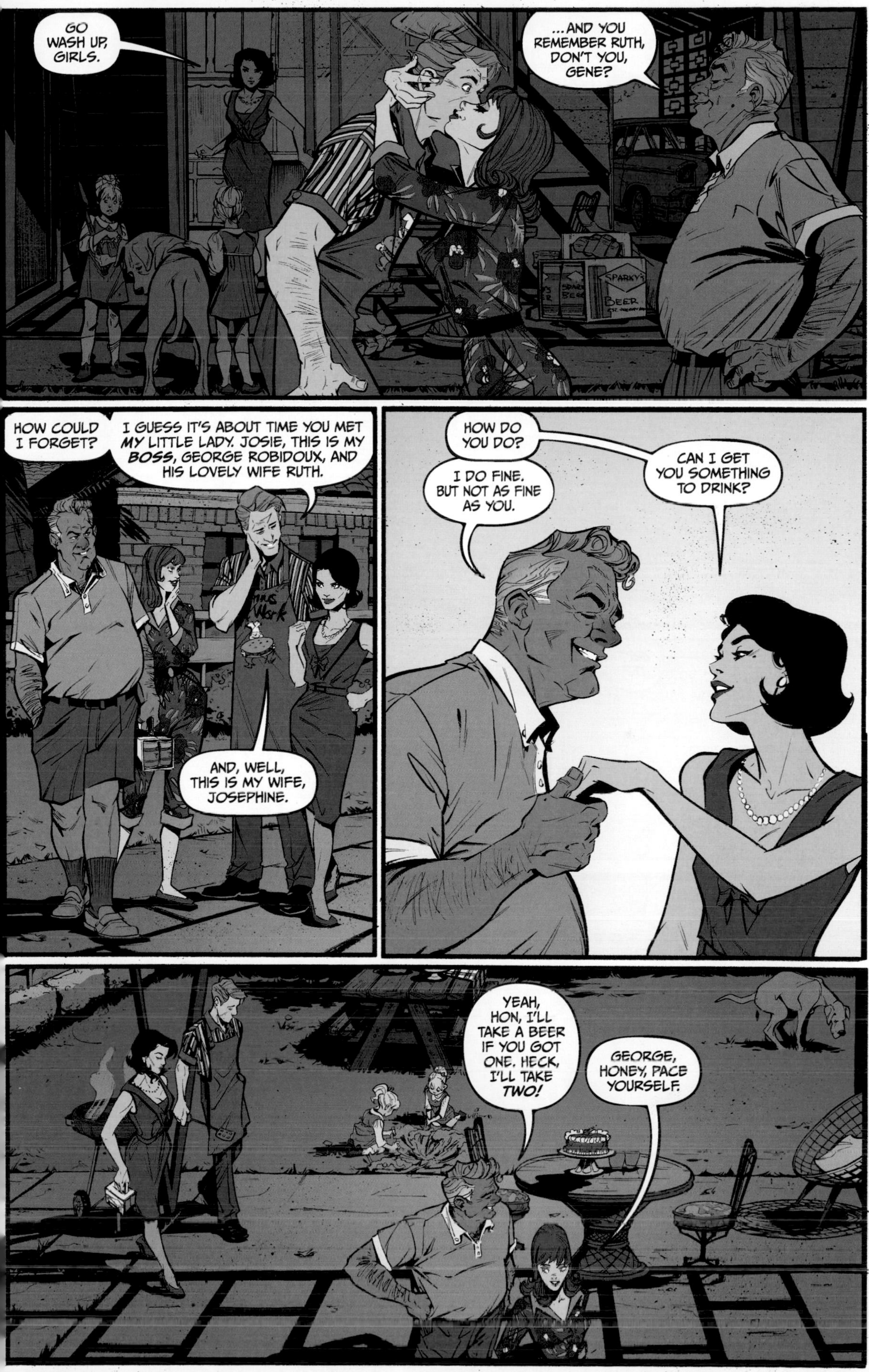
GO WASH UP, GIRLS.
...AND YOU REMEMBER RUTH, DON'T YOU, GENE?
HOW COULD I FORGET?
I GUESS IT'S ABOUT TIME YOU MET MY LITTLE LADY. JOSIE, THIS IS MY BOSS, GEORGE ROBIDOUX, AND HIS LOVELY WIFE RUTH.
AND, WELL, THIS IS MY WIFE, JOSEPHINE.
HOW DO YOU DO?
I DO FINE. BUT NOT AS FINE AS YOU.
CAN I GET YOU SOMETHING TO DRINK?
YEAH, HON, I'LL TAKE A BEER IF YOU GOT ONE. HECK, I'LL TAKE TWO!
GEORGE, HONEY, PACE YOURSELF.

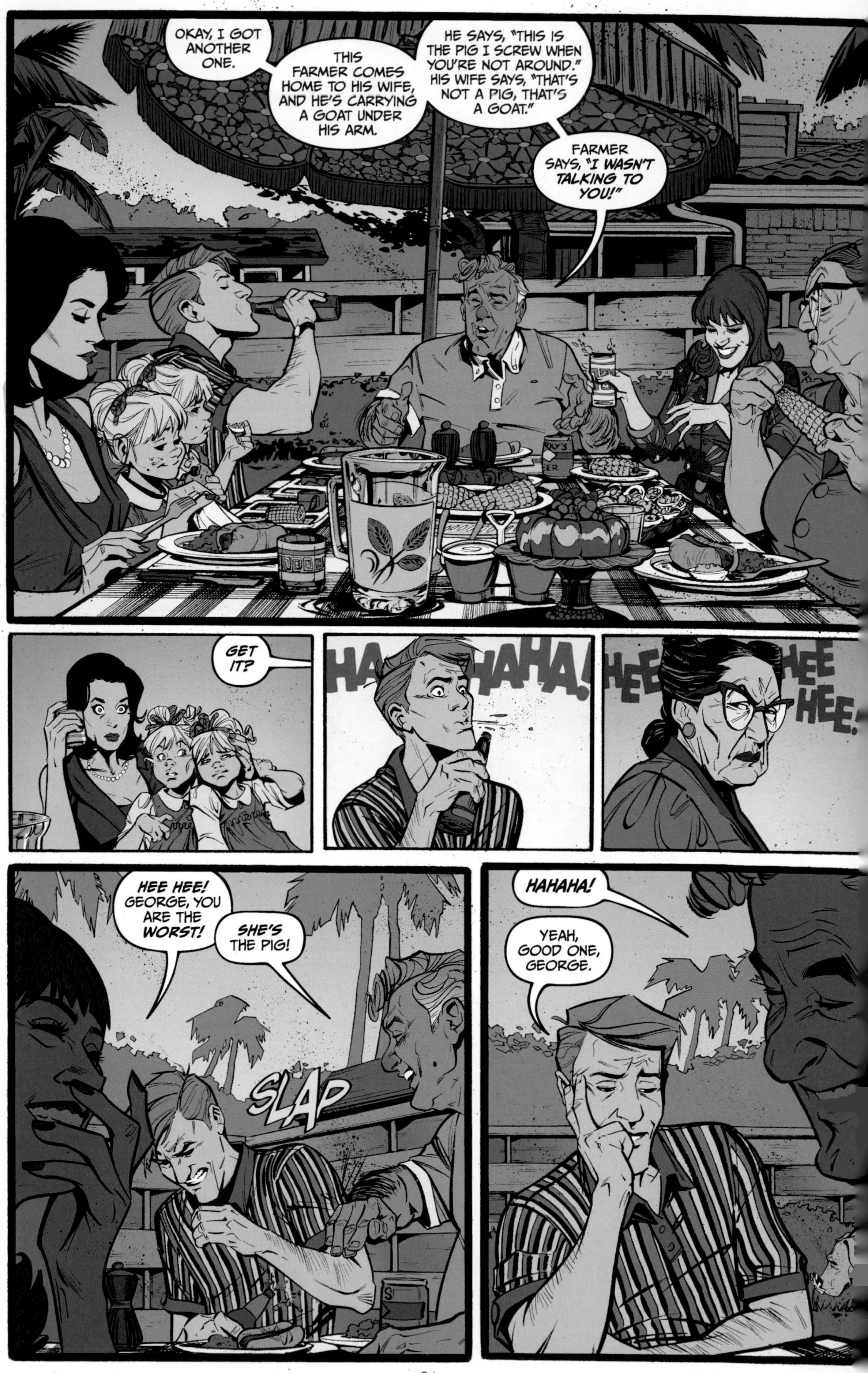
OKAY, I GOT ANOTHER ONE.
THIS FARMER COMES HOME TO HIS WIFE, AND HE'S CARRYING A GOAT UNDER HIS ARM.
HE SAYS, "THIS IS THE PIG I SCREW WHEN YOU'RE NOT AROUND." HIS WIFE SAYS, "THAT'S NOT A PIG, THAT'S A GOAT."
FARMER SAYS, "I WASN'T TALKING TO YOU!"
GET IT?
HA HAHA!
HEE HEE HEE!
HEE HEE! GEORGE, YOU ARE THE WORST!
SHE'S THE PIG!
SLAP
HAHAHA!
YEAH, GOOD ONE, GEORGE.

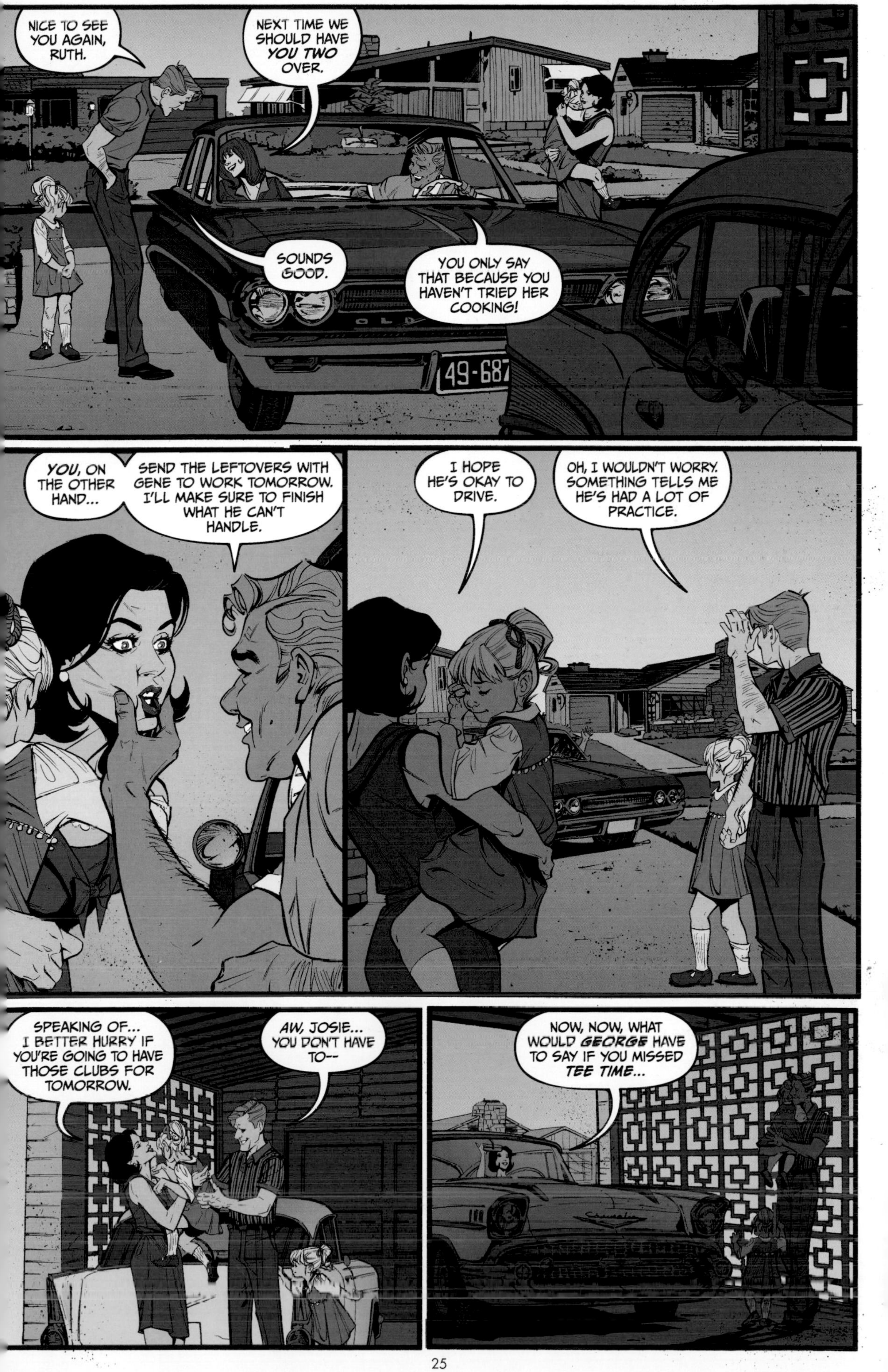
NICE TO SEE YOU AGAIN, RUTH.
NEXT TIME WE SHOULD HAVE YOU TWO OVER.
SOUNDS GOOD.
YOU ONLY SAY THAT BECAUSE YOU HAVEN'T TRIED HER COOKING!
49-687
YOU, ON THE OTHER HAND...
SEND THE LEFTOVERS WITH GENE TO WORK TOMORROW. I'LL MAKE SURE TO FINISH WHAT HE CAN'T HANDLE.
I HOPE HE'S OKAY TO DRIVE.
OH, I WOULDN'T WORRY. SOMETHING TELLS ME HE'S HAD A LOT OF PRACTICE.
SPEAKING OF... I BETTER HURRY IF YOU'RE GOING TO HAVE THOSE CLUBS FOR TOMORROW.
AW, JOSIE... YOU DON'T HAVE TO--
NOW, NOW, WHAT WOULD GEORGE HAVE TO SAY IF YOU MISSED TEE TIME...

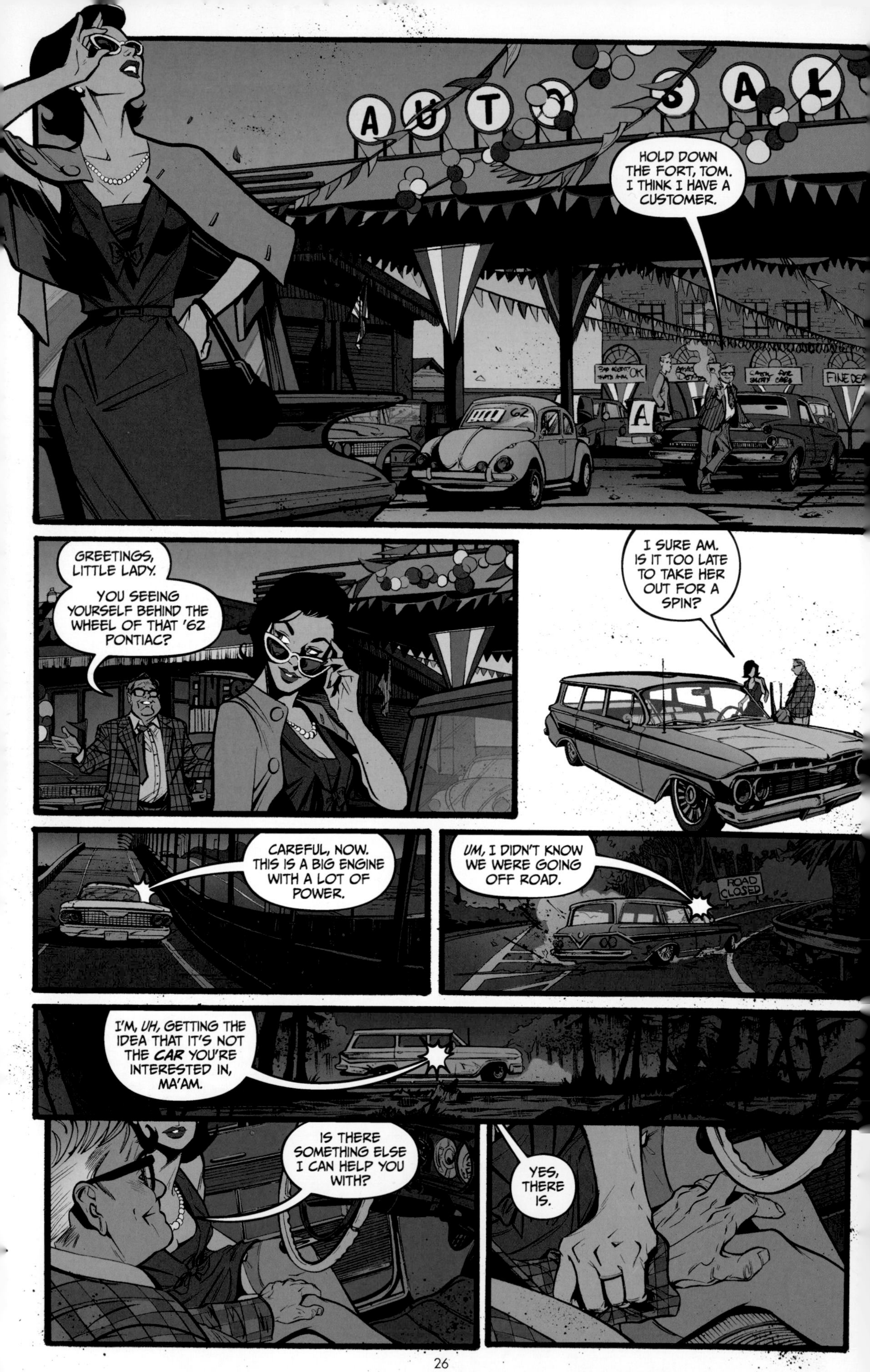
AUTO SAL
HOLD DOWN THE FORT, TOM. I THINK I HAVE A CUSTOMER.
GREETINGS, LITTLE LADY.
YOU SEEING YOURSELF BEHIND THE WHEEL OF THAT '62 PONTIAC?
I SURE AM. IS IT TOO LATE TO TAKE HER OUT FOR A SPIN?
CAREFUL, NOW. THIS IS A BIG ENGINE WITH A LOT OF POWER.
UM, I DIDN'T KNOW WE WERE GOING OFF ROAD.
ROAD CLOSED
I'M, UH, GETTING THE IDEA THAT IT'S NOT THE CAR YOU'RE INTERESTED IN, MA'AM.
IS THERE SOMETHING ELSE I CAN HELP YOU WITH?
YES, THERE IS.

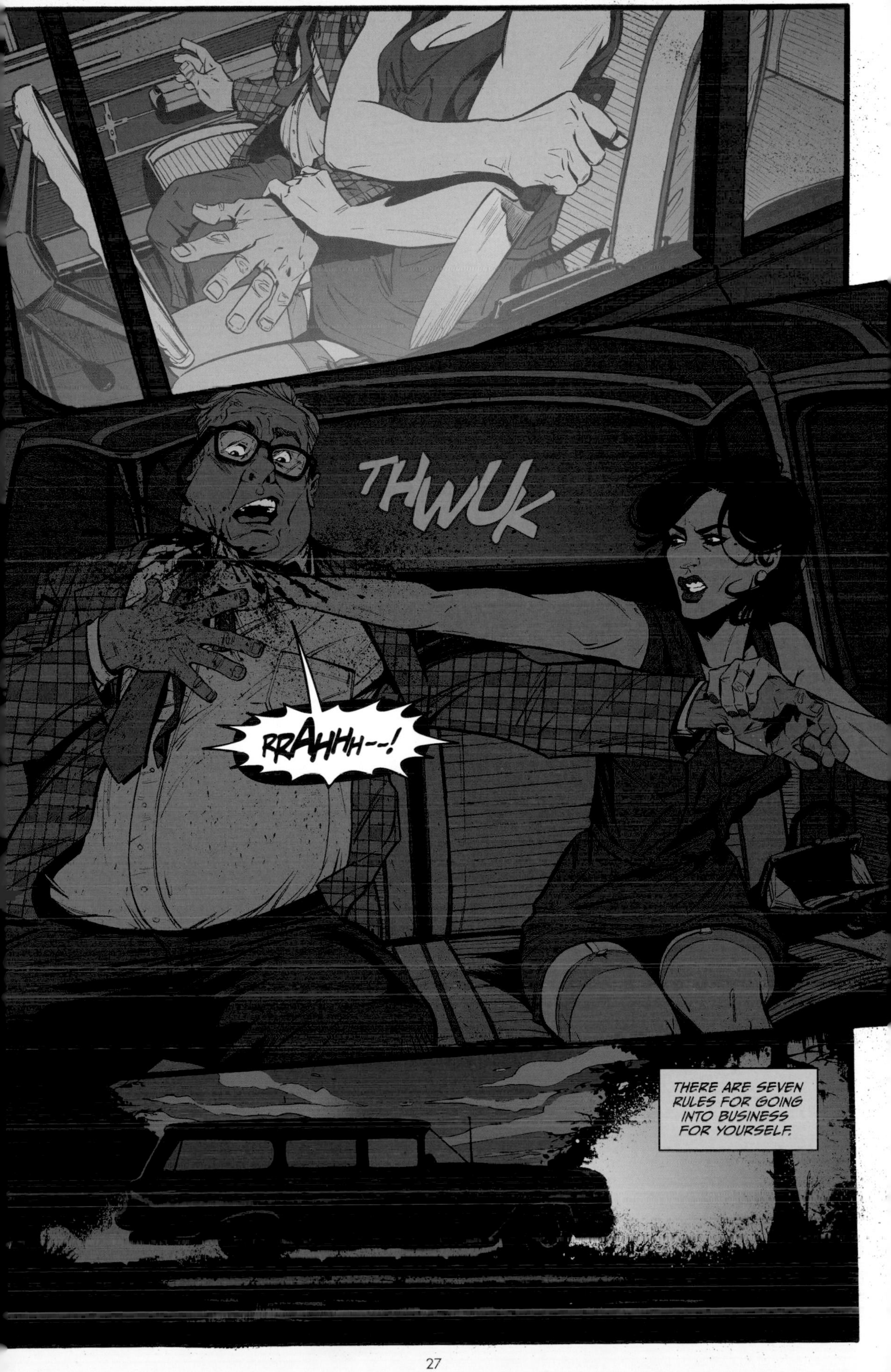
THWUK
RRAHHH--!
THERE ARE SEVEN RULES FOR GOING INTO BUSINESS FOR YOURSELF.

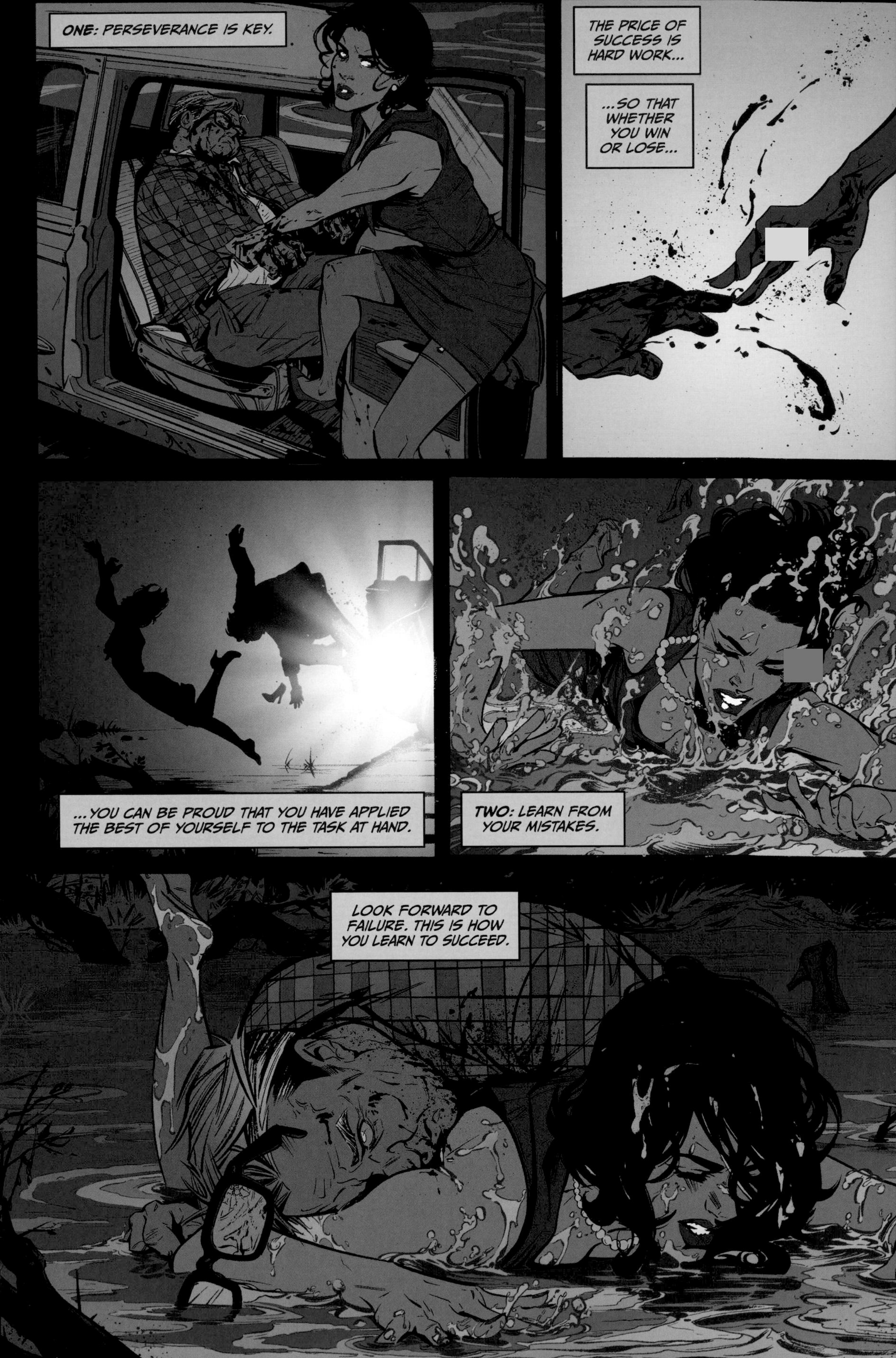
ONE: PERSEVERANCE IS KEY.
THE PRICE OF SUCCESS IS HARD WORK...
...SO THAT WHETHER YOU WIN OR LOSE...
...YOU CAN BE PROUD THAT YOU HAVE APPLIED THE BEST OF YOURSELF TO THE TASK AT HAND.
TWO: LEARN FROM YOUR MISTAKES.
LOOK FORWARD TO FAILURE. THIS IS HOW YOU LEARN TO SUCCEED.

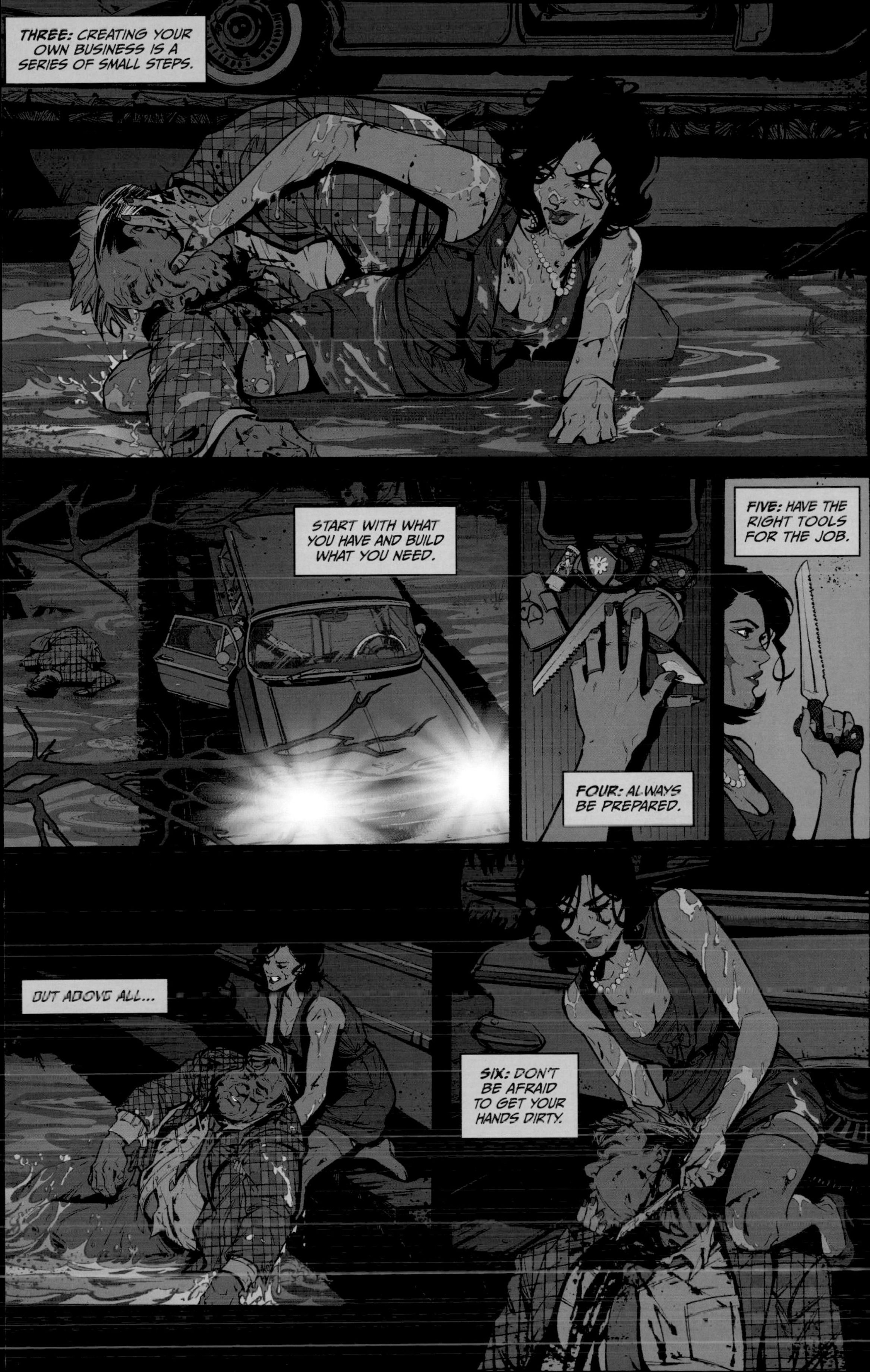
THREE: CREATING YOUR OWN BUSINESS IS A SERIES OF SMALL STEPS.
START WITH WHAT YOU HAVE AND BUILD WHAT YOU NEED.
FOUR: ALWAYS BE PREPARED.
FIVE: HAVE THE RIGHT TOOLS FOR THE JOB.
BUT ABOVE ALL...
SIX: DON'T BE AFRAID TO GET YOUR HANDS DIRTY.

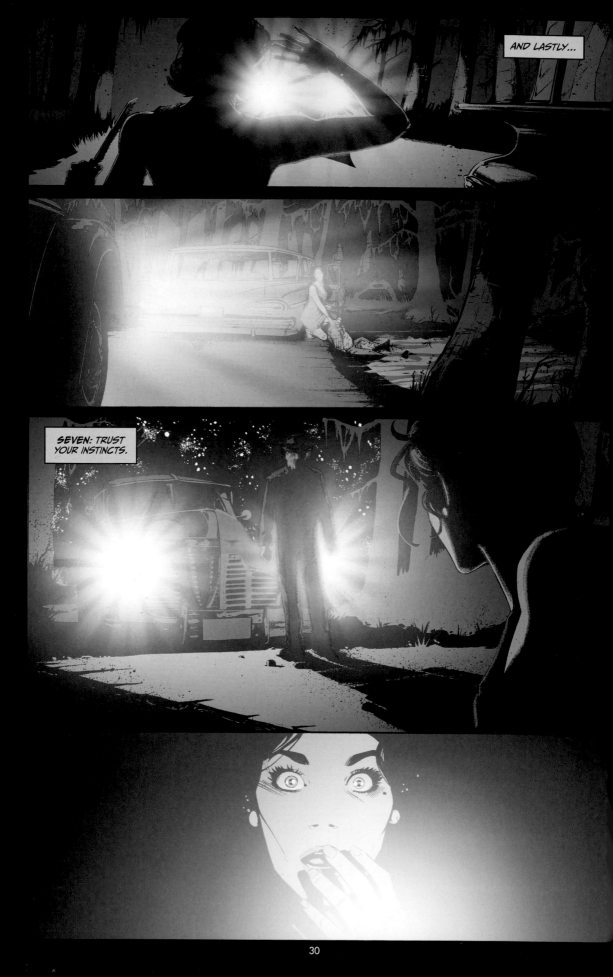

AND LASTLY...

SEVEN: TRUST YOUR INSTINCTS.

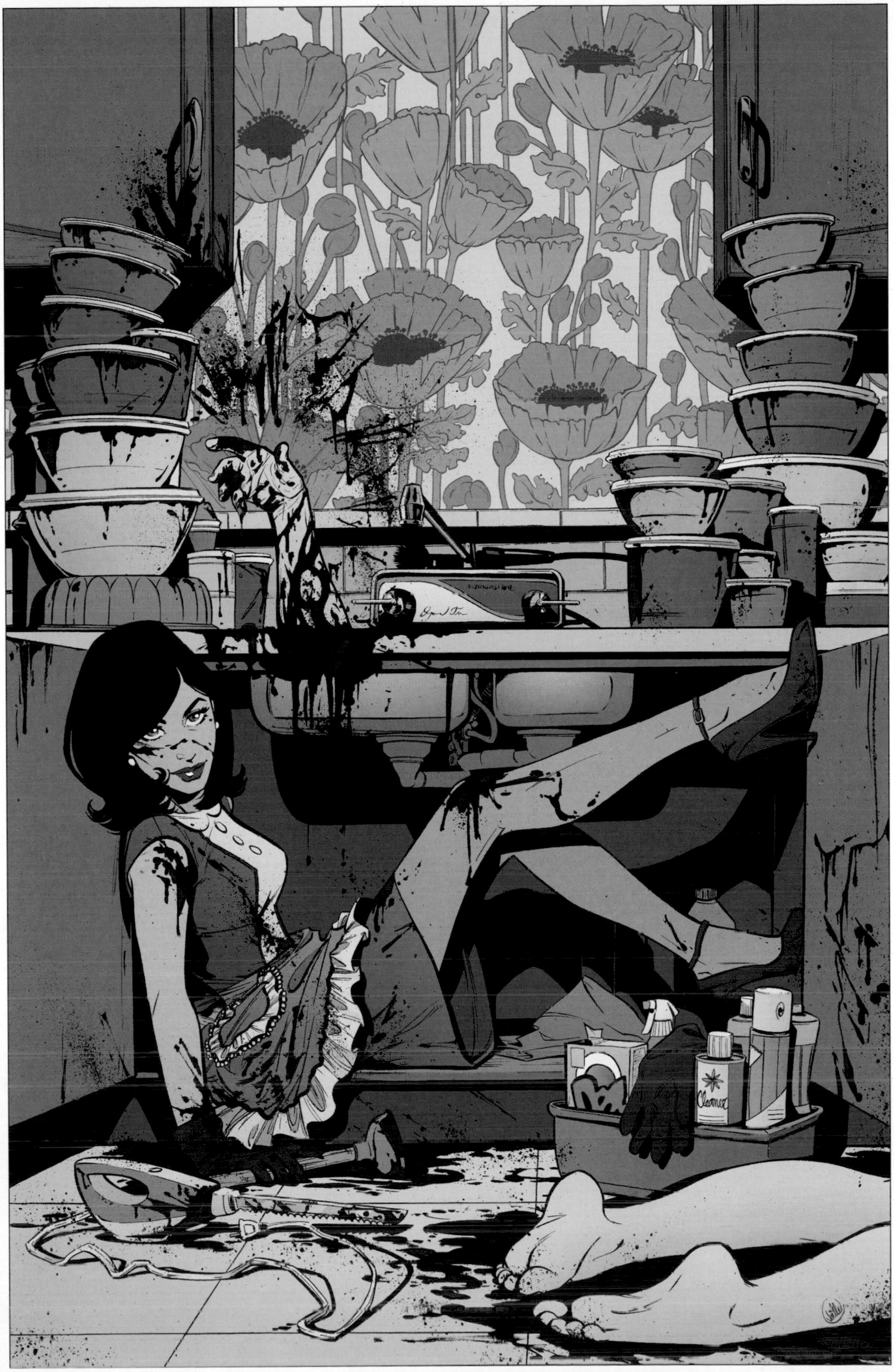

CHAPTER TWO

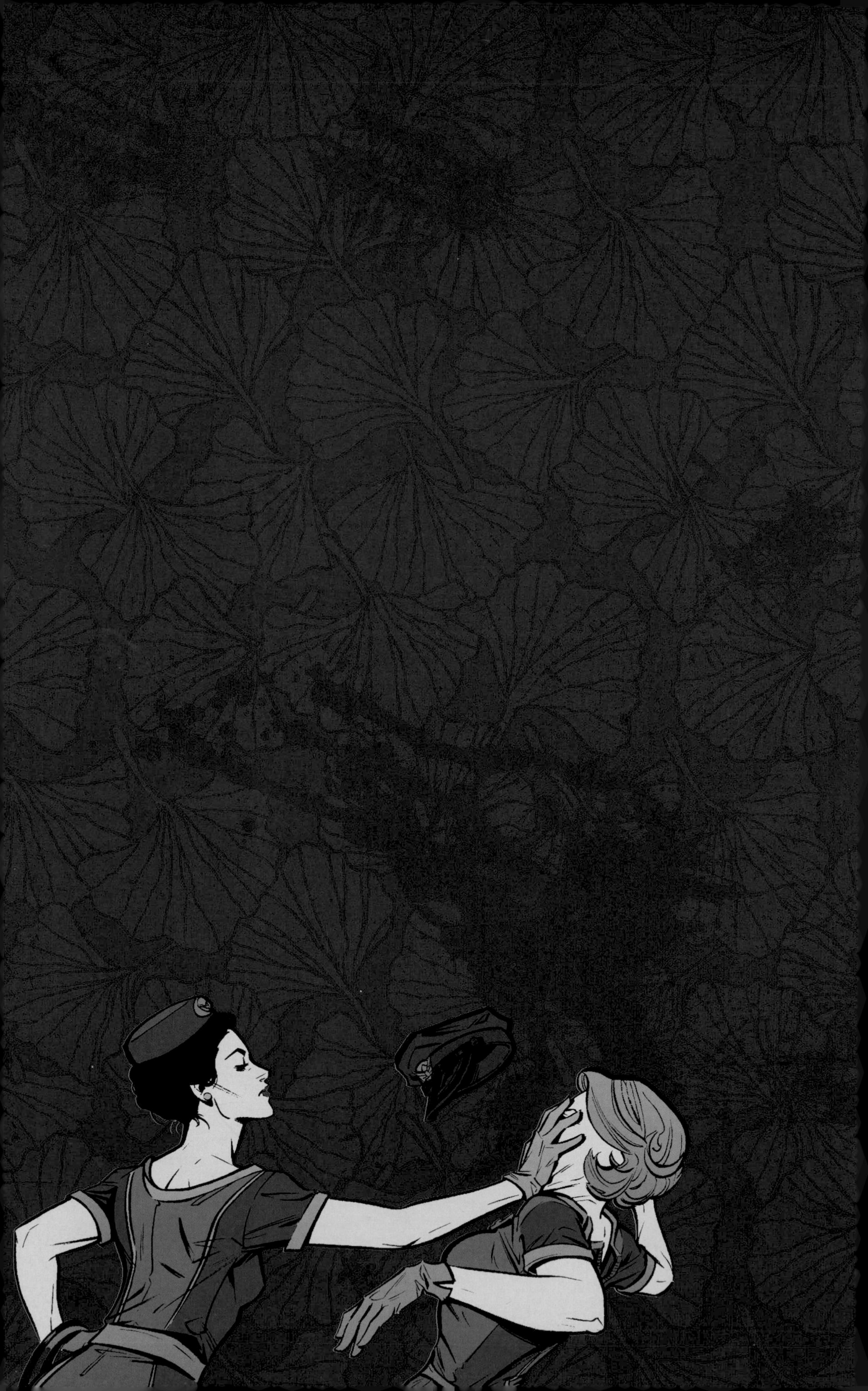

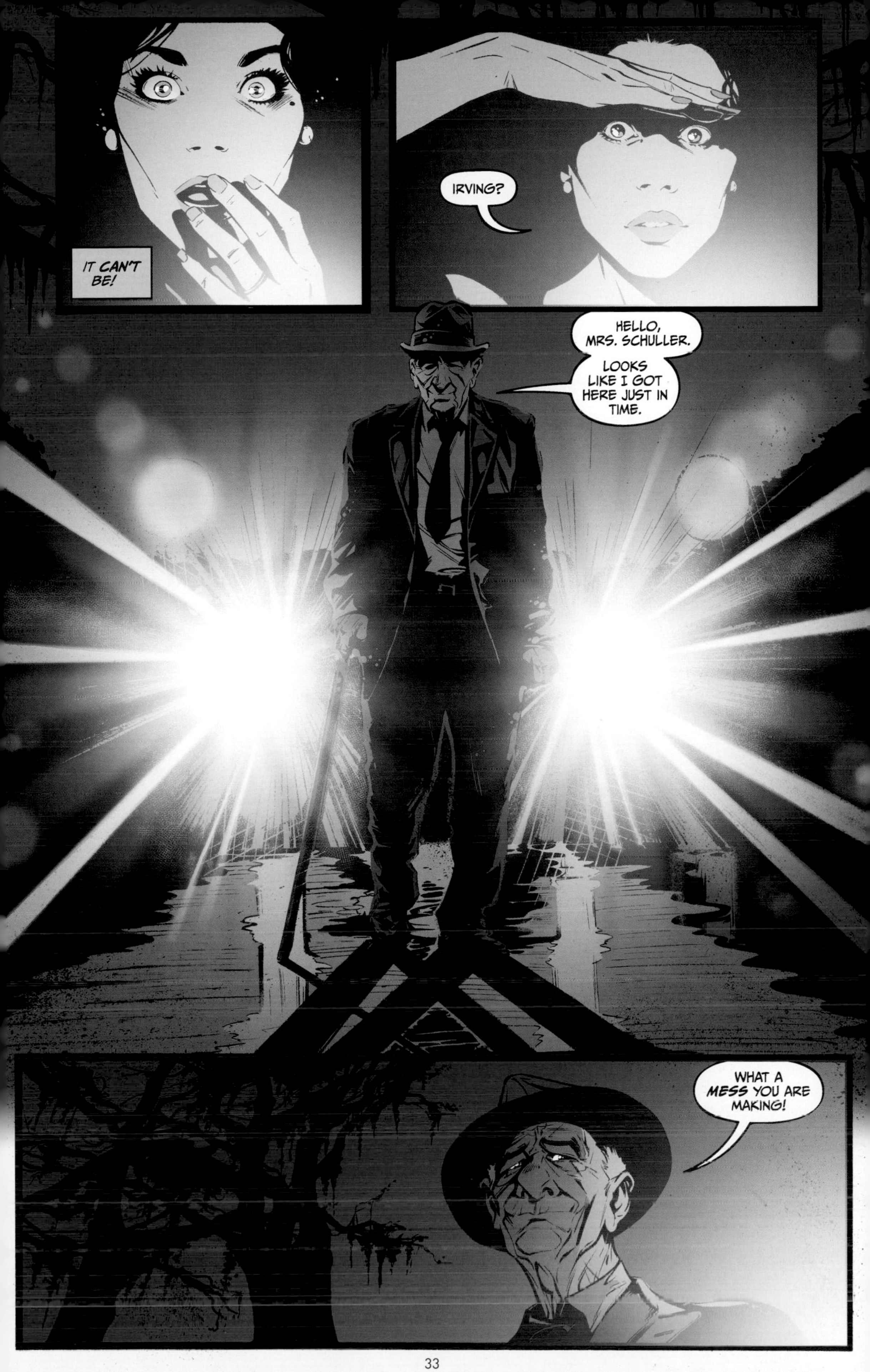
IT CAN'T BE!
IRVING?
HELLO, MRS. SCHULLER.
LOOKS LIKE I GOT HERE JUST IN TIME.
WHAT A MESS YOU ARE MAKING!

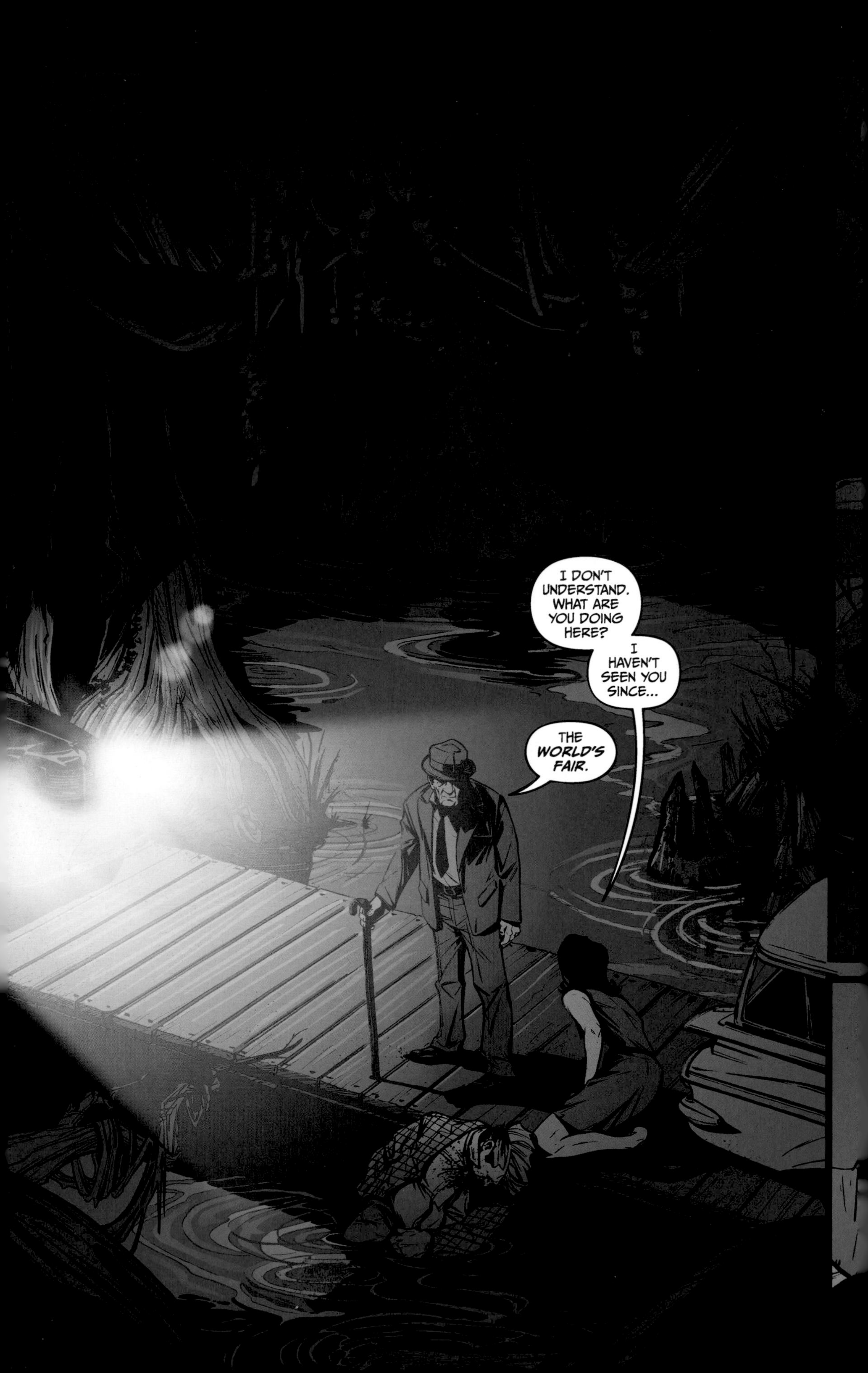
I DON'T UNDERSTAND. WHAT ARE YOU DOING HERE?
I HAVEN'T SEEN YOU SINCE...
THE *WORLD'S FAIR.*

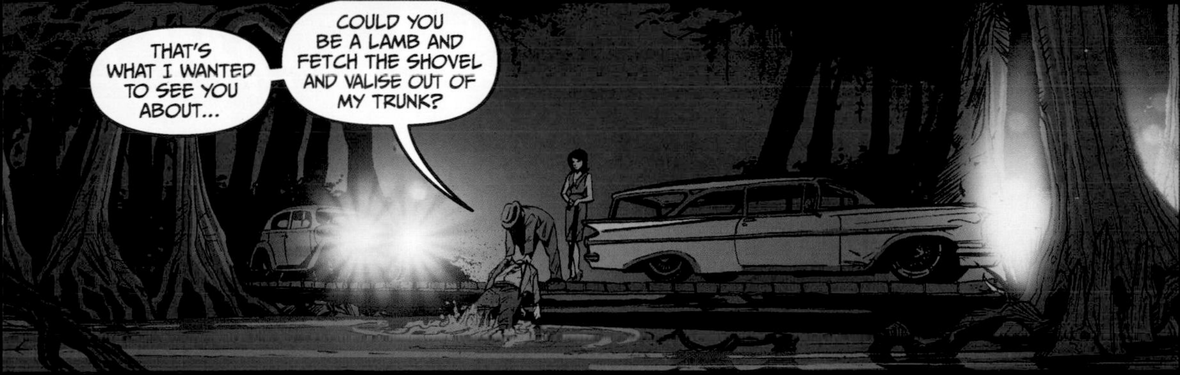
THAT'S WHAT I WANTED TO SEE YOU ABOUT...
COULD YOU BE A LAMB AND FETCH THE SHOVEL AND VALISE OUT OF MY TRUNK?

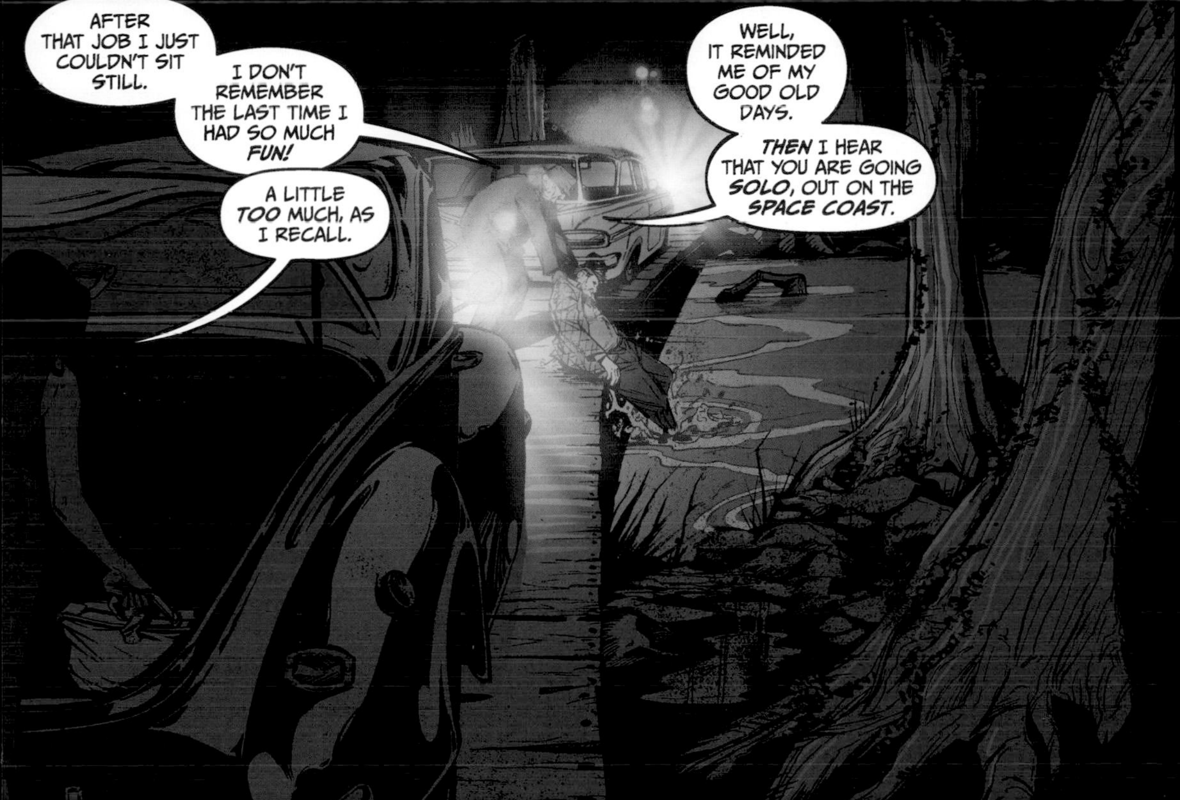
AFTER THAT JOB I JUST COULDN'T SIT STILL.
I DON'T REMEMBER THE LAST TIME I HAD SO MUCH FUN!
A LITTLE TOO MUCH, AS I RECALL.
WELL, IT REMINDED ME OF MY GOOD OLD DAYS.
THEN I HEAR THAT YOU ARE GOING SOLO, OUT ON THE SPACE COAST.

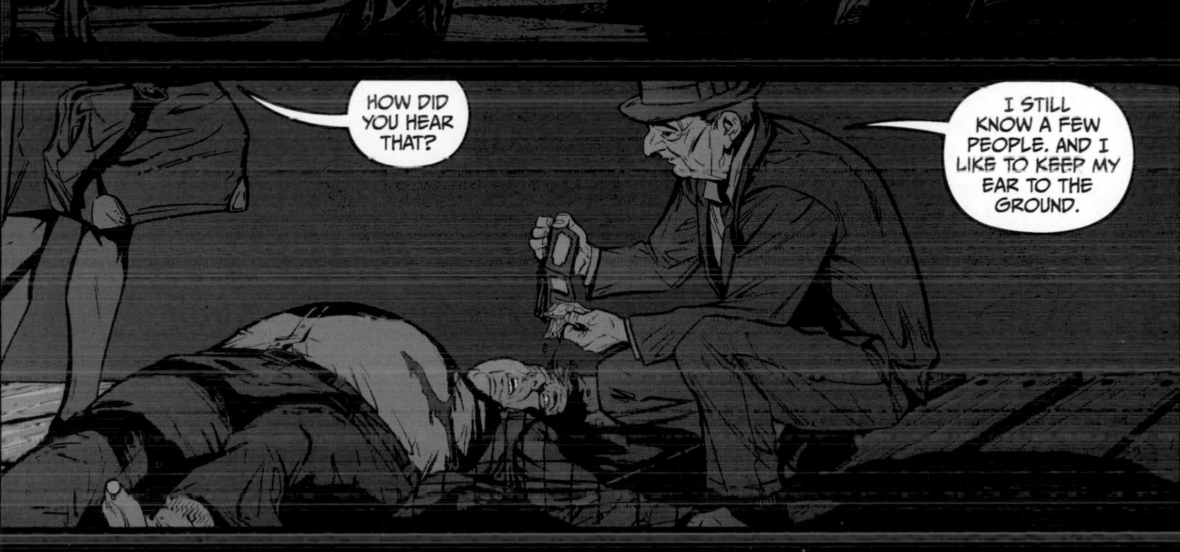
HOW DID YOU HEAR THAT?
I STILL KNOW A FEW PEOPLE. AND I LIKE TO KEEP MY EAR TO THE GROUND.

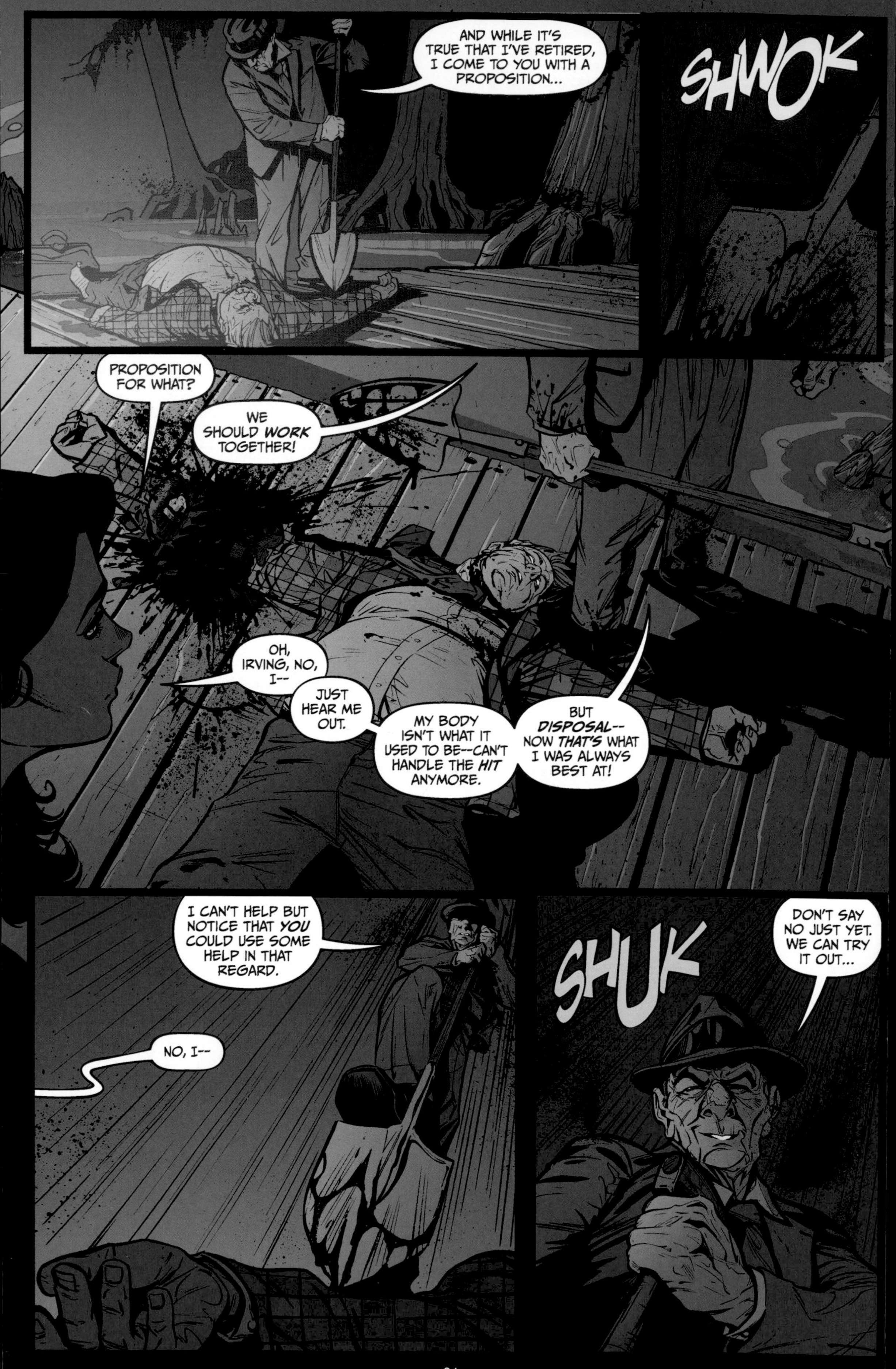
AND WHILE IT'S TRUE THAT I'VE RETIRED, I COME TO YOU WITH A PROPOSITION...
SHWOK
PROPOSITION FOR WHAT?
WE SHOULD WORK TOGETHER!
OH, IRVING, NO, I--
JUST HEAR ME OUT.
MY BODY ISN'T WHAT IT USED TO BE--CAN'T HANDLE THE HIT ANYMORE.
BUT DISPOSAL-- NOW THAT'S WHAT I WAS ALWAYS BEST AT!
I CAN'T HELP BUT NOTICE THAT YOU COULD USE SOME HELP IN THAT REGARD.
NO, I--
SHUK
DON'T SAY NO JUST YET. WE CAN TRY IT OUT...

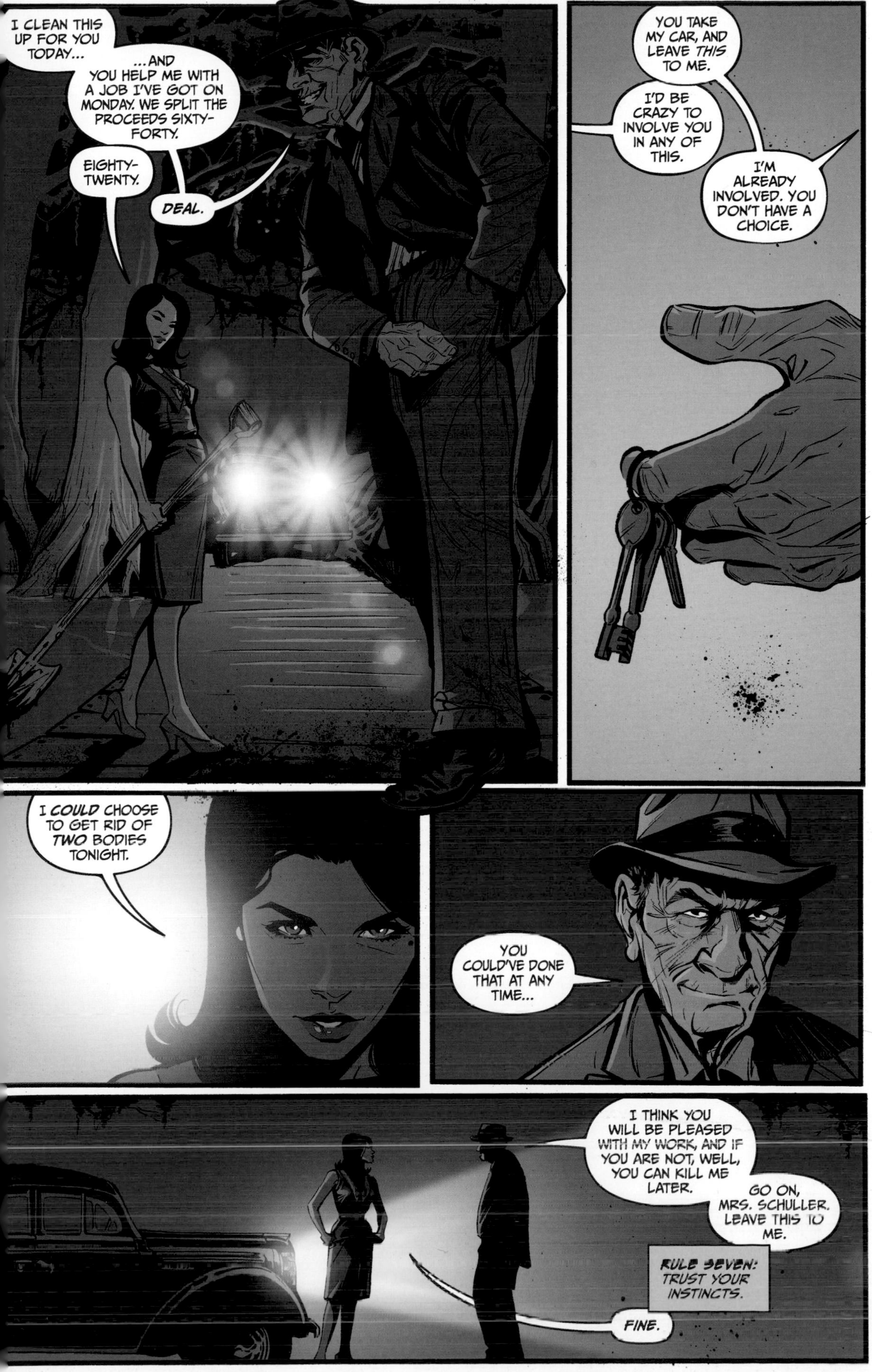
I CLEAN THIS UP FOR YOU TODAY...
...AND YOU HELP ME WITH A JOB I'VE GOT ON MONDAY. WE SPLIT THE PROCEEDS SIXTY-FORTY.
EIGHTY-TWENTY.
DEAL.
YOU TAKE MY CAR, AND LEAVE *THIS* TO ME.
I'D BE CRAZY TO INVOLVE YOU IN ANY OF THIS.
I'M ALREADY INVOLVED. YOU DON'T HAVE A CHOICE.
I *COULD* CHOOSE TO GET RID OF *TWO* BODIES TONIGHT.
YOU COULD'VE DONE THAT AT ANY TIME...
I THINK YOU WILL BE PLEASED WITH MY WORK, AND IF YOU ARE NOT, WELL, YOU CAN KILL ME LATER.
GO ON, MRS. SCHULLER. LEAVE THIS TO ME.
RULE SEVEN: TRUST YOUR INSTINCTS.
FINE.

AEROJET GENERAL

Annual Christmas Bash at the Beach

THERE JUST NEVER IS ENOUGH TIME TO KNOW IF YOUR INSTINCTS ARE CORRECT.

ONE MINUTE, LIFE SEEMS DROLL AND ENDLESS.

THEN OUT OF NOWHERE THINGS SPEED UP, AND UNTIL IT'S ALL OVER I'LL NEVER KNOW IF I GOT IT RIGHT.

OH GENE, I *TOLD* YOU ALL THE OTHER WIVES WOULD BE WEARING BIKINIS!

YOU DON'T THINK MY SUIT IS TOO OLD FASHIONED, DO YOU?

NOT AT ALL-- YOU LOOK LOVELY, DEAR.

IS THAT GEORGE?

YES, AND IT LOOKS LIKE HE'S SPOTTED US!

HEY!

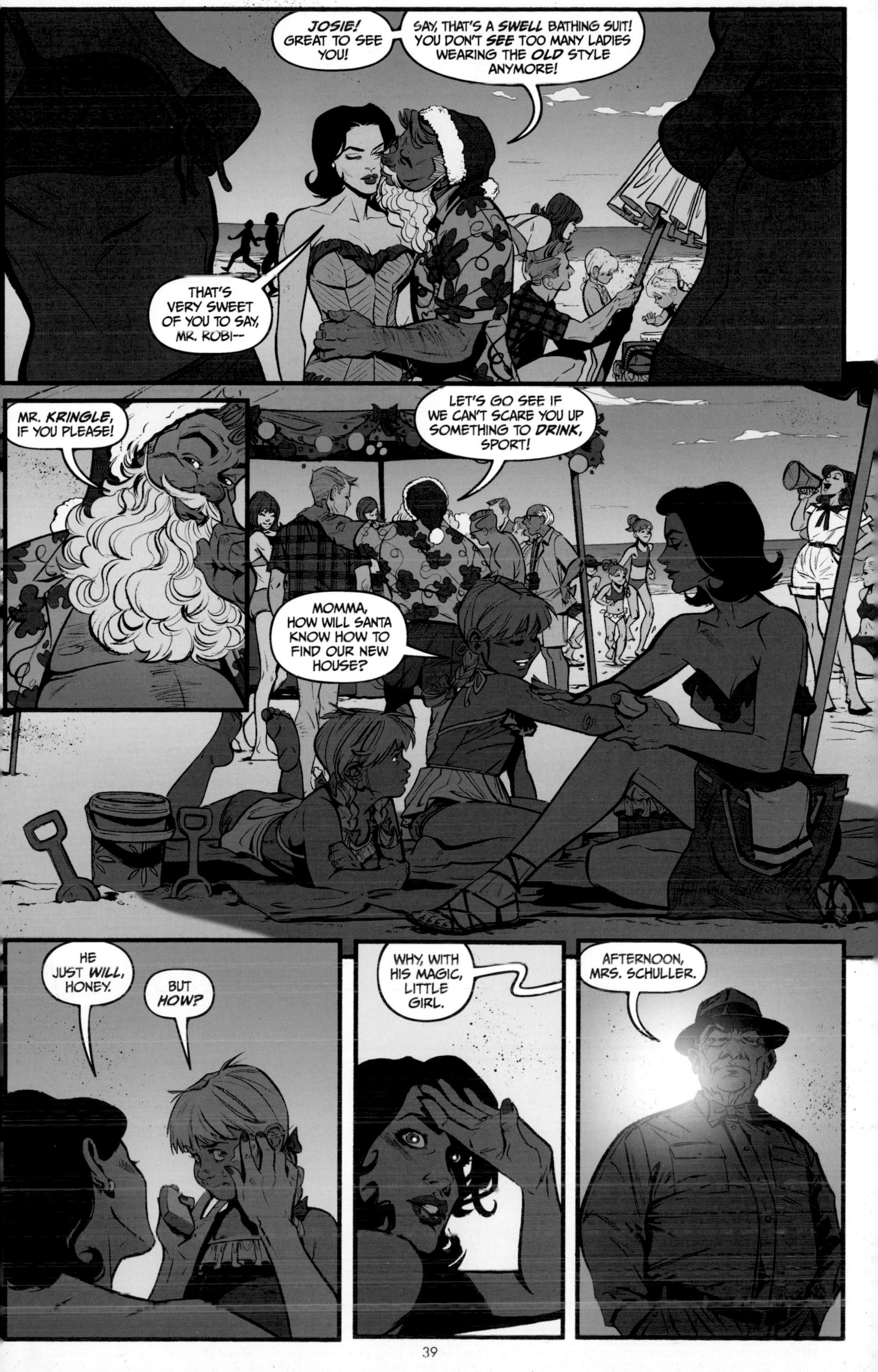
JOSIE! GREAT TO SEE YOU!
SAY, THAT'S A SWELL BATHING SUIT! YOU DON'T SEE TOO MANY LADIES WEARING THE OLD STYLE ANYMORE!
THAT'S VERY SWEET OF YOU TO SAY, MR. ROBI--
MR. KRINGLE, IF YOU PLEASE!
LET'S GO SEE IF WE CAN'T SCARE YOU UP SOMETHING TO DRINK, SPORT!
MOMMA, HOW WILL SANTA KNOW HOW TO FIND OUR NEW HOUSE?
HE JUST WILL, HONEY.
BUT HOW?
WHY, WITH HIS MAGIC, LITTLE GIRL.
AFTERNOON, MRS. SCHULLER.

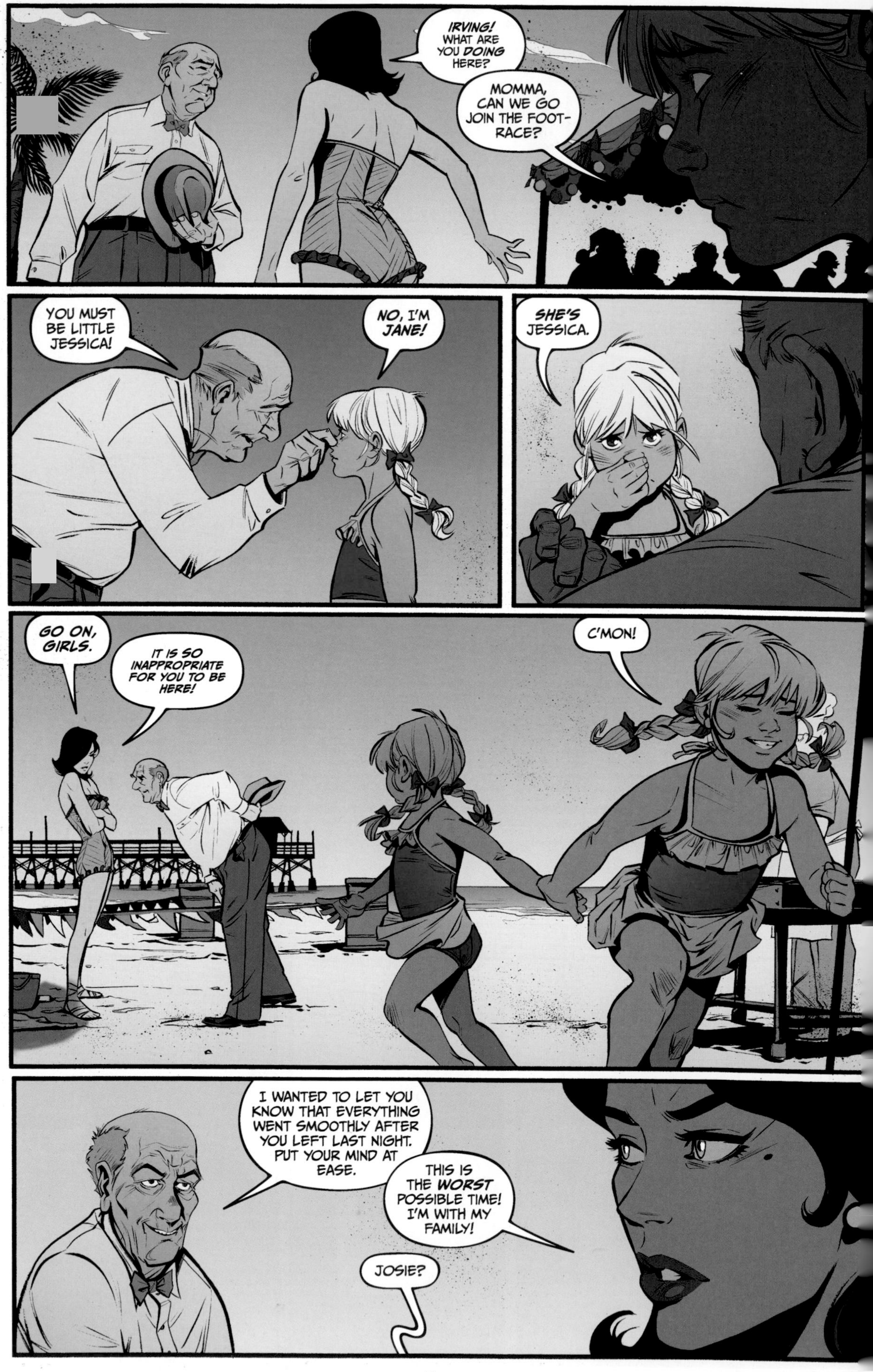
IRVING! WHAT ARE YOU DOING HERE?
MOMMA, CAN WE GO JOIN THE FOOT-RACE?
YOU MUST BE LITTLE JESSICA!
NO, I'M JANE!
SHE'S JESSICA.
GO ON, GIRLS.
IT IS SO INAPPROPRIATE FOR YOU TO BE HERE!
C'MON!
I WANTED TO LET YOU KNOW THAT EVERYTHING WENT SMOOTHLY AFTER YOU LEFT LAST NIGHT. PUT YOUR MIND AT EASE.
THIS IS THE WORST POSSIBLE TIME! I'M WITH MY FAMILY!
JOSIE?

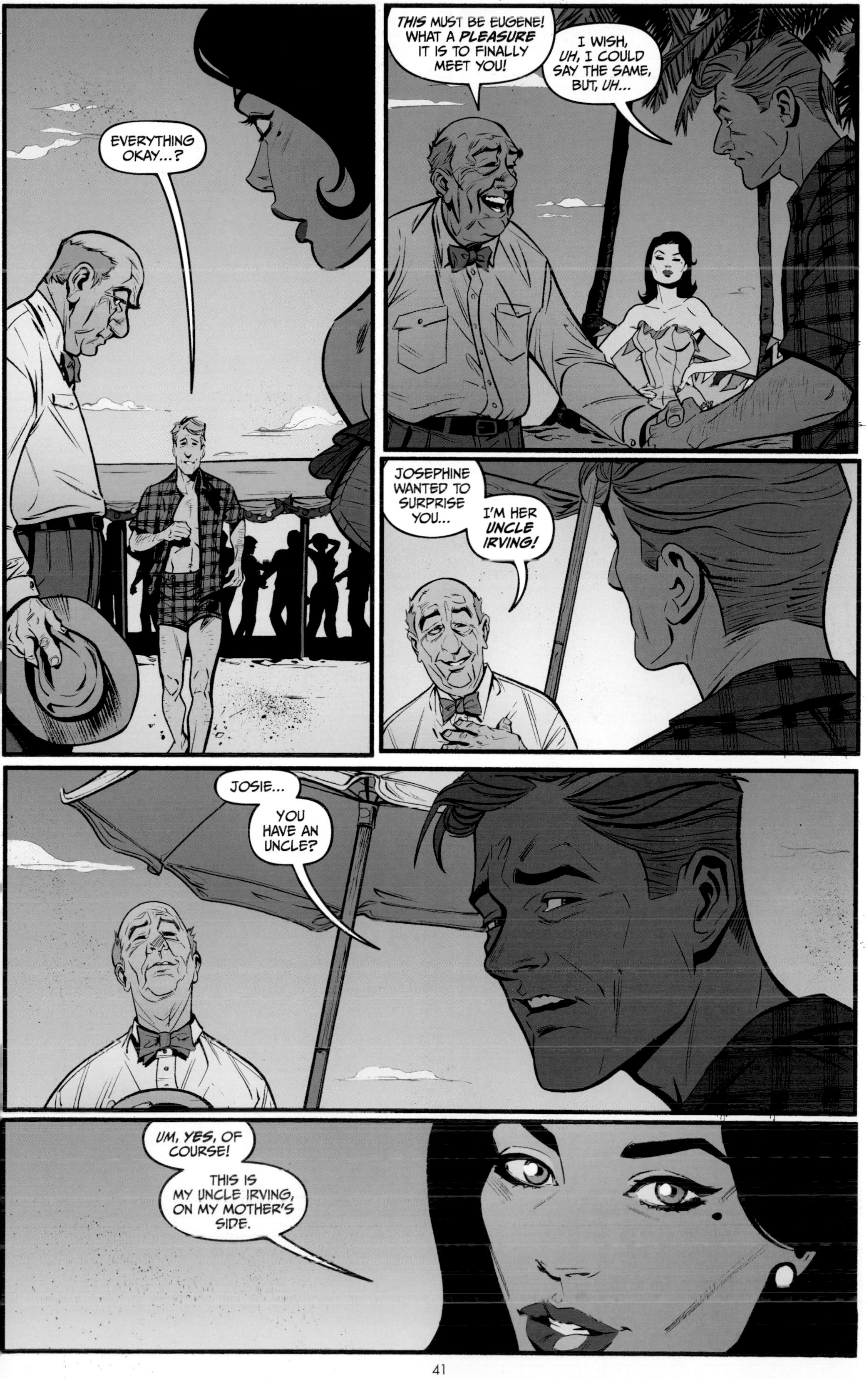
EVERYTHING OKAY...?
THIS MUST BE EUGENE! WHAT A PLEASURE IT IS TO FINALLY MEET YOU!
I WISH, UH, I COULD SAY THE SAME, BUT, UH...
JOSEPHINE WANTED TO SURPRISE YOU...
I'M HER UNCLE IRVING!
JOSIE...
YOU HAVE AN UNCLE?
UM, YES, OF COURSE!
THIS IS MY UNCLE IRVING, ON MY MOTHER'S SIDE.

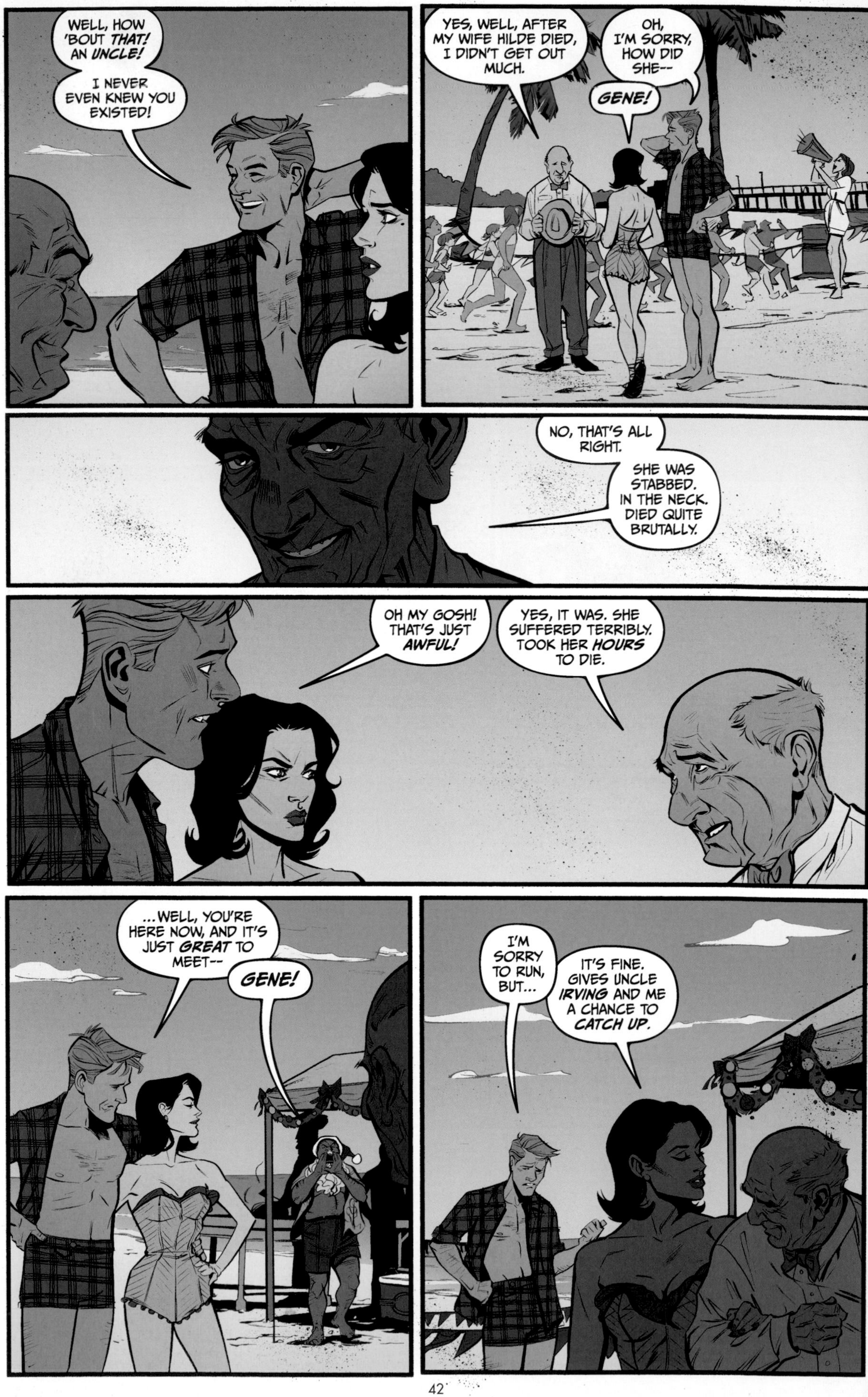
WELL, HOW 'BOUT THAT! AN UNCLE!
I NEVER EVEN KNEW YOU EXISTED!
YES, WELL, AFTER MY WIFE HILDE DIED, I DIDN'T GET OUT MUCH.
OH, I'M SORRY, HOW DID SHE--
GENE!
NO, THAT'S ALL RIGHT.
SHE WAS STABBED. IN THE NECK. DIED QUITE BRUTALLY.
OH MY GOSH! THAT'S JUST AWFUL!
YES, IT WAS. SHE SUFFERED TERRIBLY. TOOK HER HOURS TO DIE.
...WELL, YOU'RE HERE NOW, AND IT'S JUST GREAT TO MEET--
GENE!
I'M SORRY TO RUN, BUT...
IT'S FINE. GIVES UNCLE IRVING AND ME A CHANCE TO CATCH UP.

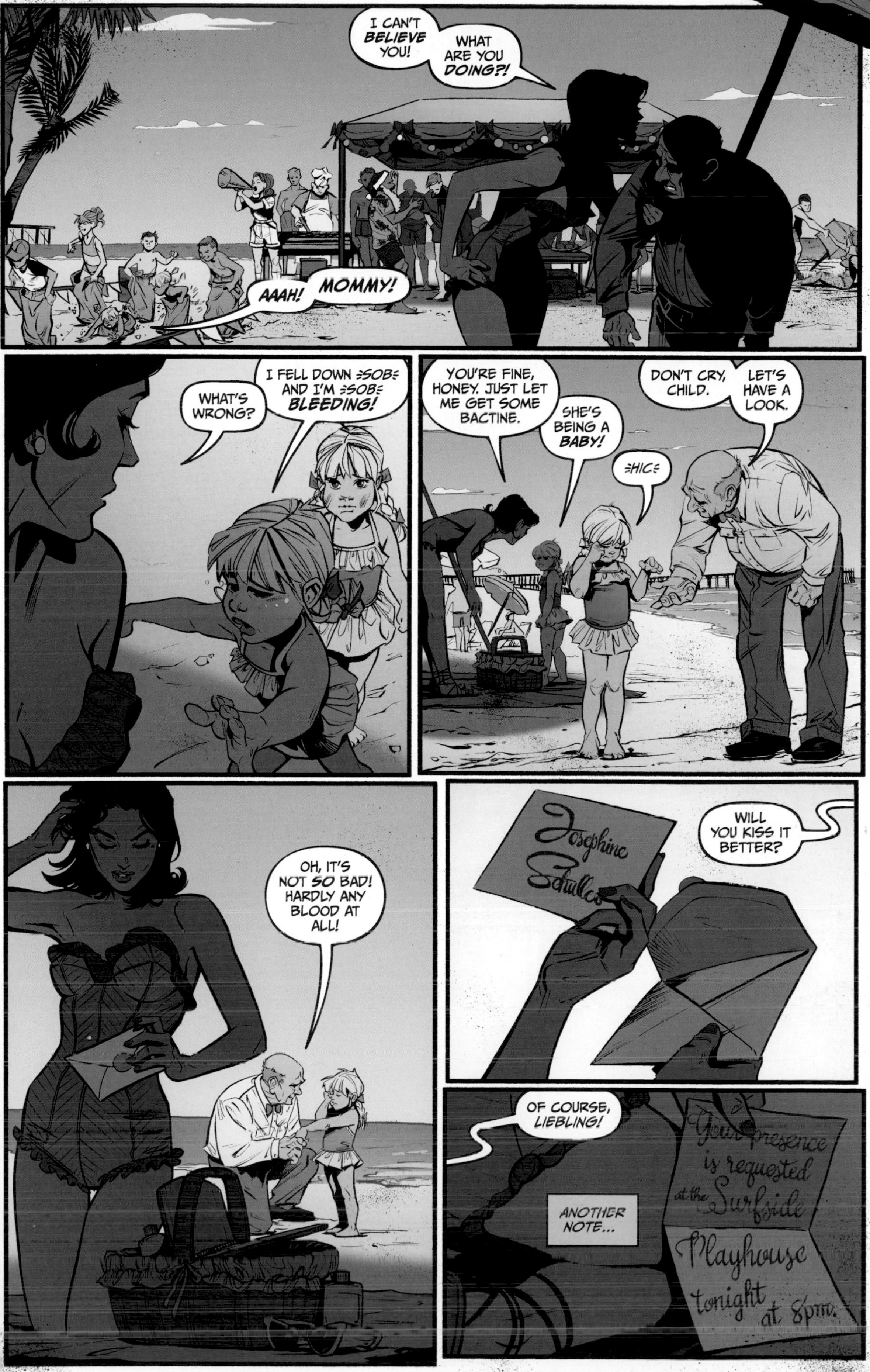
I CAN'T BELIEVE YOU!
WHAT ARE YOU DOING?!
AAAH!
MOMMY!
WHAT'S WRONG?
I FELL DOWN *SOB* AND I'M *SOB* BLEEDING!
YOU'RE FINE, HONEY. JUST LET ME GET SOME BACTINE.
SHE'S BEING A BABY!
HIC
DON'T CRY, CHILD.
LET'S HAVE A LOOK.
OH, IT'S NOT SO BAD! HARDLY ANY BLOOD AT ALL!
Josephine Schuller
WILL YOU KISS IT BETTER?
OF COURSE, LIEBLING!
ANOTHER NOTE...
Your presence is requested at the Surfside Playhouse tonight at 8pm.

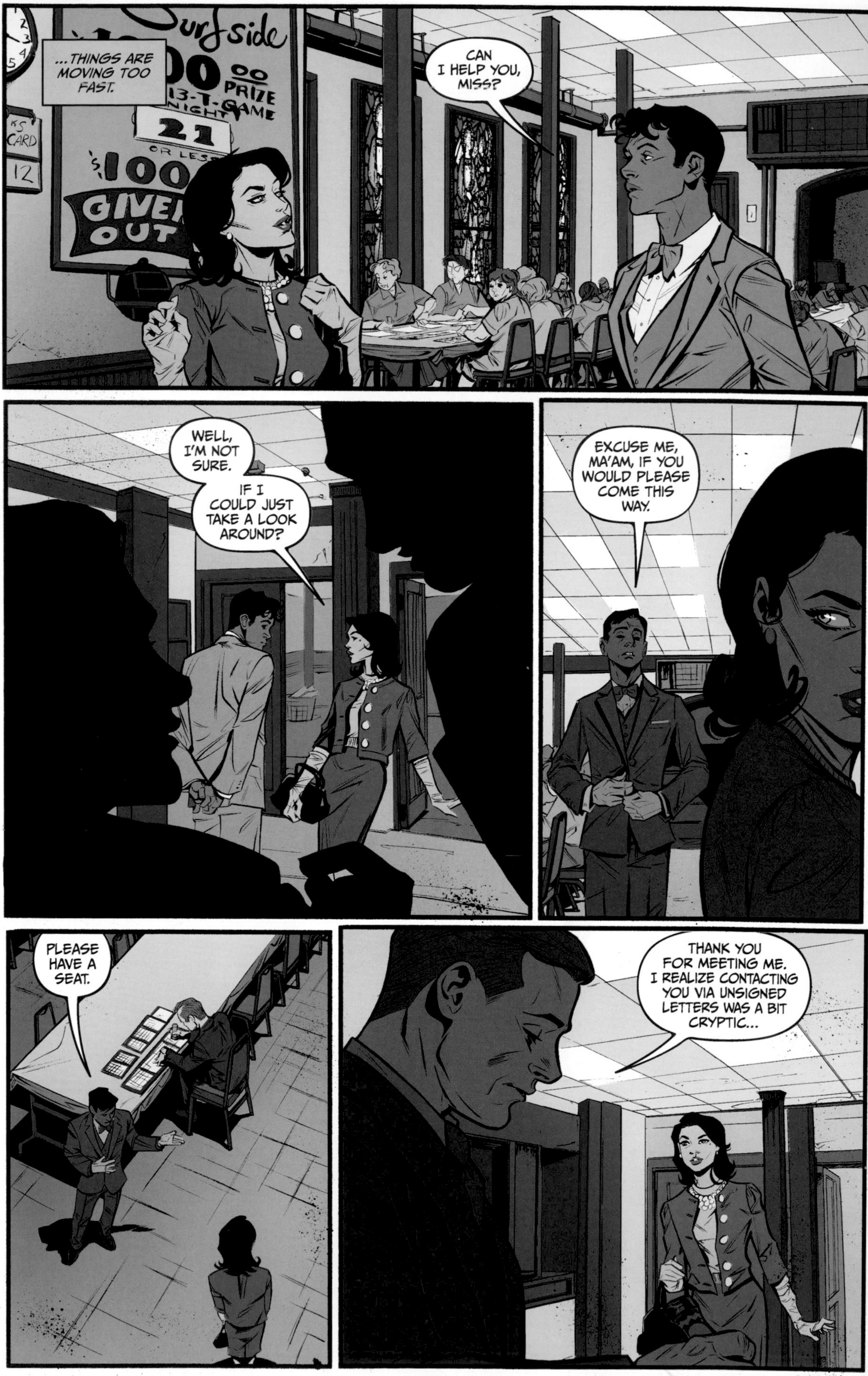

Surfside
00 00 PRIZE
13-T-GAME
NIGHT
21
OR LESS
$100
GIVEN OUT
12
...THINGS ARE MOVING TOO FAST.
CAN I HELP YOU, MISS?
WELL, I'M NOT SURE.
IF I COULD JUST TAKE A LOOK AROUND?
EXCUSE ME, MA'AM, IF YOU WOULD PLEASE COME THIS WAY.
PLEASE HAVE A SEAT.
THANK YOU FOR MEETING ME. I REALIZE CONTACTING YOU VIA UNSIGNED LETTERS WAS A BIT CRYPTIC...

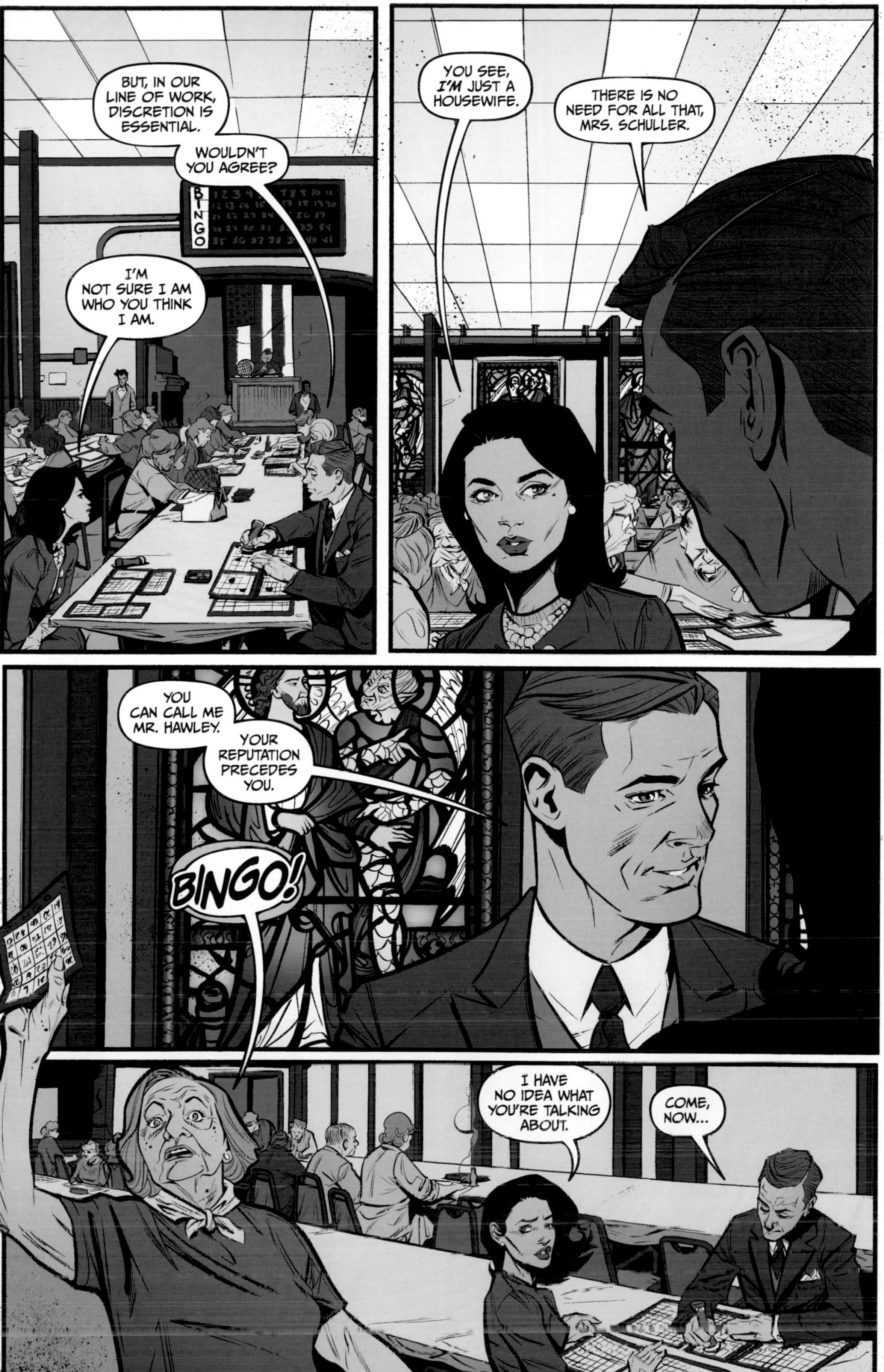

BUT, IN OUR LINE OF WORK, DISCRETION IS ESSENTIAL.
WOULDN'T YOU AGREE?
BINGO
I'M NOT SURE I AM WHO YOU THINK I AM.
YOU SEE, *I'M* JUST A HOUSEWIFE.
THERE IS NO NEED FOR ALL THAT, MRS. SCHULLER.
YOU CAN CALL ME MR. HAWLEY.
YOUR REPUTATION PRECEDES YOU.
BINGO!
I HAVE NO IDEA WHAT YOU'RE TALKING ABOUT.
COME, NOW...

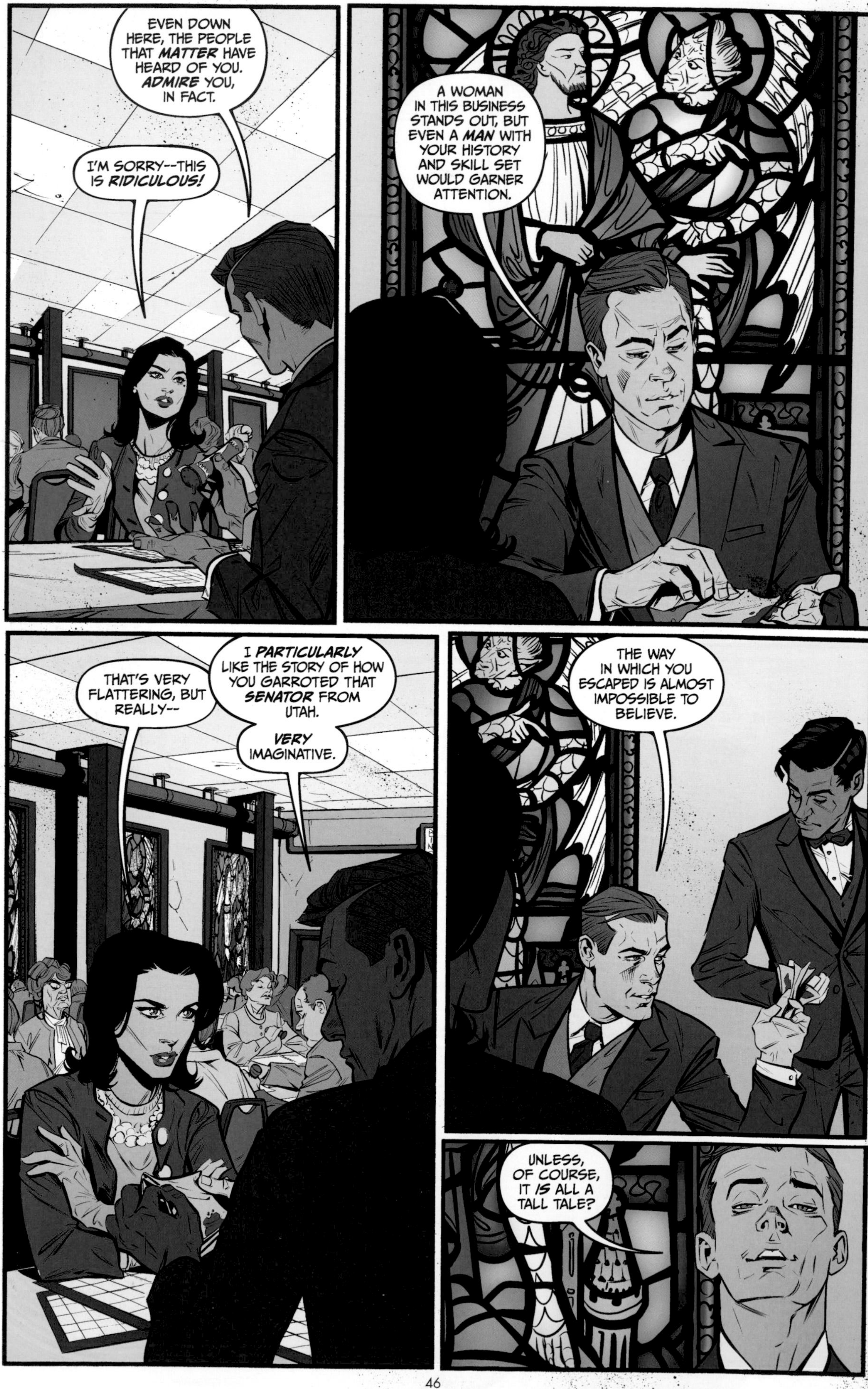
EVEN DOWN HERE, THE PEOPLE THAT MATTER HAVE HEARD OF YOU. ADMIRE YOU, IN FACT.
I'M SORRY--THIS IS RIDICULOUS!
A WOMAN IN THIS BUSINESS STANDS OUT, BUT EVEN A MAN WITH YOUR HISTORY AND SKILL SET WOULD GARNER ATTENTION.
THAT'S VERY FLATTERING, BUT REALLY--
I PARTICULARLY LIKE THE STORY OF HOW YOU GARROTED THAT SENATOR FROM UTAH.
VERY IMAGINATIVE.
THE WAY IN WHICH YOU ESCAPED IS ALMOST IMPOSSIBLE TO BELIEVE.
UNLESS, OF COURSE, IT IS ALL A TALL TALE?

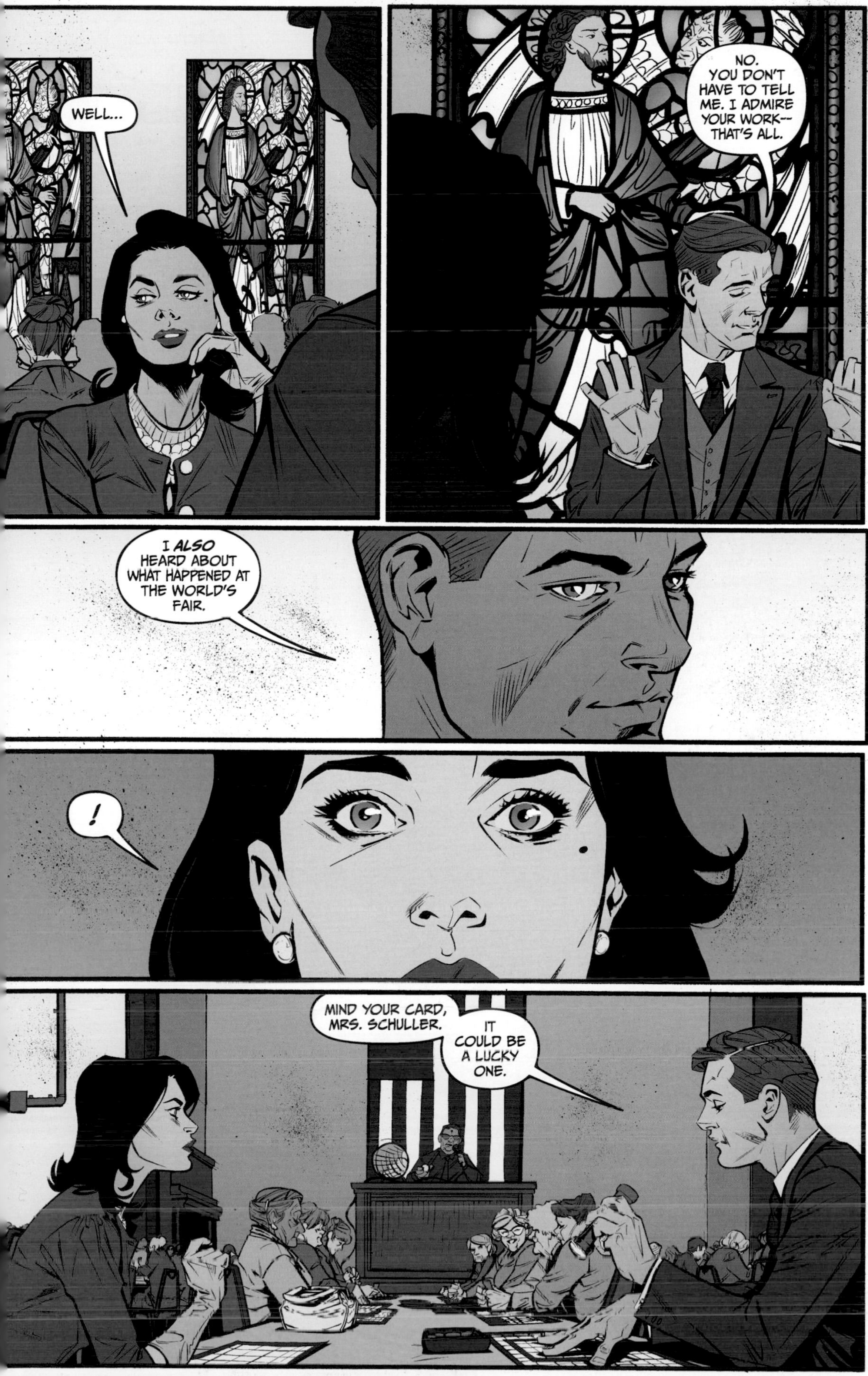
WELL...
NO. YOU DON'T HAVE TO TELL ME. I ADMIRE YOUR WORK-- THAT'S ALL.
I *ALSO* HEARD ABOUT WHAT HAPPENED AT THE WORLD'S FAIR.
!
MIND YOUR CARD, MRS. SCHULLER.
IT COULD BE A LUCKY ONE.

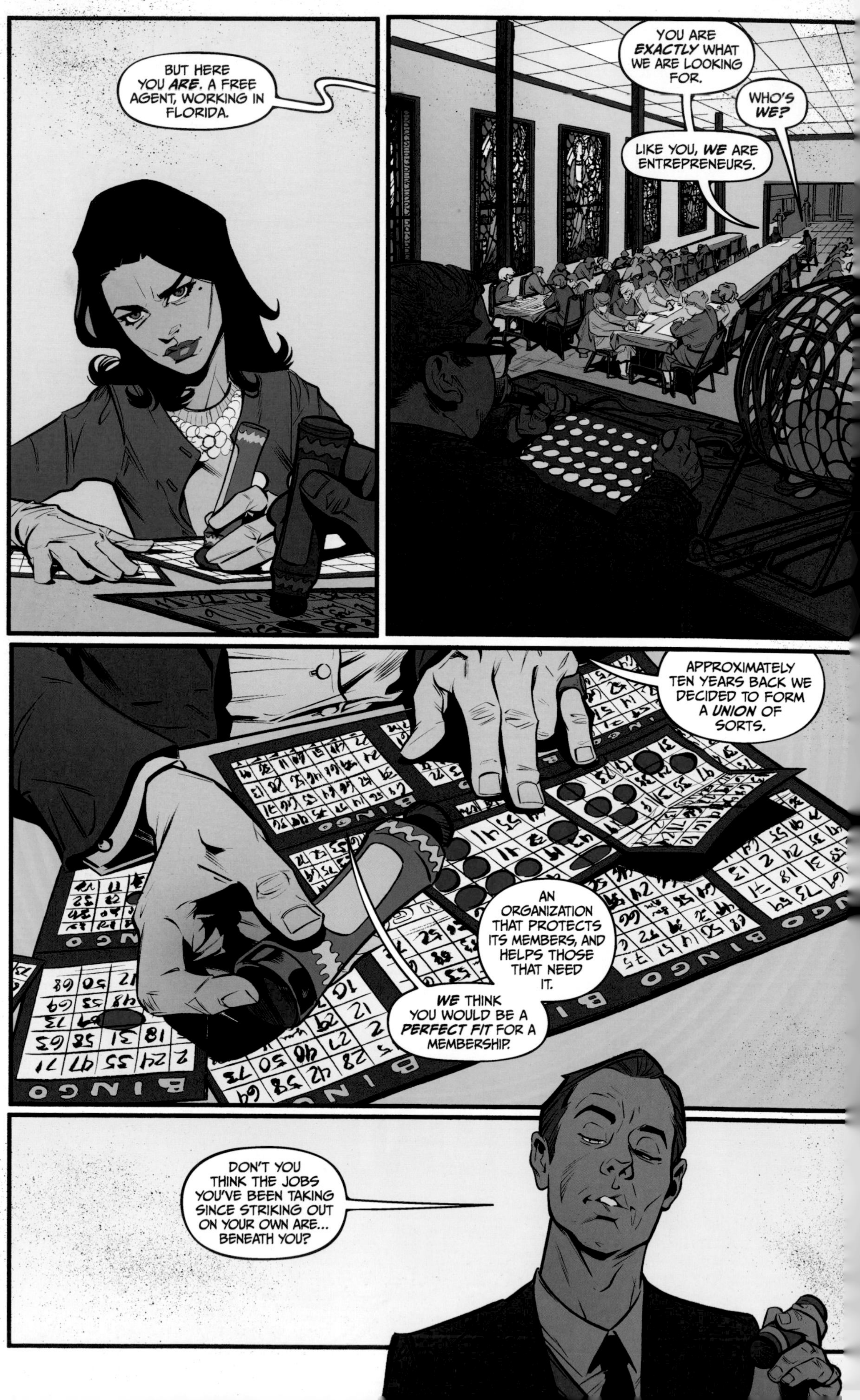
BUT HERE YOU ARE. A FREE AGENT, WORKING IN FLORIDA.
YOU ARE EXACTLY WHAT WE ARE LOOKING FOR.
WHO'S WE?
LIKE YOU, WE ARE ENTREPRENEURS.
APPROXIMATELY TEN YEARS BACK WE DECIDED TO FORM A UNION OF SORTS.
AN ORGANIZATION THAT PROTECTS ITS MEMBERS, AND HELPS THOSE THAT NEED IT.
WE THINK YOU WOULD BE A PERFECT FIT FOR A MEMBERSHIP.
DON'T YOU THINK THE JOBS YOU'VE BEEN TAKING SINCE STRIKING OUT ON YOUR OWN ARE... BENEATH YOU?

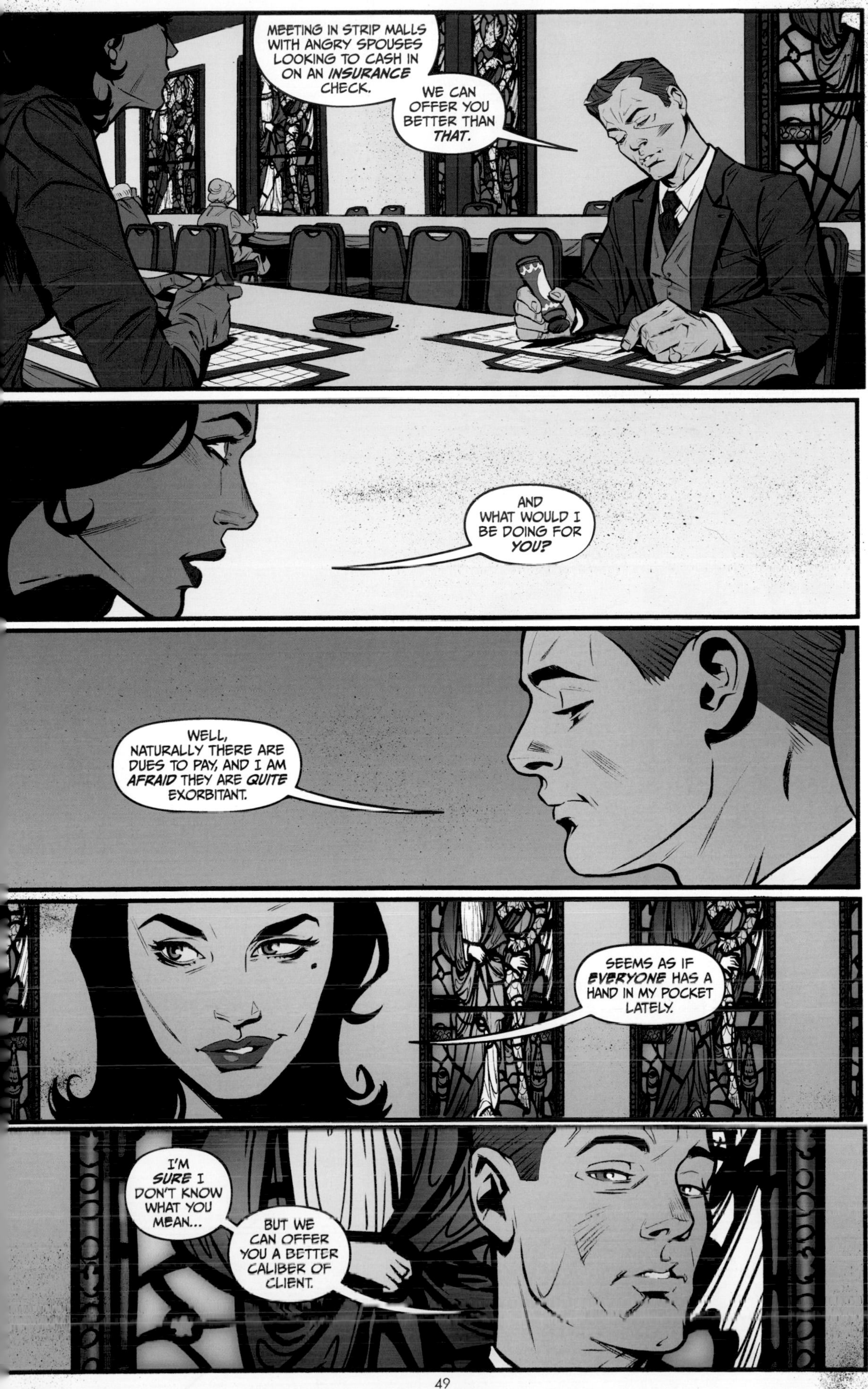
MEETING IN STRIP MALLS WITH ANGRY SPOUSES LOOKING TO CASH IN ON AN INSURANCE CHECK.
WE CAN OFFER YOU BETTER THAN THAT.
AND WHAT WOULD I BE DOING FOR YOU?
WELL, NATURALLY THERE ARE DUES TO PAY, AND I AM AFRAID THEY ARE QUITE EXORBITANT.
SEEMS AS IF EVERYONE HAS A HAND IN MY POCKET LATELY.
I'M SURE I DON'T KNOW WHAT YOU MEAN...
BUT WE CAN OFFER YOU A BETTER CALIBER OF CLIENT.

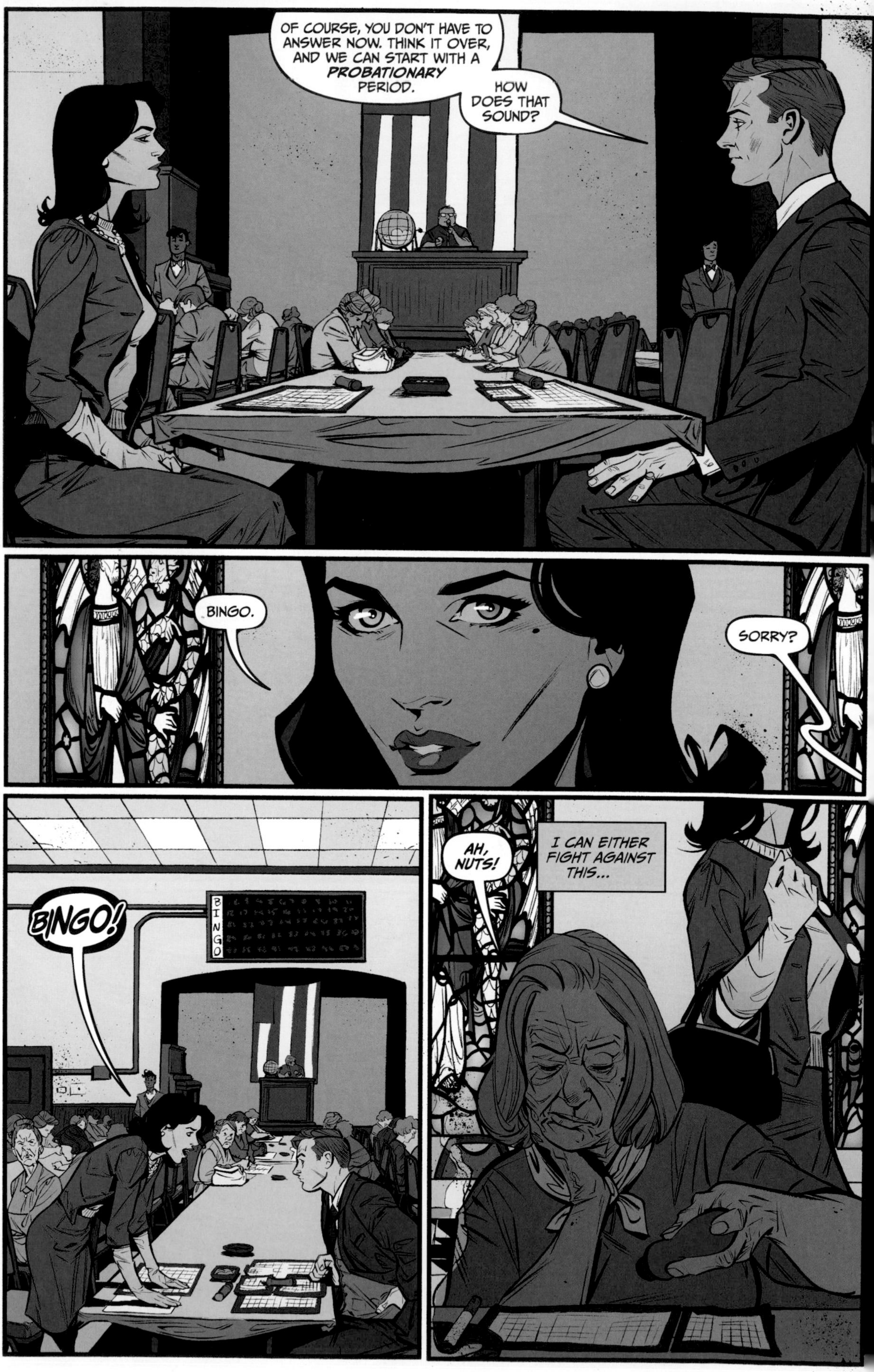
OF COURSE, YOU DON'T HAVE TO ANSWER NOW. THINK IT OVER, AND WE CAN START WITH A *PROBATIONARY* PERIOD.
HOW DOES THAT SOUND?
BINGO.
SORRY?
BINGO!
AH, NUTS!
I CAN EITHER FIGHT AGAINST THIS...

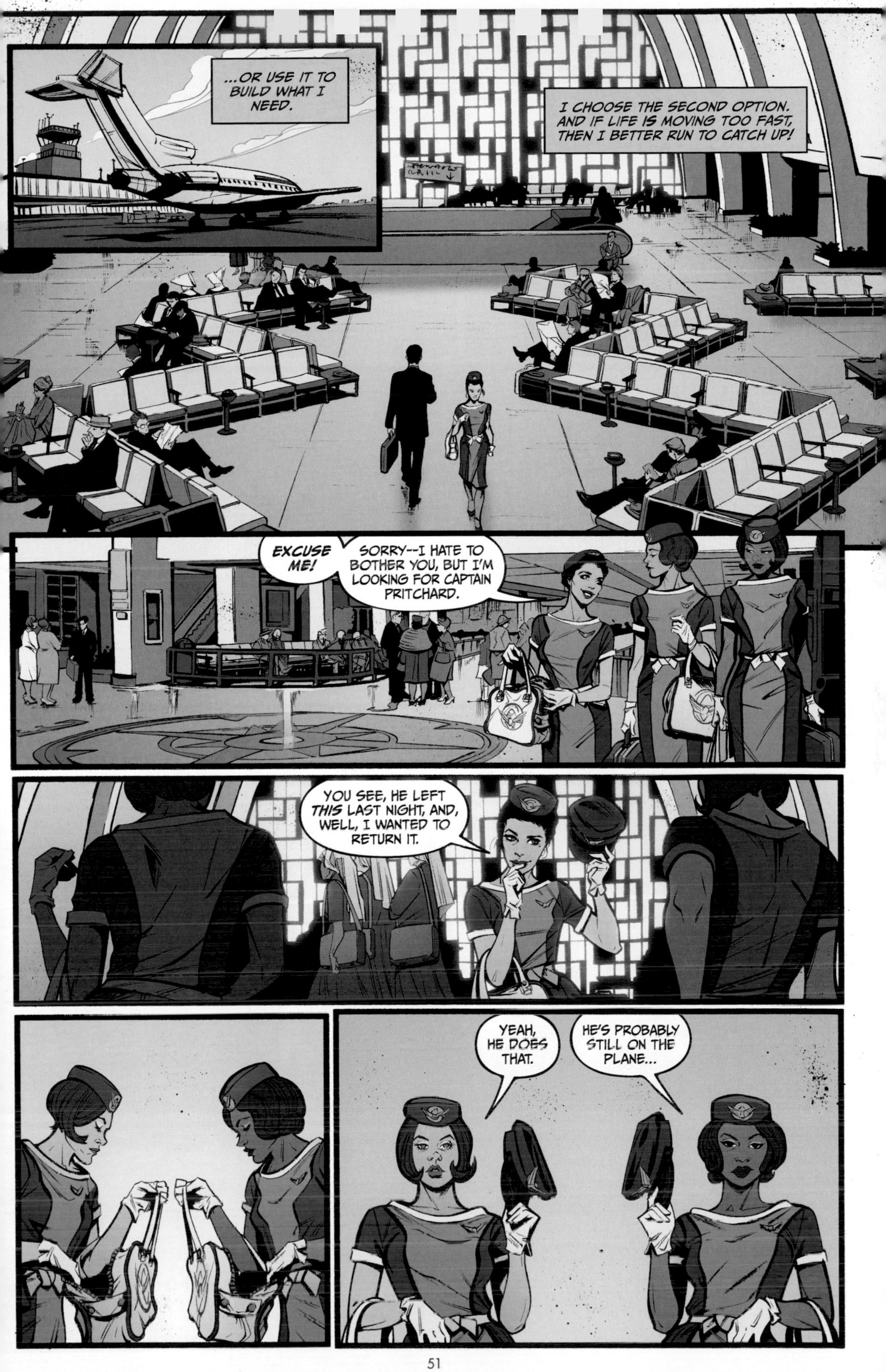
...OR USE IT TO BUILD WHAT I NEED.
I CHOOSE THE SECOND OPTION. AND IF LIFE IS MOVING TOO FAST, THEN I BETTER RUN TO CATCH UP!
EXCUSE ME!
SORRY--I HATE TO BOTHER YOU, BUT I'M LOOKING FOR CAPTAIN PRITCHARD.
YOU SEE, HE LEFT THIS LAST NIGHT, AND, WELL, I WANTED TO RETURN IT.
YEAH, HE DOES THAT.
HE'S PROBABLY STILL ON THE PLANE...

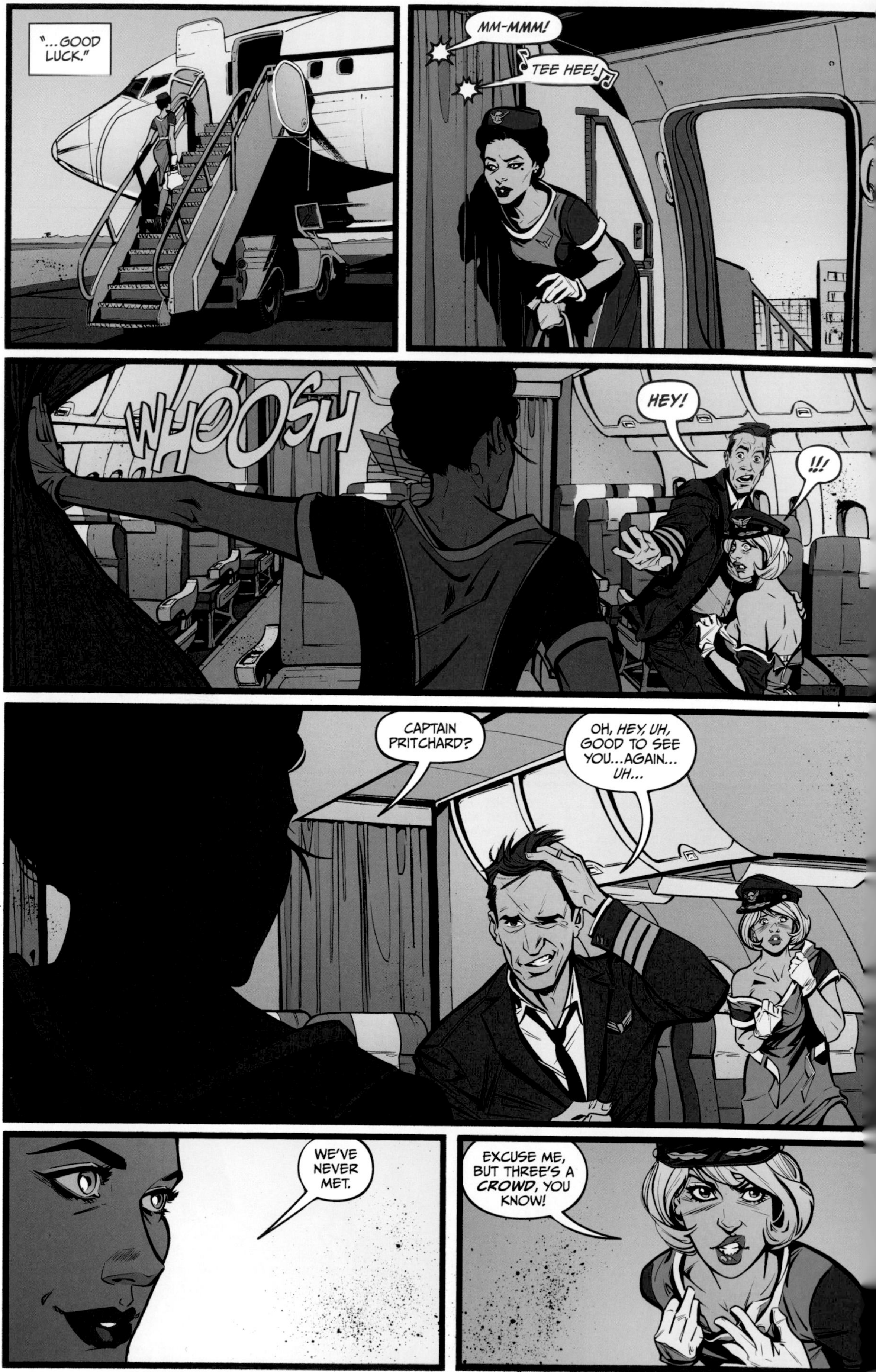
"...GOOD LUCK."
MM-MMM!
TEE HEE!
WHOOSH
HEY!
!!!
CAPTAIN PRITCHARD?
OH, HEY, UH, GOOD TO SEE YOU...AGAIN... UH...
WE'VE NEVER MET.
EXCUSE ME, BUT THREE'S A CROWD, YOU KNOW!

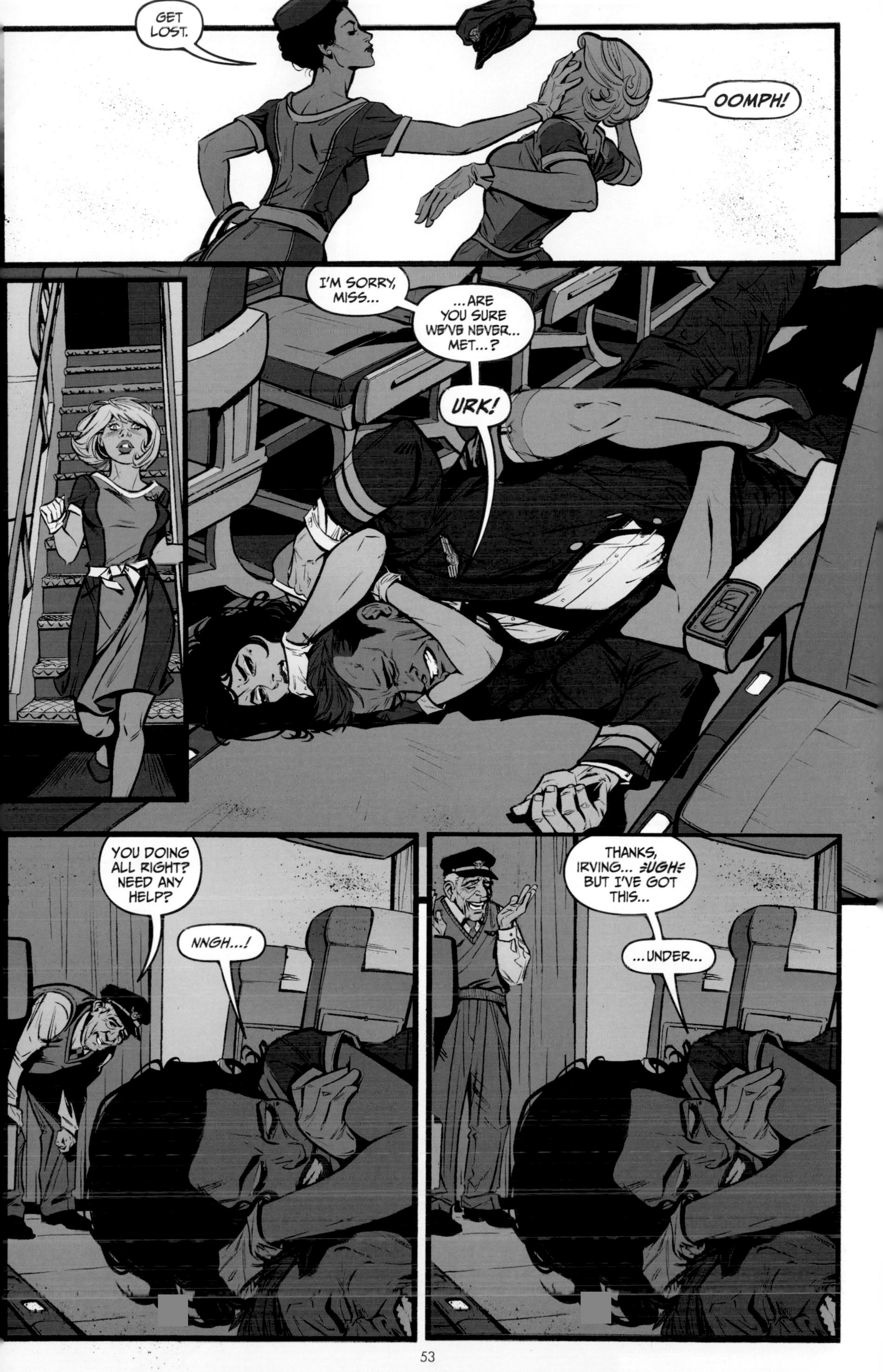
GET LOST.
OOMPH!
I'M SORRY, MISS...
...ARE YOU SURE WE'VE NEVER... MET...?
URK!
YOU DOING ALL RIGHT? NEED ANY HELP?
NNGH...!
THANKS, IRVING... UGH BUT I'VE GOT THIS...
...UNDER...

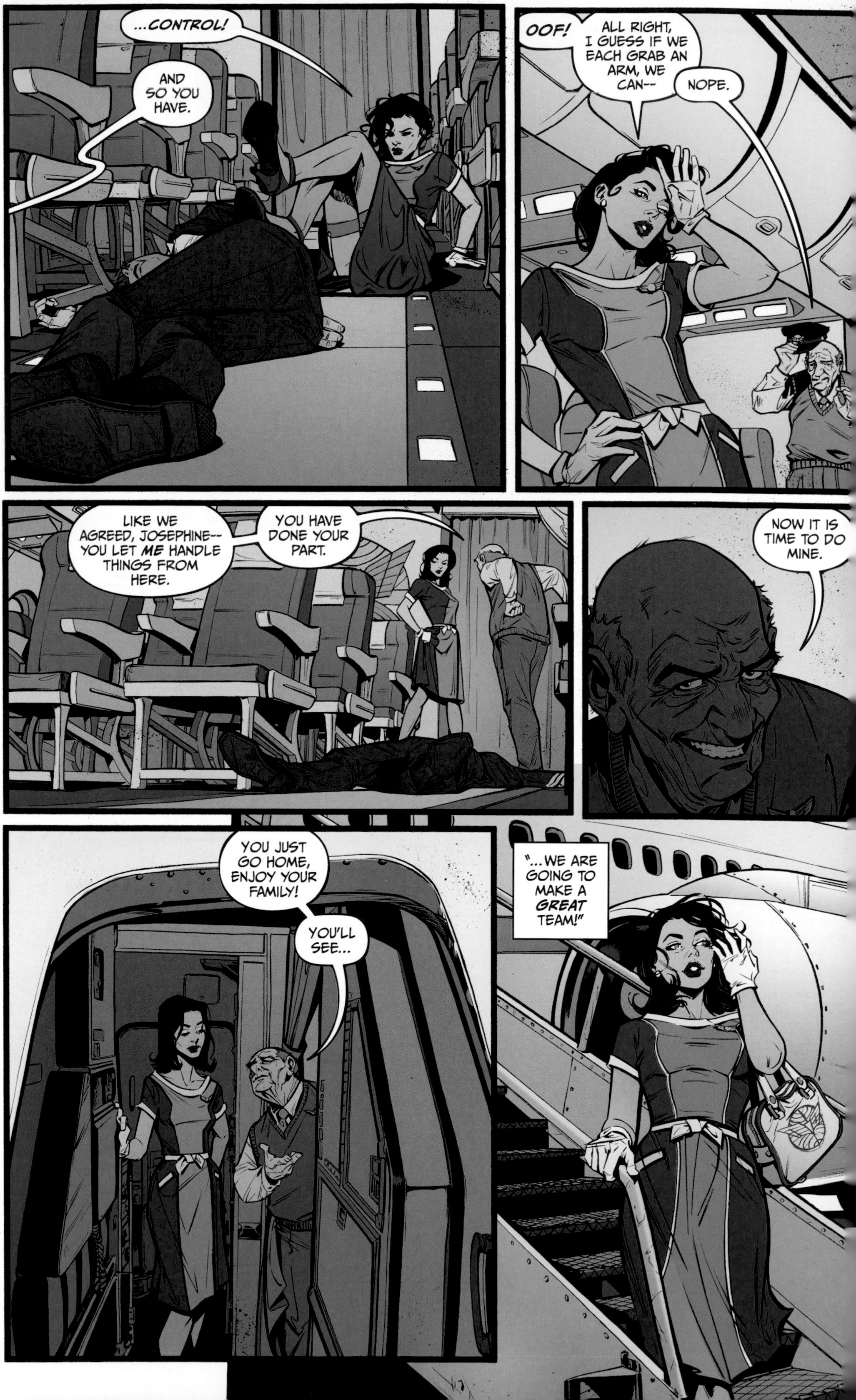
...CONTROL!
AND SO YOU HAVE.
OOF!
ALL RIGHT, I GUESS IF WE EACH GRAB AN ARM, WE CAN--
NOPE.
LIKE WE AGREED, JOSEPHINE-- YOU LET **ME** HANDLE THINGS FROM HERE.
YOU HAVE DONE YOUR PART.
NOW IT IS TIME TO DO MINE.
YOU JUST GO HOME, ENJOY YOUR FAMILY!
YOU'LL SEE...
"...WE ARE GOING TO MAKE A ***GREAT*** TEAM!"

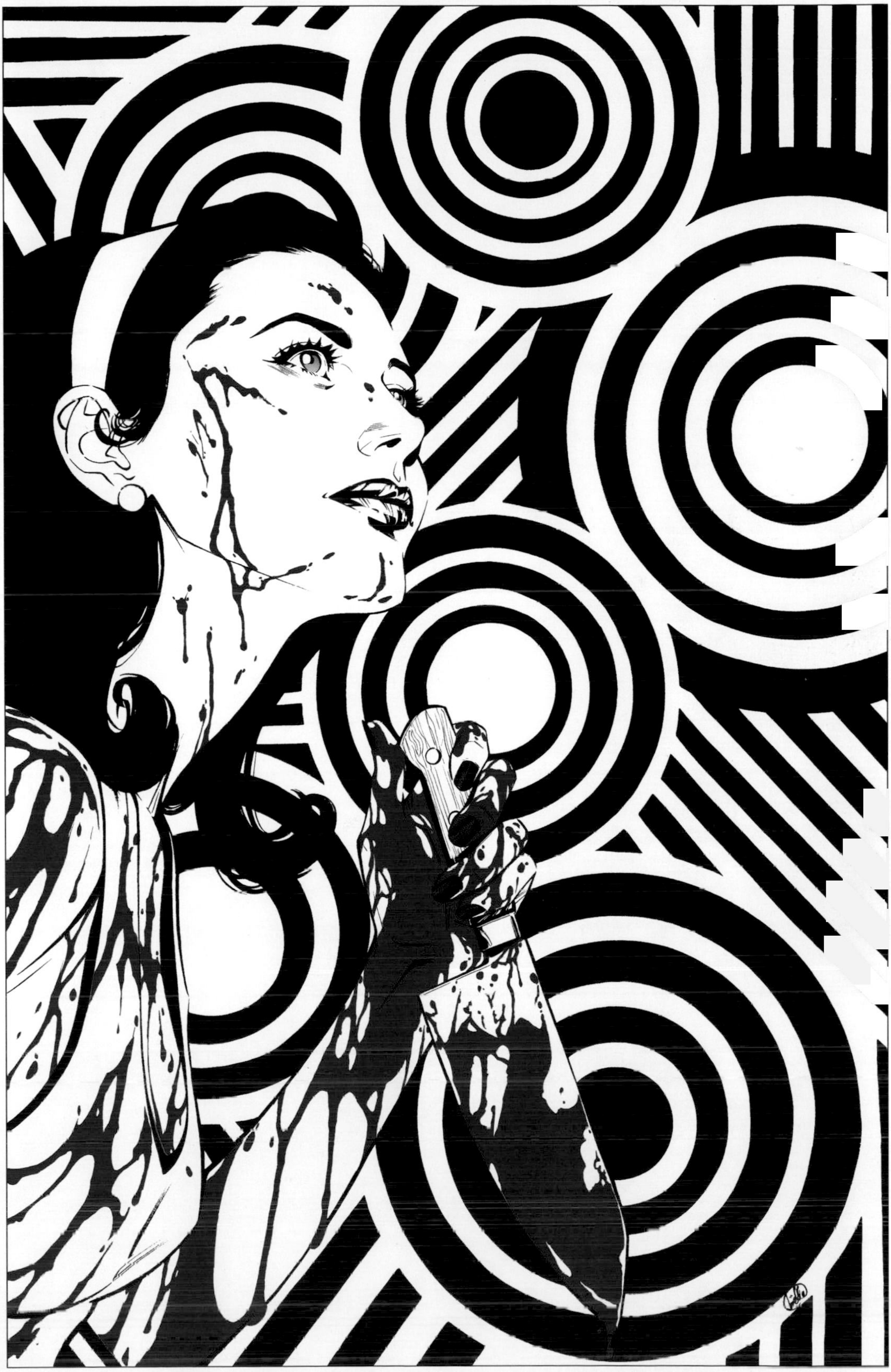

CHAPTER THREE

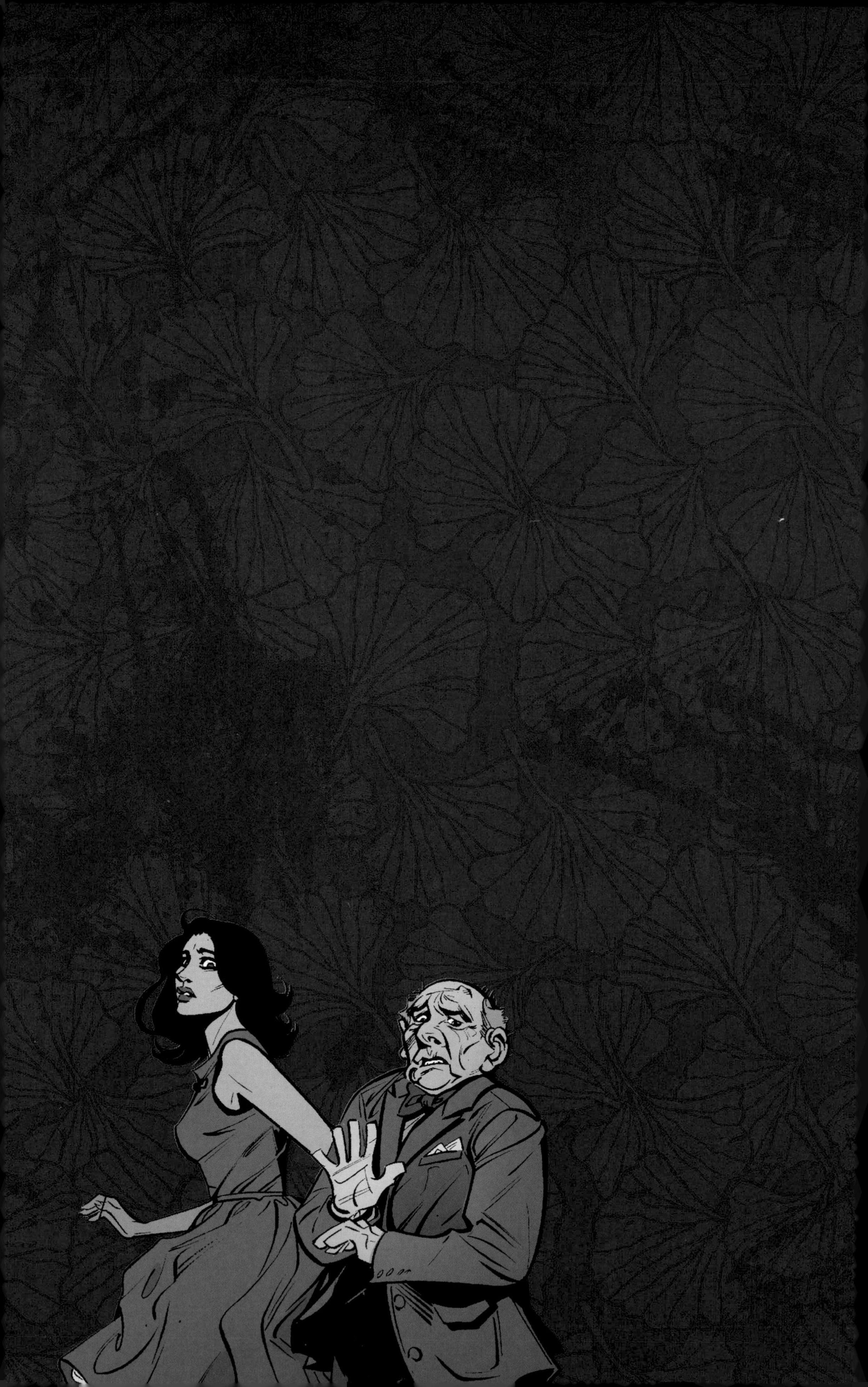

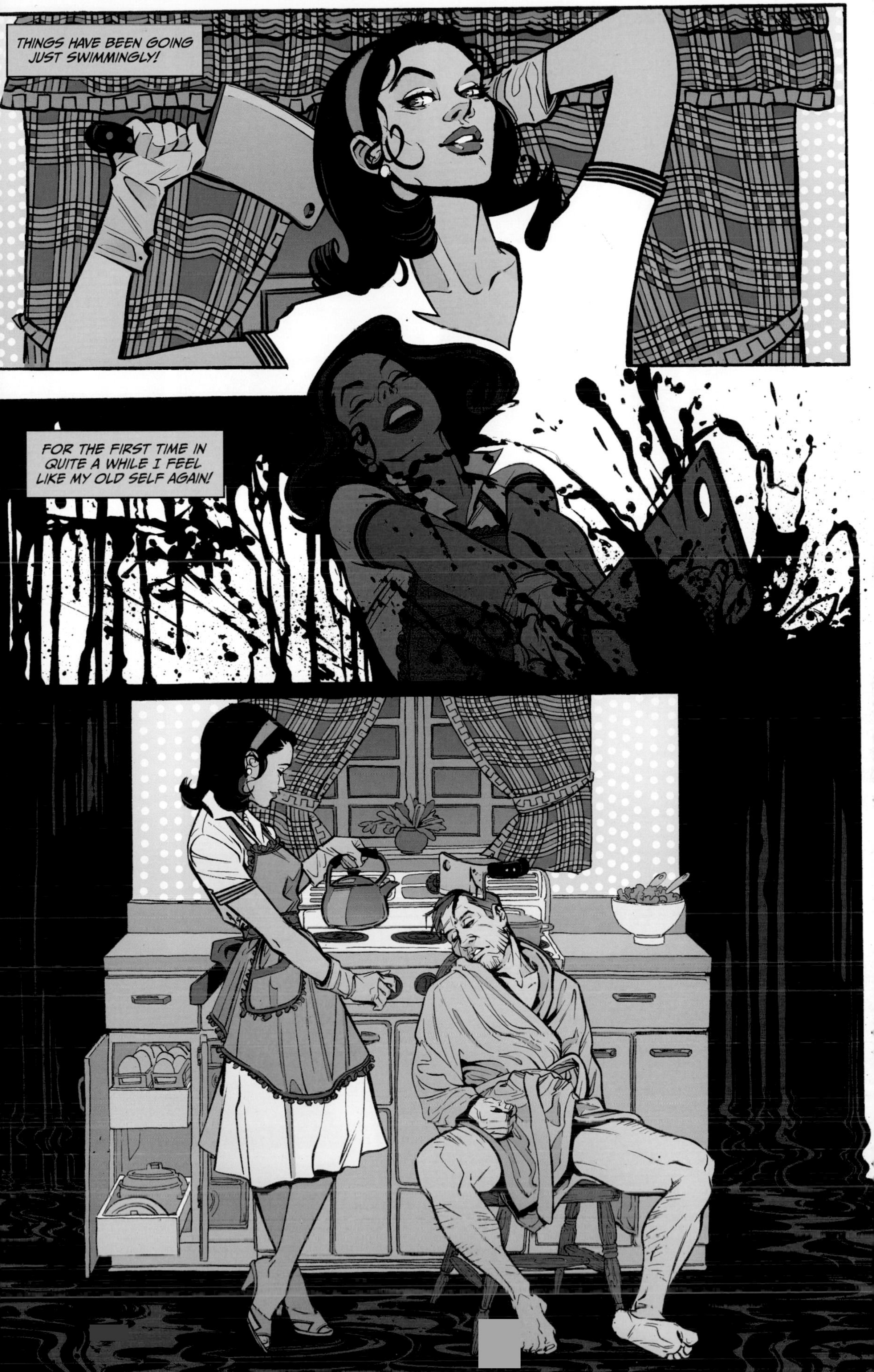
THINGS HAVE BEEN GOING JUST SWIMMINGLY!
FOR THE FIRST TIME IN QUITE A WHILE I FEEL LIKE MY OLD SELF AGAIN!

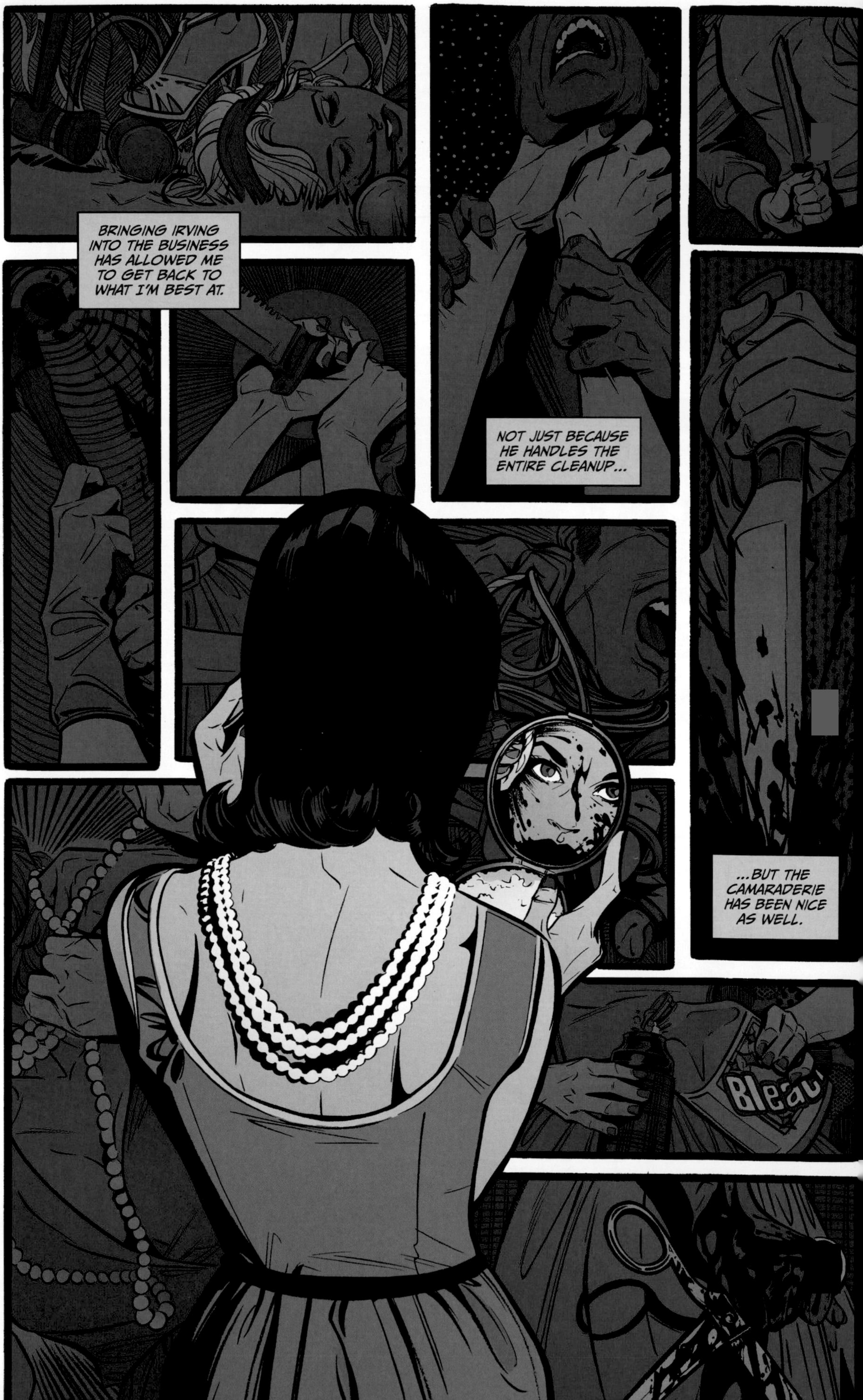
BRINGING IRVING INTO THE BUSINESS HAS ALLOWED ME TO GET BACK TO WHAT I'M BEST AT.
NOT JUST BECAUSE HE HANDLES THE ENTIRE CLEANUP...
...BUT THE CAMARADERIE HAS BEEN NICE AS WELL.

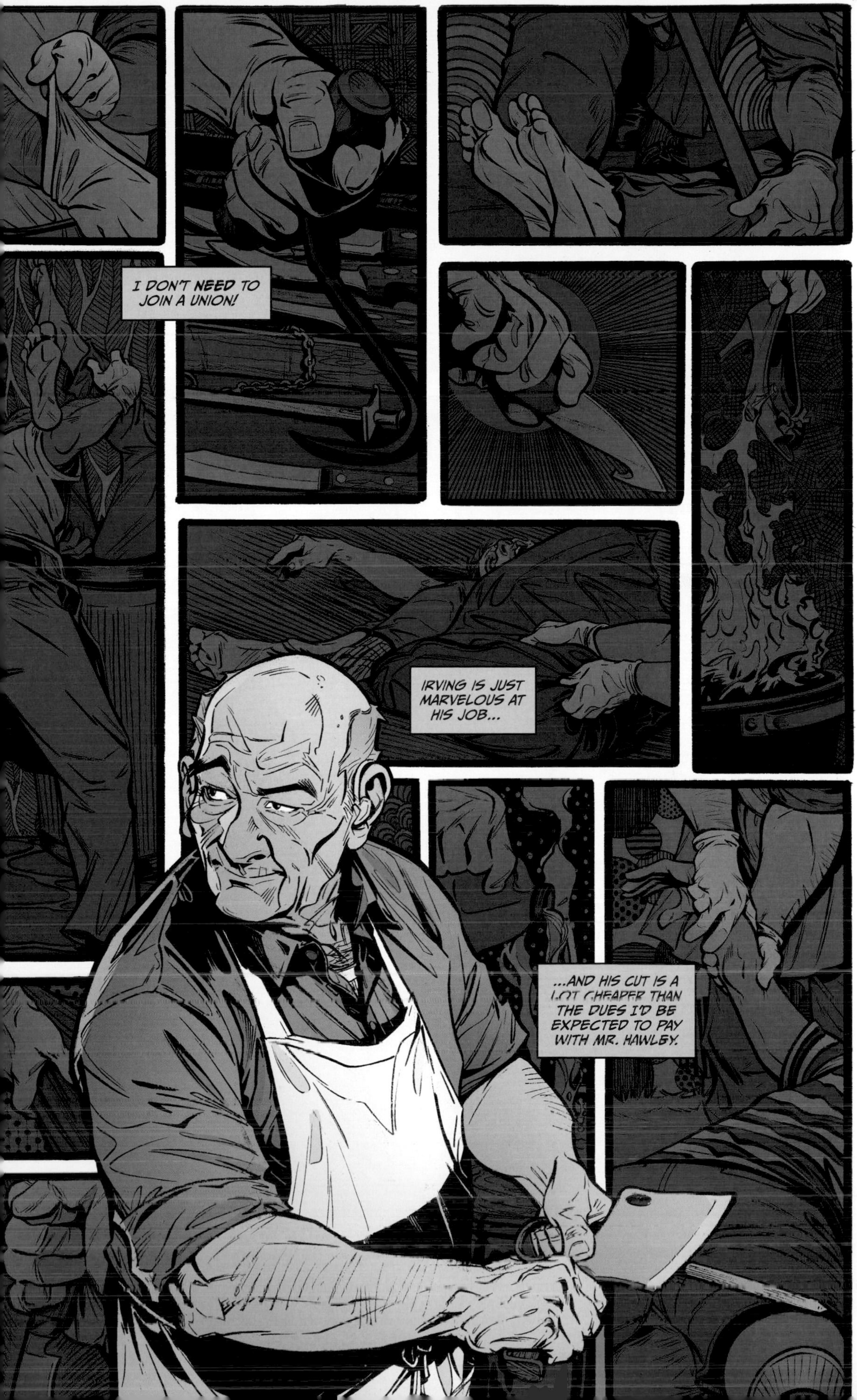
I DON'T NEED TO JOIN A UNION!
IRVING IS JUST MARVELOUS AT HIS JOB...
...AND HIS CUT IS A LOT CHEAPER THAN THE DUES I'D BE EXPECTED TO PAY WITH MR. HAWLEY.

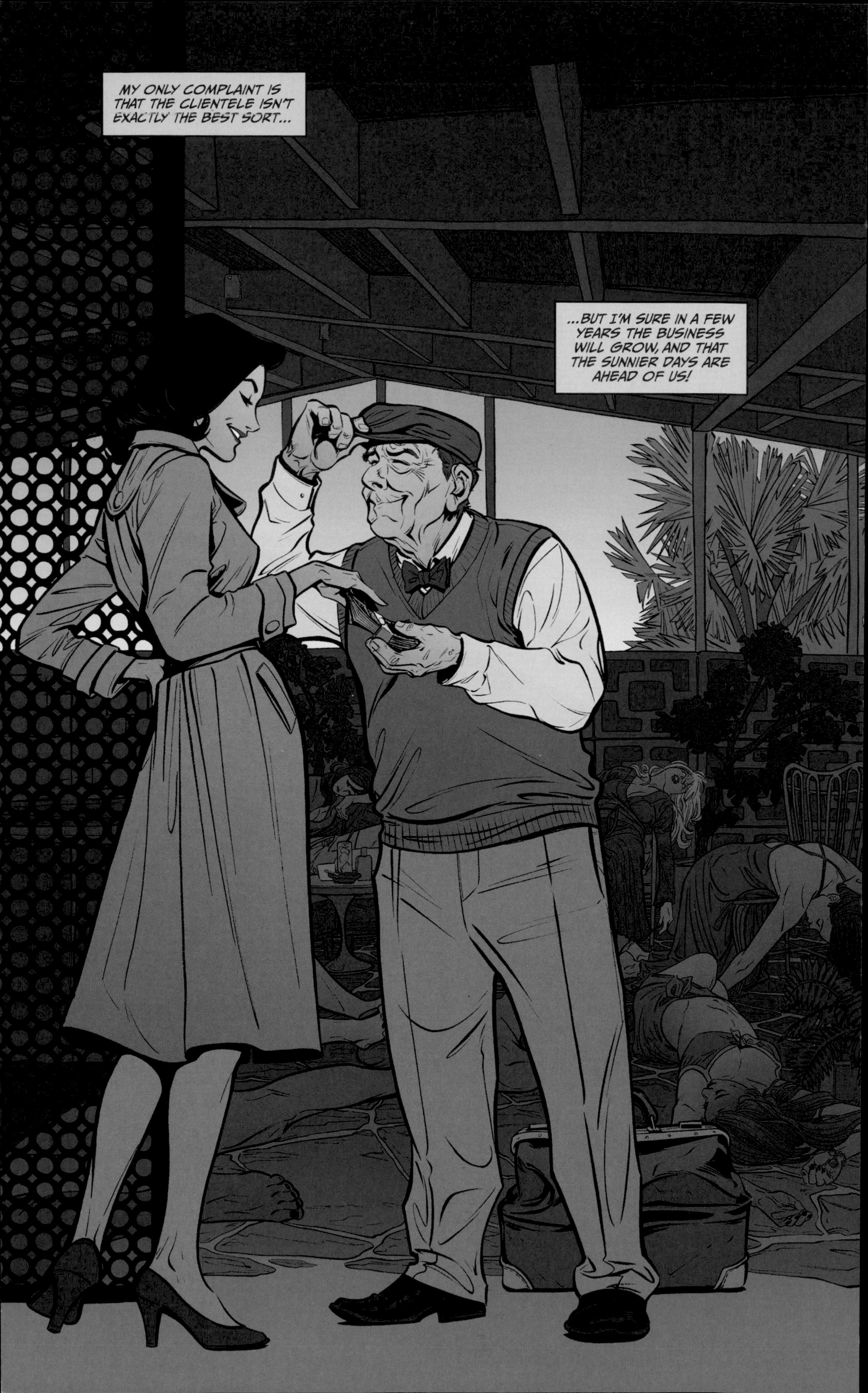
MY ONLY COMPLAINT IS THAT THE CLIENTELE ISN'T EXACTLY THE BEST SORT...
...BUT I'M SURE IN A FEW YEARS THE BUSINESS WILL GROW, AND THAT THE SUNNIER DAYS ARE AHEAD OF US!

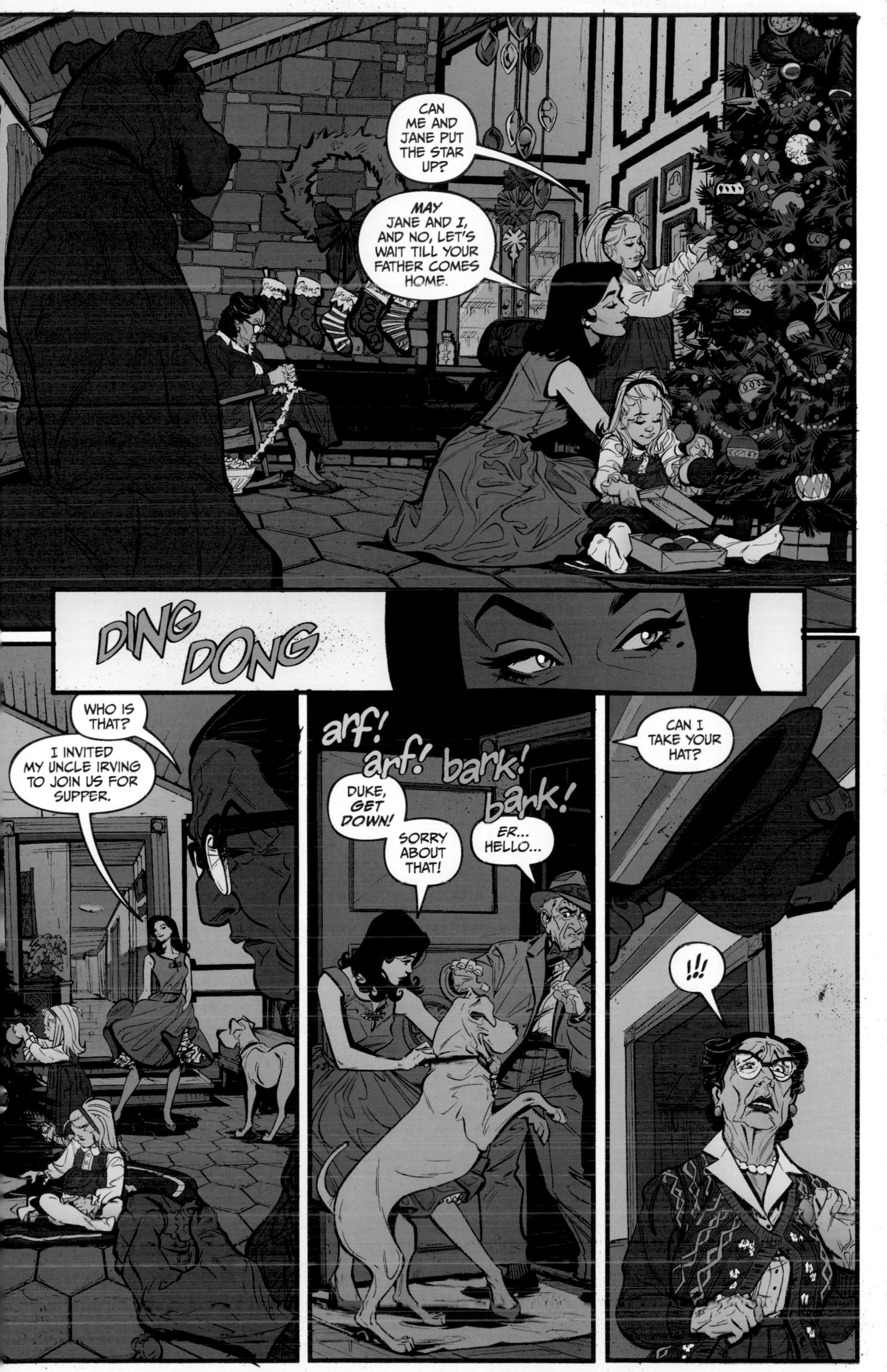

CAN ME AND JANE PUT THE STAR UP?
MAY JANE AND I, AND NO, LET'S WAIT TILL YOUR FATHER COMES HOME.
DING DONG
WHO IS THAT?
I INVITED MY UNCLE IRVING TO JOIN US FOR SUPPER.
arf! arf! bark! bark!
DUKE, GET DOWN!
SORRY ABOUT THAT!
ER... HELLO...
CAN I TAKE YOUR HAT?
!!!

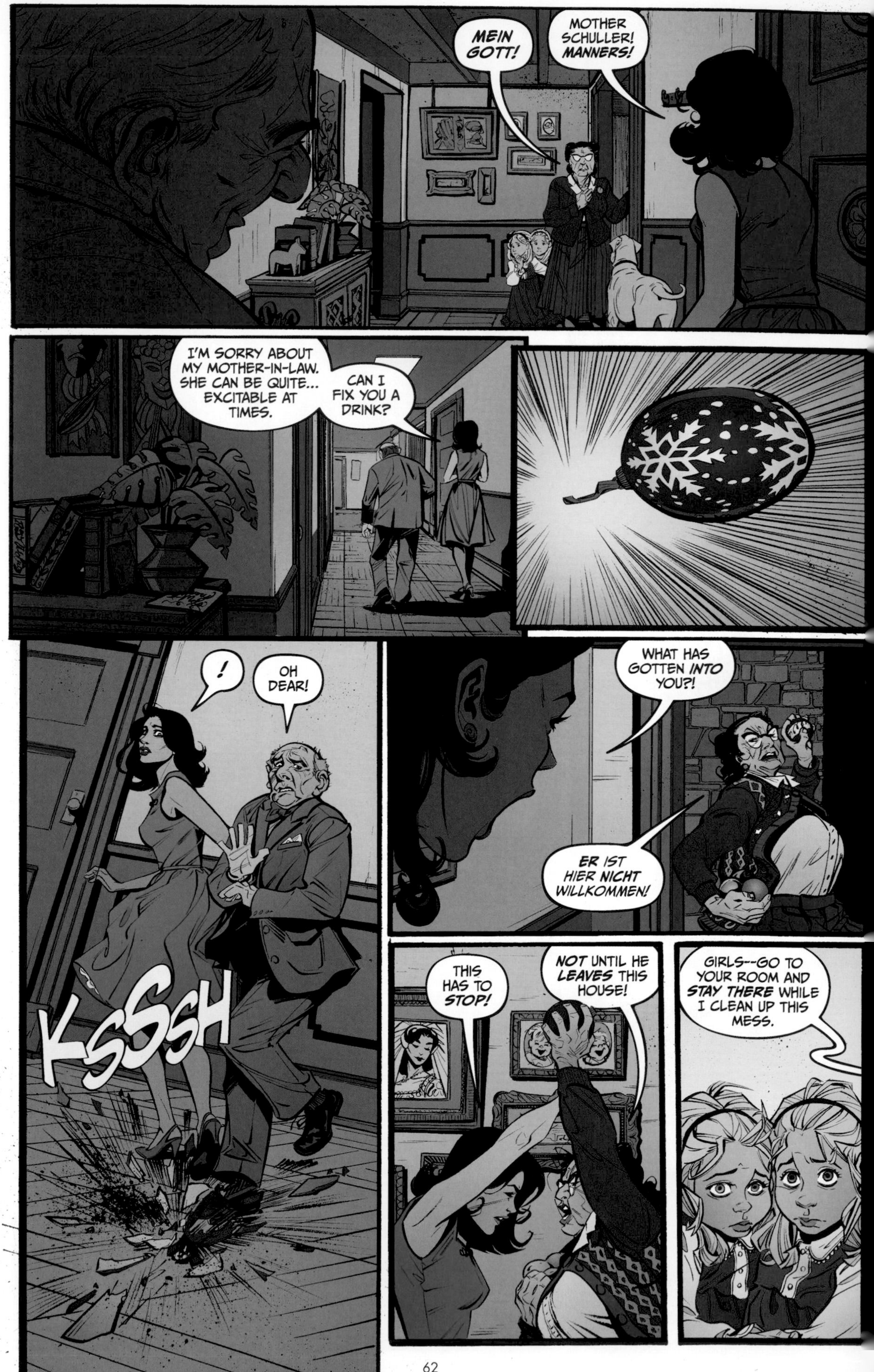
MEIN GOTT!
MOTHER SCHULLER! MANNERS!
I'M SORRY ABOUT MY MOTHER-IN-LAW. SHE CAN BE QUITE... EXCITABLE AT TIMES.
CAN I FIX YOU A DRINK?
!
OH DEAR!
KSSSH
WHAT HAS GOTTEN INTO YOU?!
ER IST HIER NICHT WILLKOMMEN!
THIS HAS TO STOP!
NOT UNTIL HE LEAVES THIS HOUSE!
GIRLS--GO TO YOUR ROOM AND STAY THERE WHILE I CLEAN UP THIS MESS.

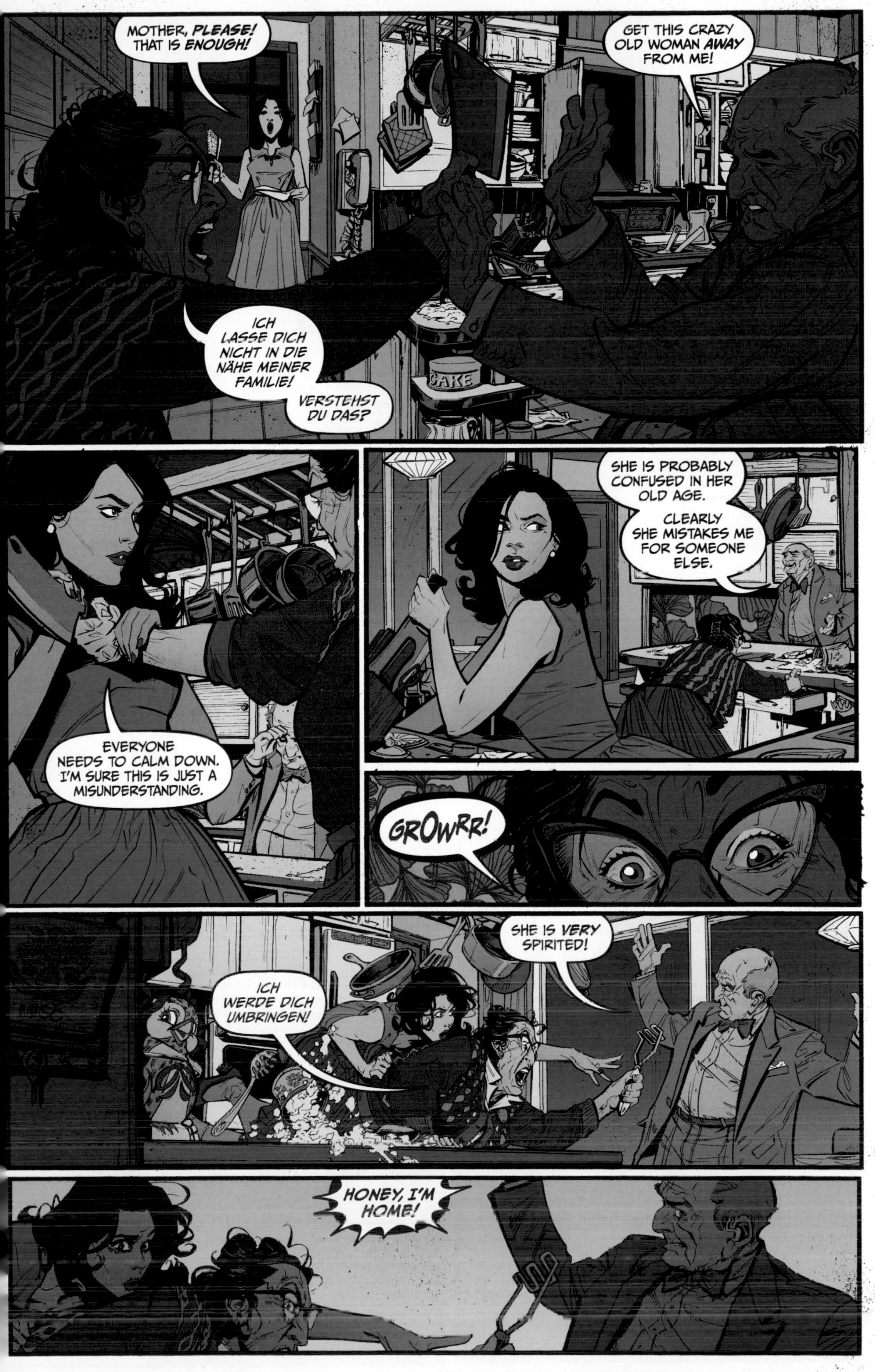
MOTHER, PLEASE! THAT IS ENOUGH!
GET THIS CRAZY OLD WOMAN AWAY FROM ME!
ICH LASSE DICH NICHT IN DIE NÄHE MEINER FAMILIE!
VERSTEHST DU DAS?
EVERYONE NEEDS TO CALM DOWN. I'M SURE THIS IS JUST A MISUNDERSTANDING.
SHE IS PROBABLY CONFUSED IN HER OLD AGE.
CLEARLY SHE MISTAKES ME FOR SOMEONE ELSE.
GROWRR!
SHE IS VERY SPIRITED!
ICH WERDE DICH UMBRINGEN!
HONEY, I'M HOME!

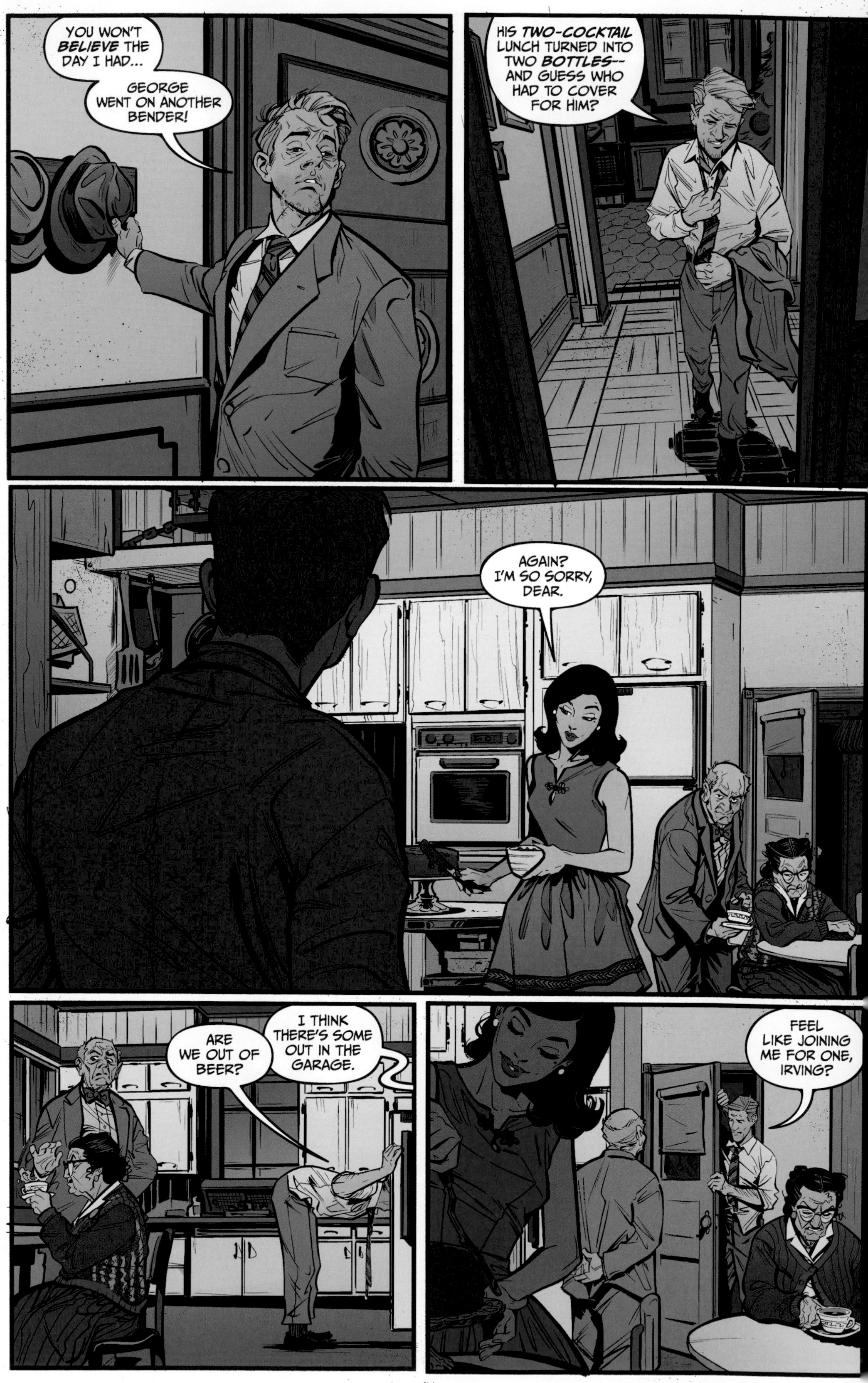
YOU WON'T *BELIEVE* THE DAY I HAD...
GEORGE WENT ON ANOTHER BENDER!
HIS *TWO-COCKTAIL* LUNCH TURNED INTO TWO *BOTTLES*-- AND GUESS WHO HAD TO COVER FOR HIM?
AGAIN? I'M SO SORRY, DEAR.
ARE WE OUT OF BEER?
I THINK THERE'S SOME OUT IN THE GARAGE.
FEEL LIKE JOINING ME FOR ONE, IRVING?

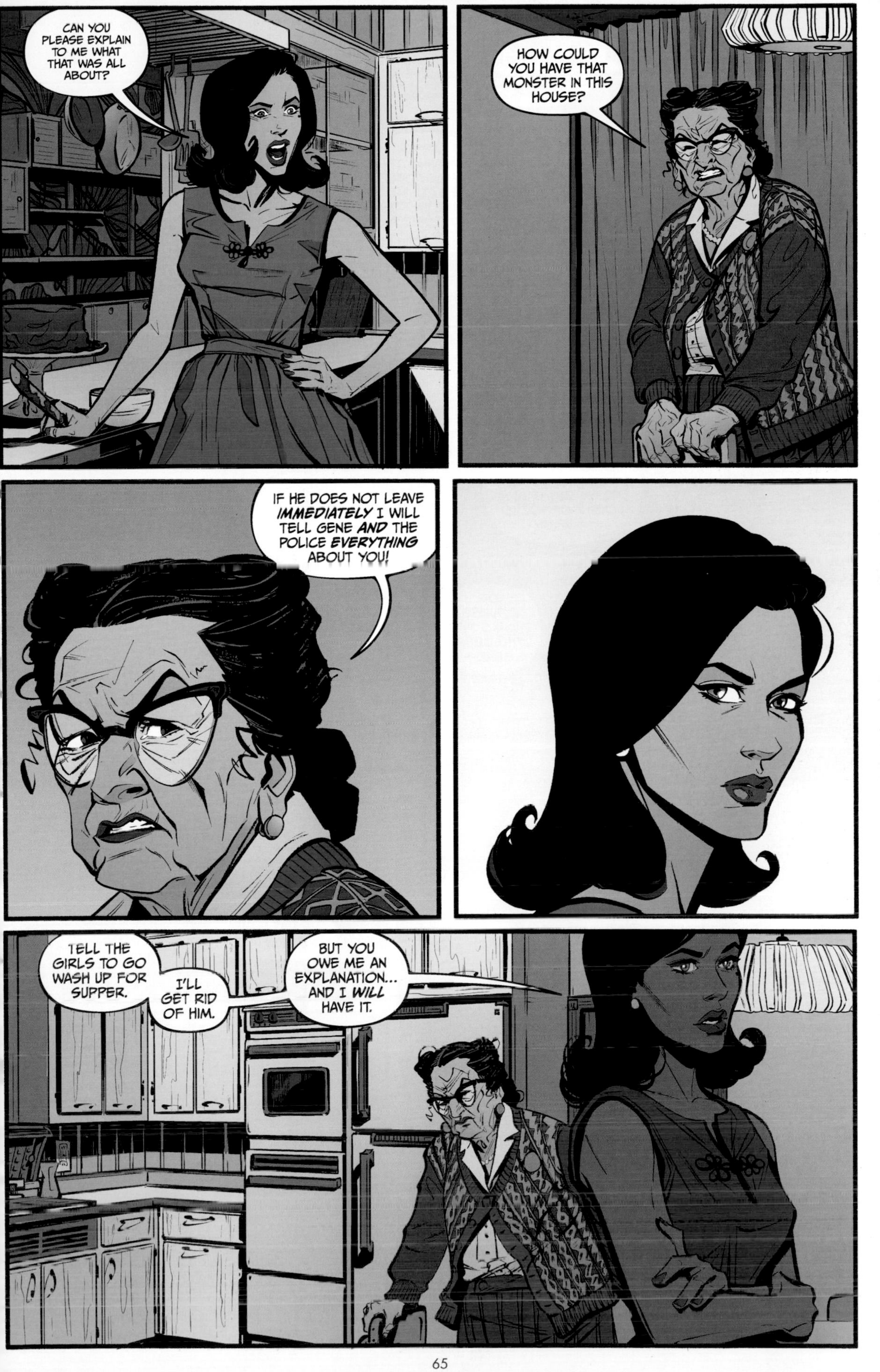
CAN YOU PLEASE EXPLAIN TO ME WHAT THAT WAS ALL ABOUT?
HOW COULD YOU HAVE THAT MONSTER IN THIS HOUSE?
IF HE DOES NOT LEAVE *IMMEDIATELY* I WILL TELL GENE *AND* THE POLICE *EVERYTHING* ABOUT YOU!
TELL THE GIRLS TO GO WASH UP FOR SUPPER.
I'LL GET RID OF HIM.
BUT YOU OWE ME AN EXPLANATION... AND I *WILL* HAVE IT.

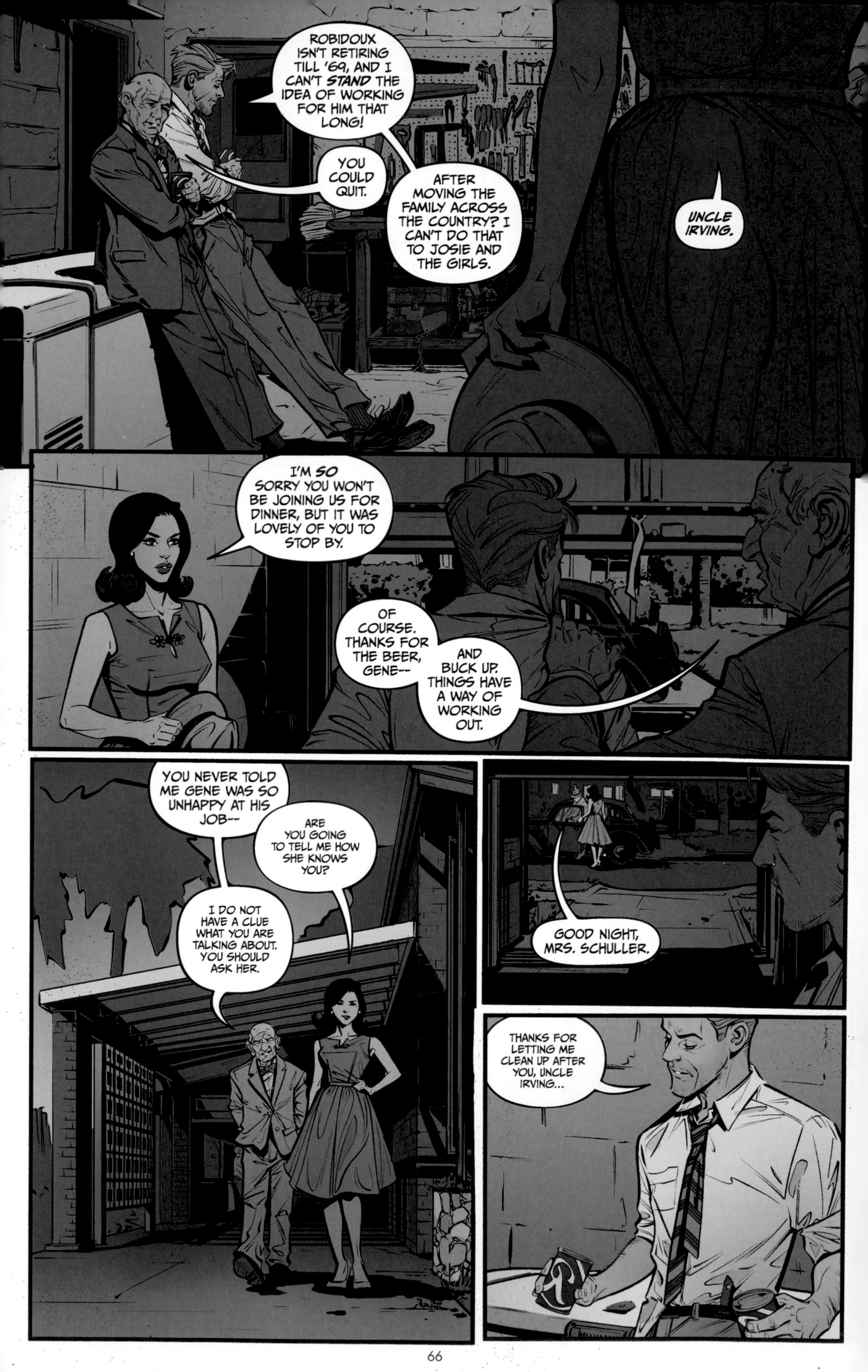
ROBIDOUX ISN'T RETIRING TILL '69, AND I CAN'T *STAND* THE IDEA OF WORKING FOR HIM THAT LONG!
YOU COULD QUIT.
AFTER MOVING THE FAMILY ACROSS THE COUNTRY? I CAN'T DO THAT TO JOSIE AND THE GIRLS.
UNCLE IRVING.
I'M *SO* SORRY YOU WON'T BE JOINING US FOR DINNER, BUT IT WAS LOVELY OF YOU TO STOP BY.
OF COURSE. THANKS FOR THE BEER, GENE--
AND BUCK UP. THINGS HAVE A WAY OF WORKING OUT.
YOU NEVER TOLD ME GENE WAS SO UNHAPPY AT HIS JOB--
ARE YOU GOING TO TELL ME HOW SHE KNOWS YOU?
I DO NOT HAVE A CLUE WHAT YOU ARE TALKING ABOUT. YOU SHOULD ASK HER.
GOOD NIGHT, MRS. SCHULLER.
THANKS FOR LETTING ME CLEAN UP AFTER YOU, UNCLE IRVING...

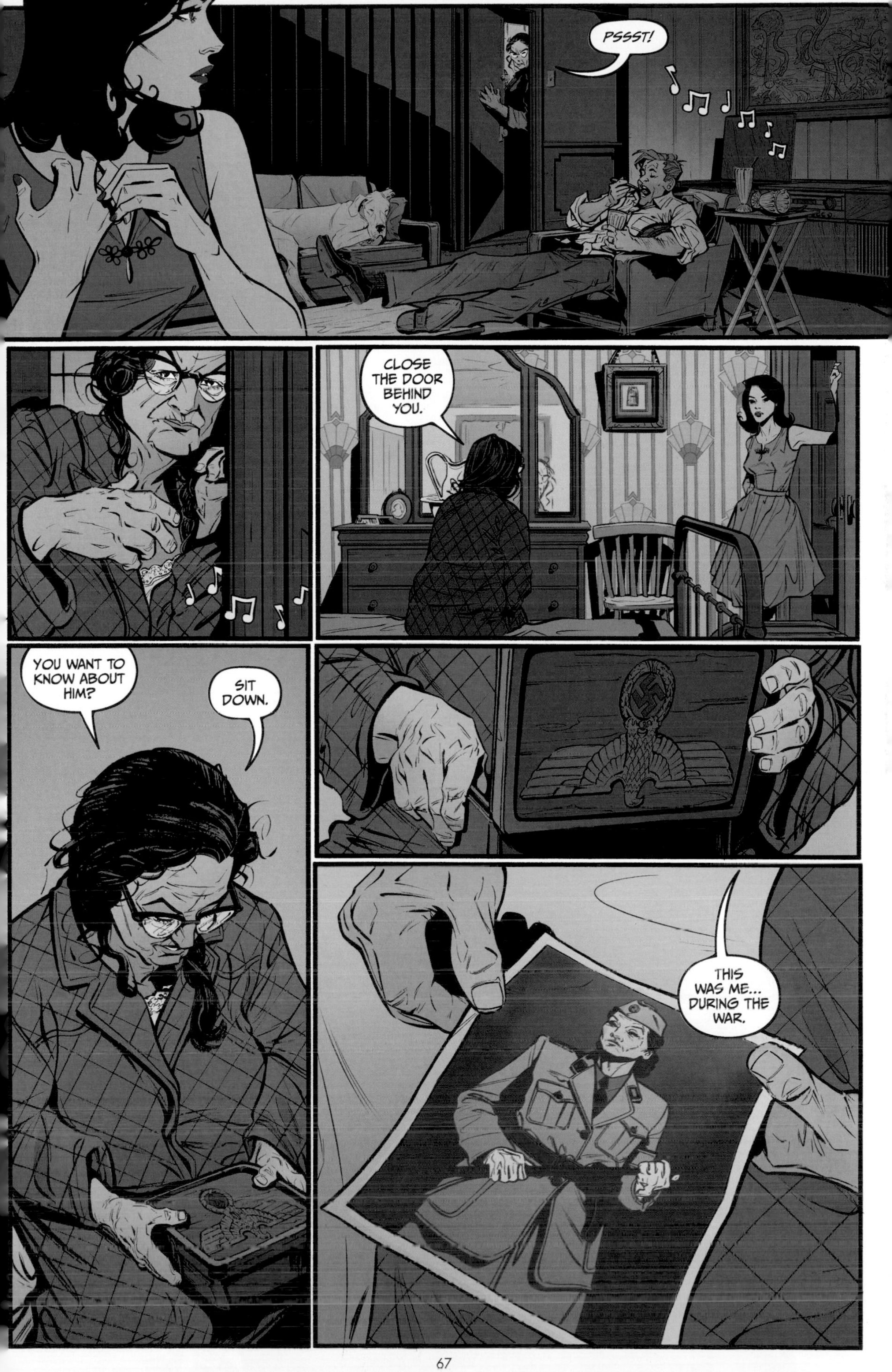
PSSST!
CLOSE THE DOOR BEHIND YOU.
YOU WANT TO KNOW ABOUT HIM?
SIT DOWN.
THIS WAS ME... DURING THE WAR.

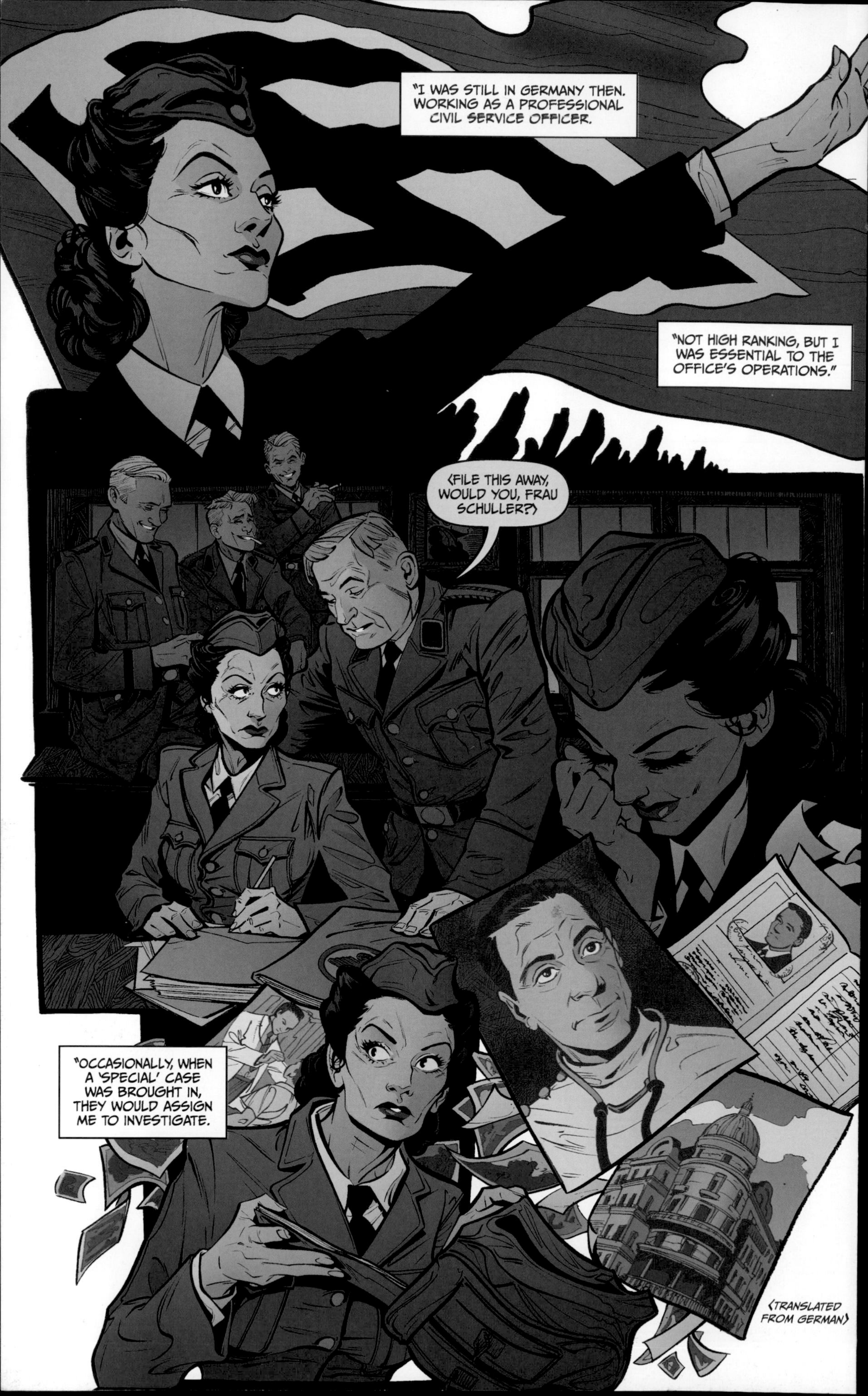
"I WAS STILL IN GERMANY THEN. WORKING AS A PROFESSIONAL CIVIL SERVICE OFFICER.
"NOT HIGH RANKING, BUT I WAS ESSENTIAL TO THE OFFICE'S OPERATIONS."
⟨FILE THIS AWAY, WOULD YOU, FRAU SCHULLER?⟩
"OCCASIONALLY, WHEN A 'SPECIAL' CASE WAS BROUGHT IN, THEY WOULD ASSIGN ME TO INVESTIGATE.
⟨TRANSLATED FROM GERMAN⟩

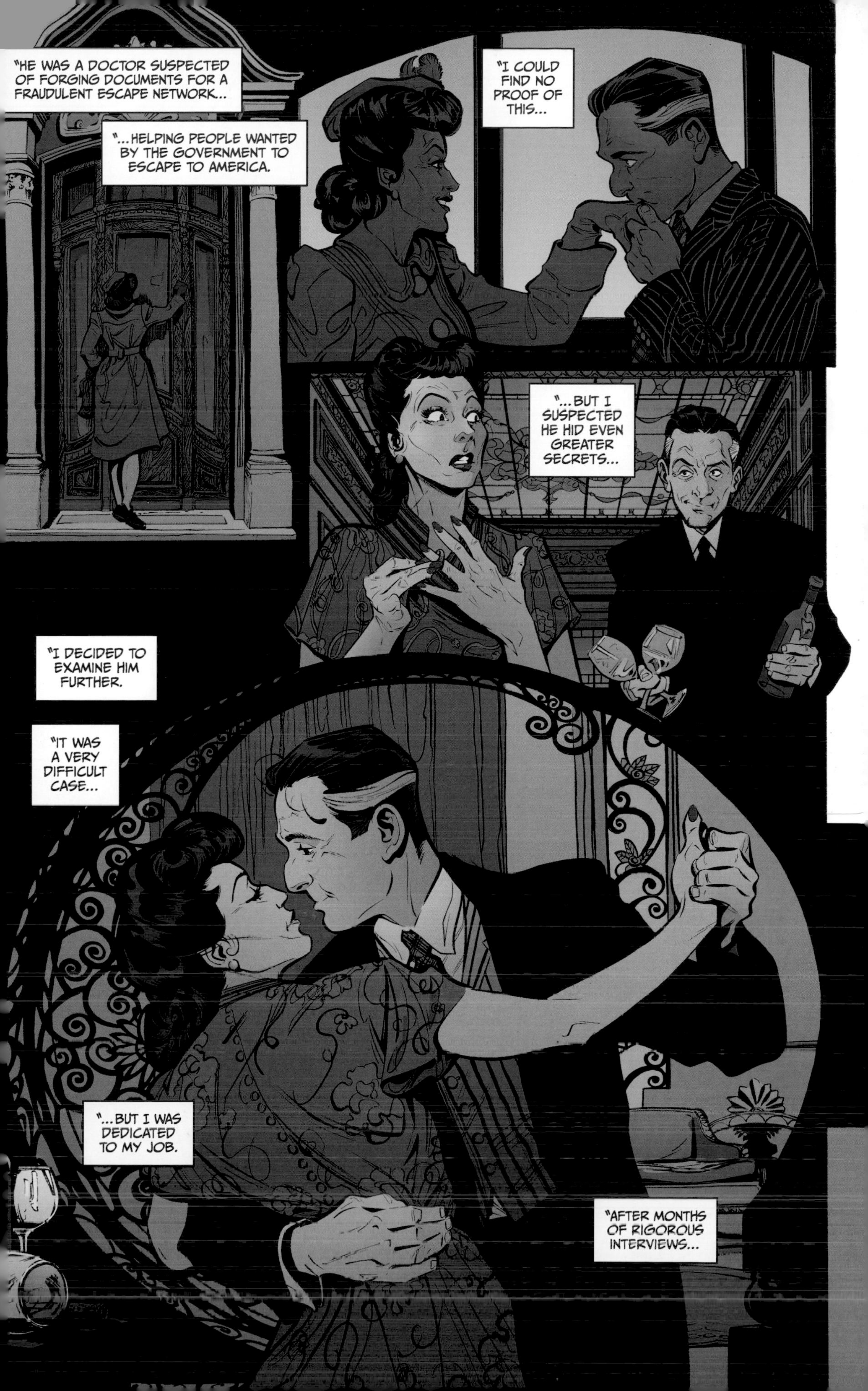
"HE WAS A DOCTOR SUSPECTED OF FORGING DOCUMENTS FOR A FRAUDULENT ESCAPE NETWORK...
"...HELPING PEOPLE WANTED BY THE GOVERNMENT TO ESCAPE TO AMERICA.
"I COULD FIND NO PROOF OF THIS...
"...BUT I SUSPECTED HE HID EVEN GREATER SECRETS...
"I DECIDED TO EXAMINE HIM FURTHER.
"IT WAS A VERY DIFFICULT CASE...
"...BUT I WAS DEDICATED TO MY JOB.
"AFTER MONTHS OF RIGOROUS INTERVIEWS...

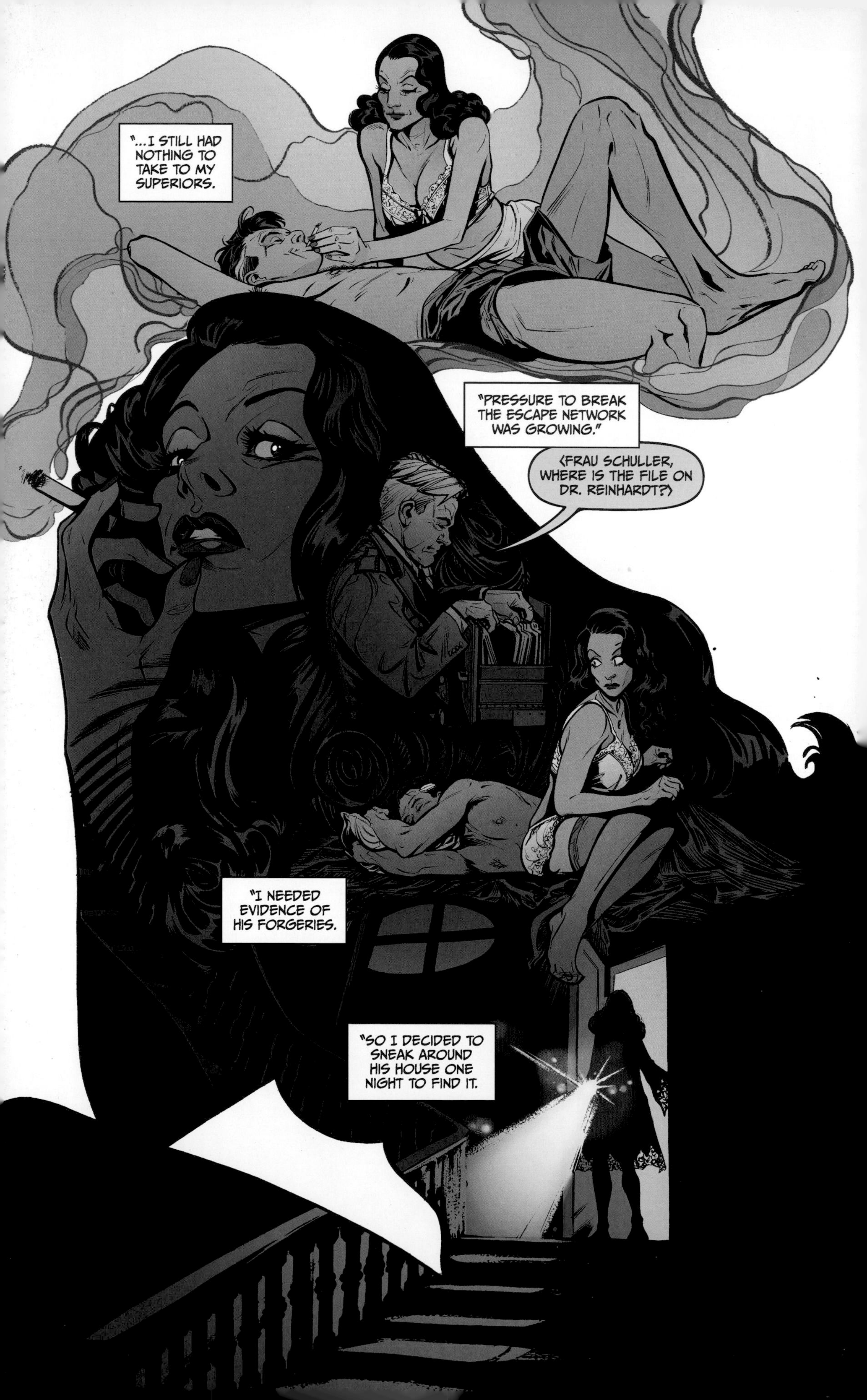
"...I STILL HAD NOTHING TO TAKE TO MY SUPERIORS.
"PRESSURE TO BREAK THE ESCAPE NETWORK WAS GROWING."
<FRAU SCHULLER, WHERE IS THE FILE ON DR. REINHARDT?>
"I NEEDED EVIDENCE OF HIS FORGERIES.
"SO I DECIDED TO SNEAK AROUND HIS HOUSE ONE NIGHT TO FIND IT.

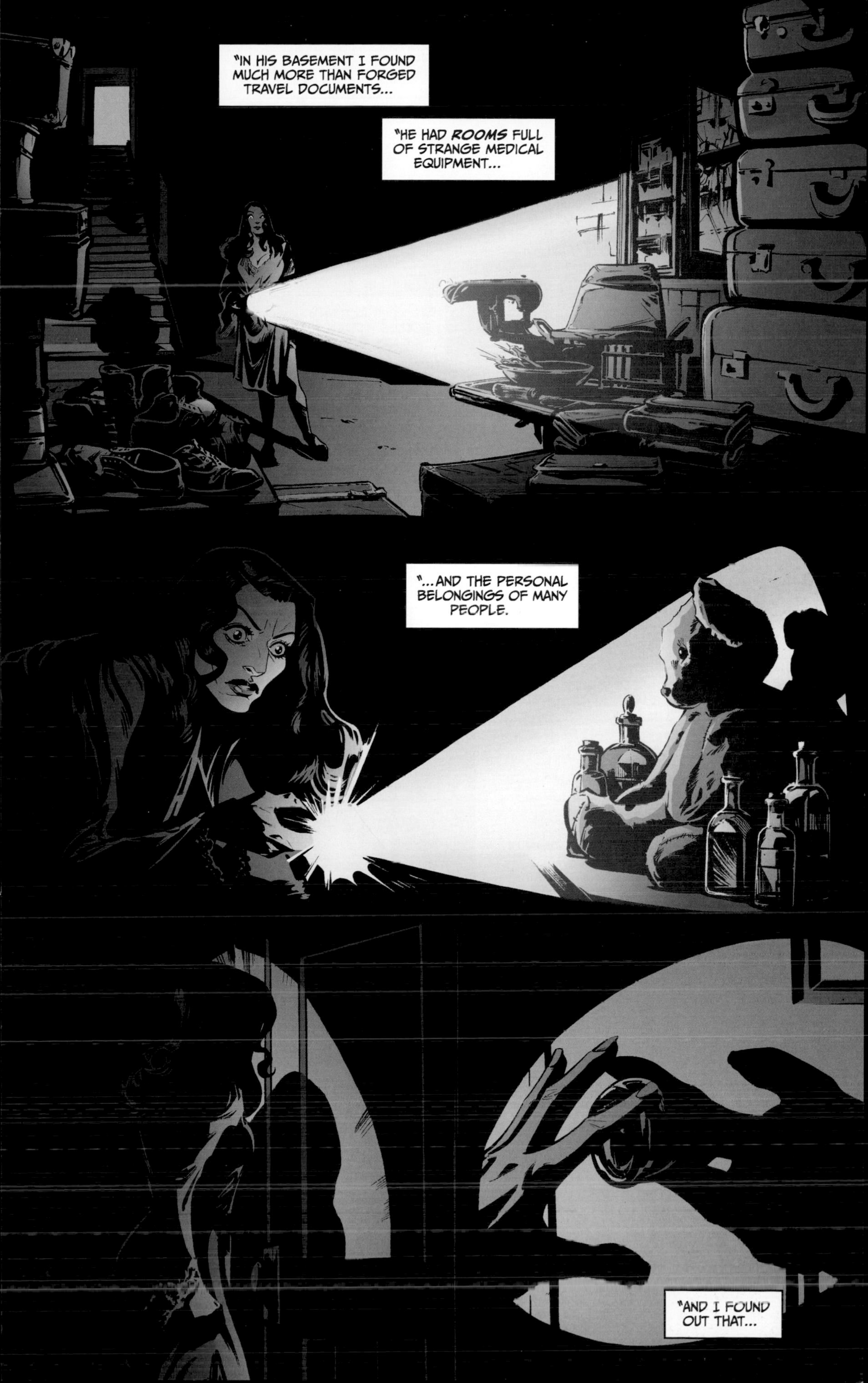
"IN HIS BASEMENT I FOUND MUCH MORE THAN FORGED TRAVEL DOCUMENTS...
"HE HAD ROOMS FULL OF STRANGE MEDICAL EQUIPMENT...
"...AND THE PERSONAL BELONGINGS OF MANY PEOPLE.
"AND I FOUND OUT THAT...

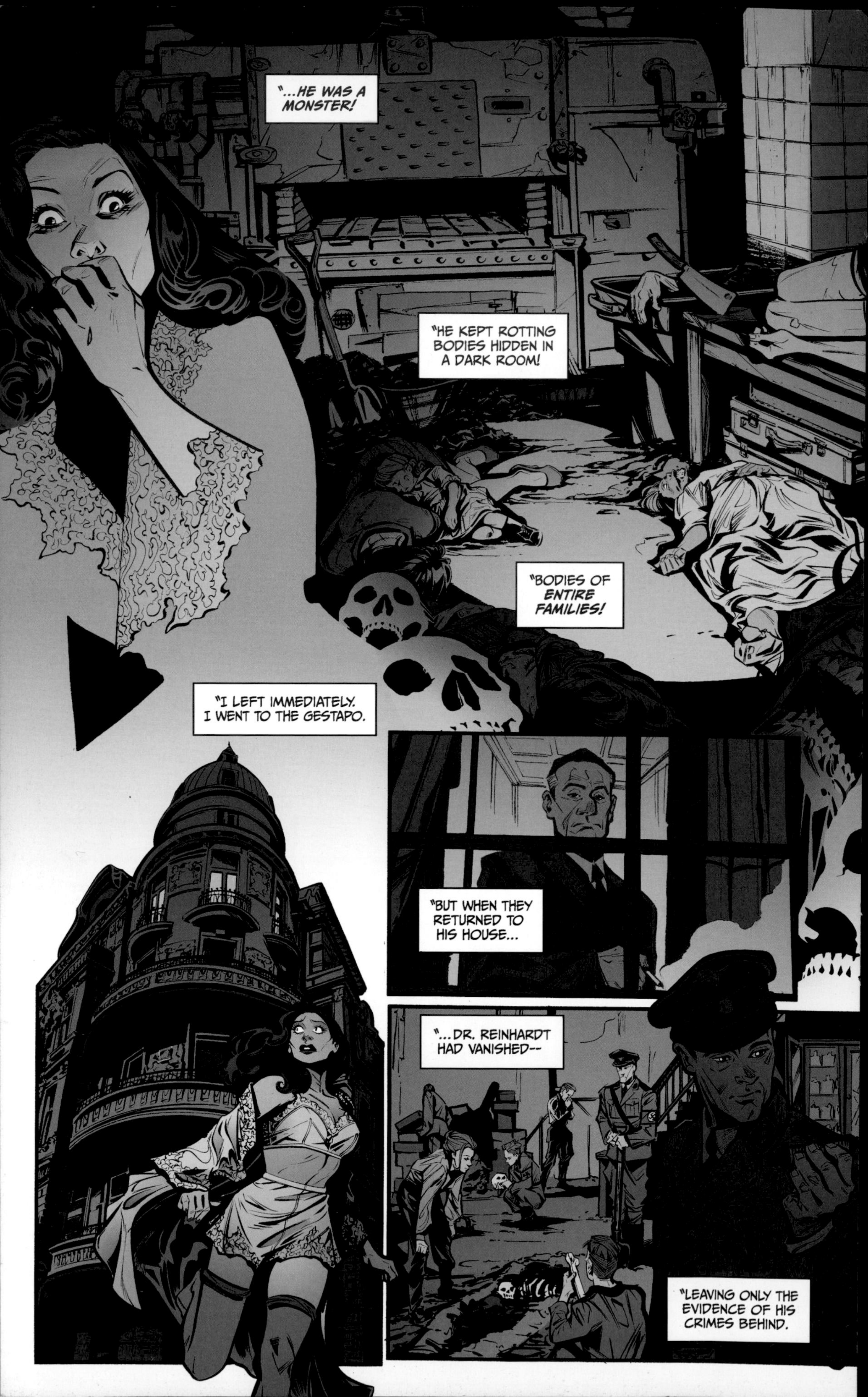
"...HE WAS A MONSTER!
"HE KEPT ROTTING BODIES HIDDEN IN A DARK ROOM!
"BODIES OF ENTIRE FAMILIES!
"I LEFT IMMEDIATELY. I WENT TO THE GESTAPO.
"BUT WHEN THEY RETURNED TO HIS HOUSE...
"...DR. REINHARDT HAD VANISHED--
"LEAVING ONLY THE EVIDENCE OF HIS CRIMES BEHIND.

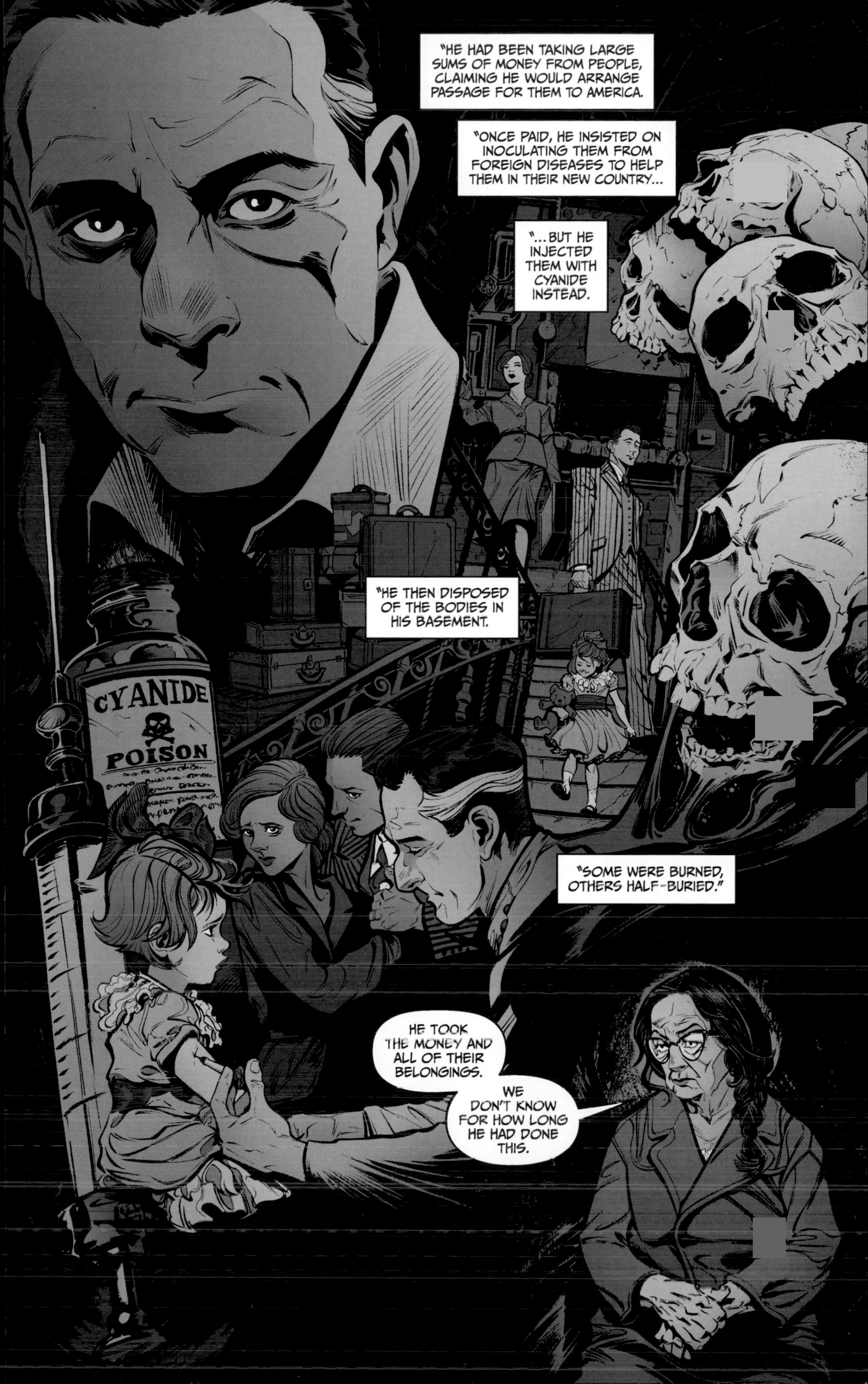
"HE HAD BEEN TAKING LARGE SUMS OF MONEY FROM PEOPLE, CLAIMING HE WOULD ARRANGE PASSAGE FOR THEM TO AMERICA.
"ONCE PAID, HE INSISTED ON INOCULATING THEM FROM FOREIGN DISEASES TO HELP THEM IN THEIR NEW COUNTRY...
"...BUT HE INJECTED THEM WITH CYANIDE INSTEAD.
"HE THEN DISPOSED OF THE BODIES IN HIS BASEMENT.
CYANIDE
POISON
"SOME WERE BURNED, OTHERS HALF-BURIED."
HE TOOK THE MONEY AND ALL OF THEIR BELONGINGS.
WE DON'T KNOW FOR HOW LONG HE HAD DONE THIS.

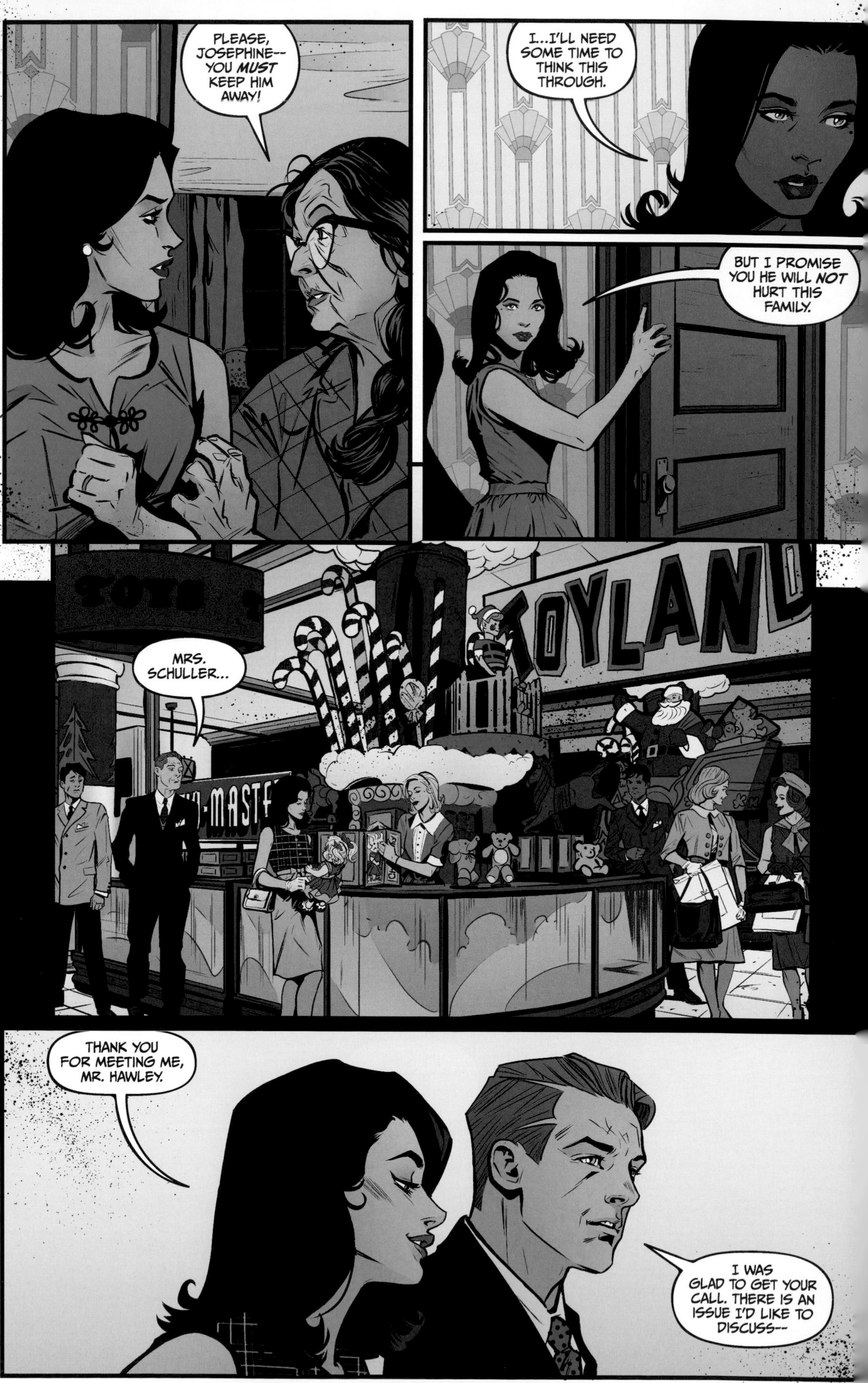
PLEASE, JOSEPHINE-- YOU MUST KEEP HIM AWAY!
I...I'LL NEED SOME TIME TO THINK THIS THROUGH.
BUT I PROMISE YOU HE WILL NOT HURT THIS FAMILY.
TOYLAND
MRS. SCHULLER...
THANK YOU FOR MEETING ME, MR. HAWLEY.
I WAS GLAD TO GET YOUR CALL. THERE IS AN ISSUE I'D LIKE TO DISCUSS--

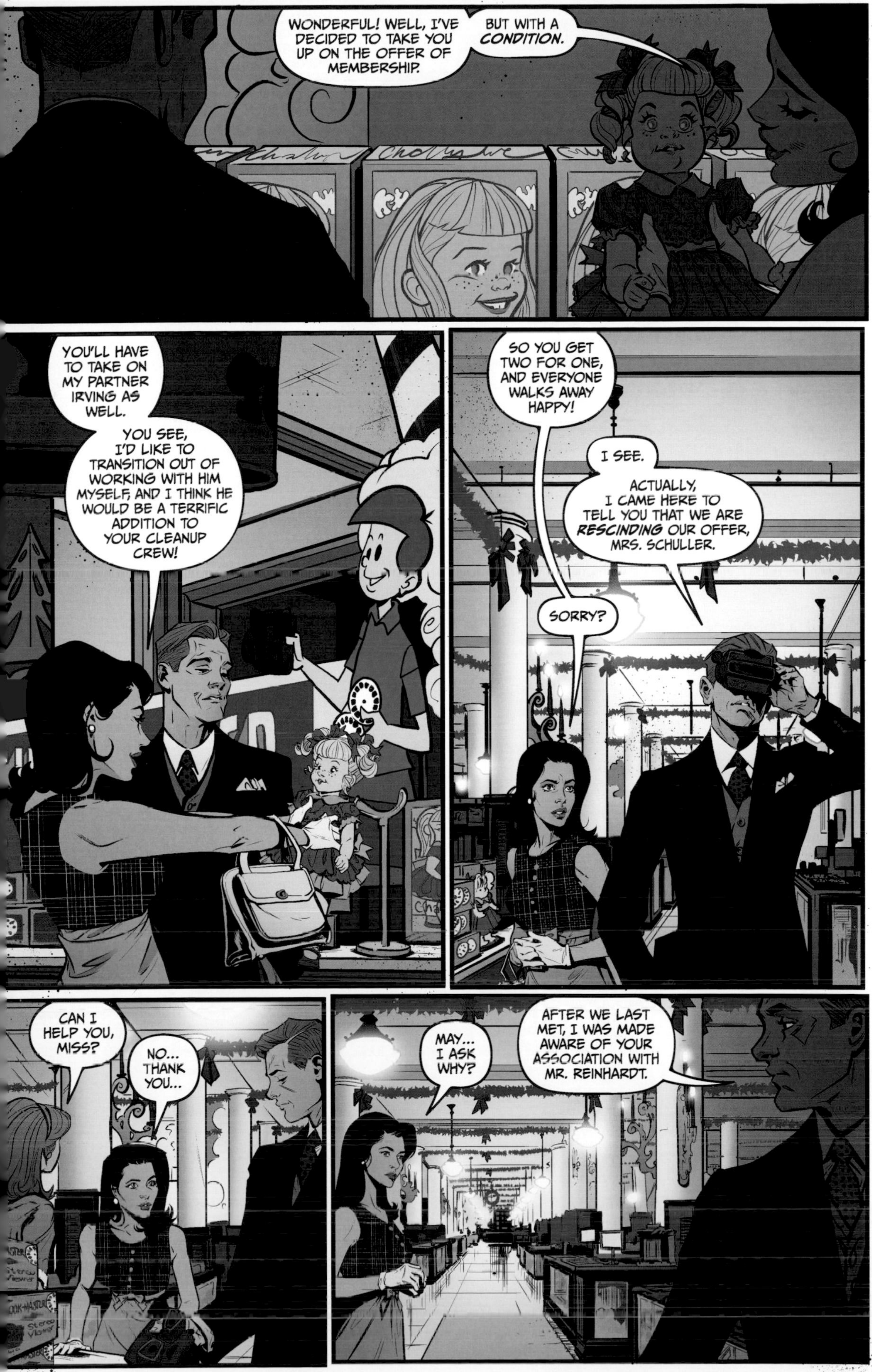
WONDERFUL! WELL, I'VE DECIDED TO TAKE YOU UP ON THE OFFER OF MEMBERSHIP.
BUT WITH A *CONDITION*.
YOU'LL HAVE TO TAKE ON MY PARTNER IRVING AS WELL.
YOU SEE, I'D LIKE TO TRANSITION OUT OF WORKING WITH HIM MYSELF, AND I THINK HE WOULD BE A TERRIFIC ADDITION TO YOUR CLEANUP CREW!
SO YOU GET TWO FOR ONE, AND EVERYONE WALKS AWAY HAPPY!
I SEE.
ACTUALLY, I CAME HERE TO TELL YOU THAT WE ARE *RESCINDING* OUR OFFER, MRS. SCHULLER.
SORRY?
CAN I HELP YOU, MISS?
NO... THANK YOU...
MAY... I ASK WHY?
AFTER WE LAST MET, I WAS MADE AWARE OF YOUR ASSOCIATION WITH MR. REINHARDT.

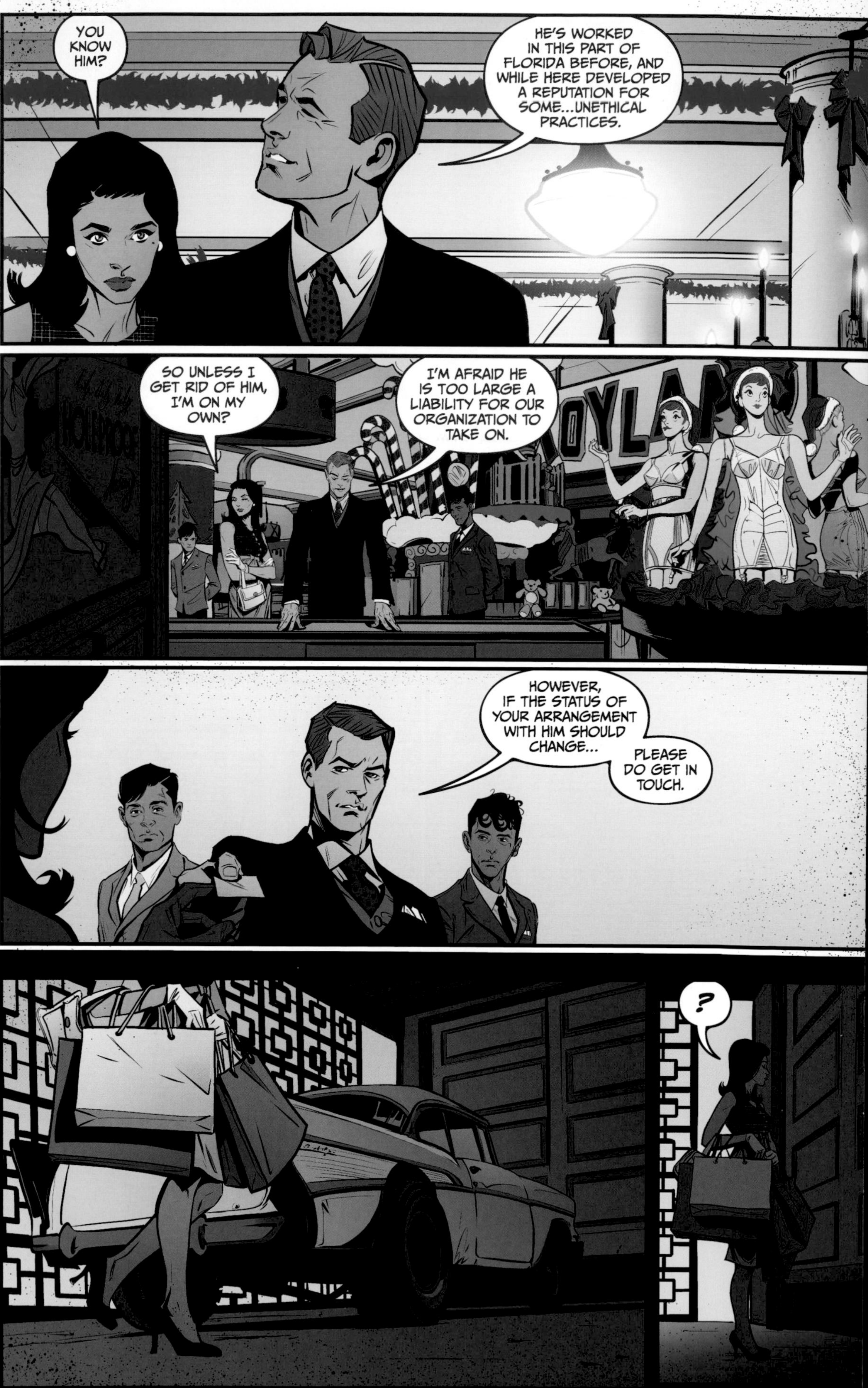

YOU KNOW HIM?
HE'S WORKED IN THIS PART OF FLORIDA BEFORE, AND WHILE HERE DEVELOPED A REPUTATION FOR SOME...UNETHICAL PRACTICES.
SO UNLESS I GET RID OF HIM, I'M ON MY OWN?
I'M AFRAID HE IS TOO LARGE A LIABILITY FOR OUR ORGANIZATION TO TAKE ON.
HOWEVER, IF THE STATUS OF YOUR ARRANGEMENT WITH HIM SHOULD CHANGE...
PLEASE DO GET IN TOUCH.
?

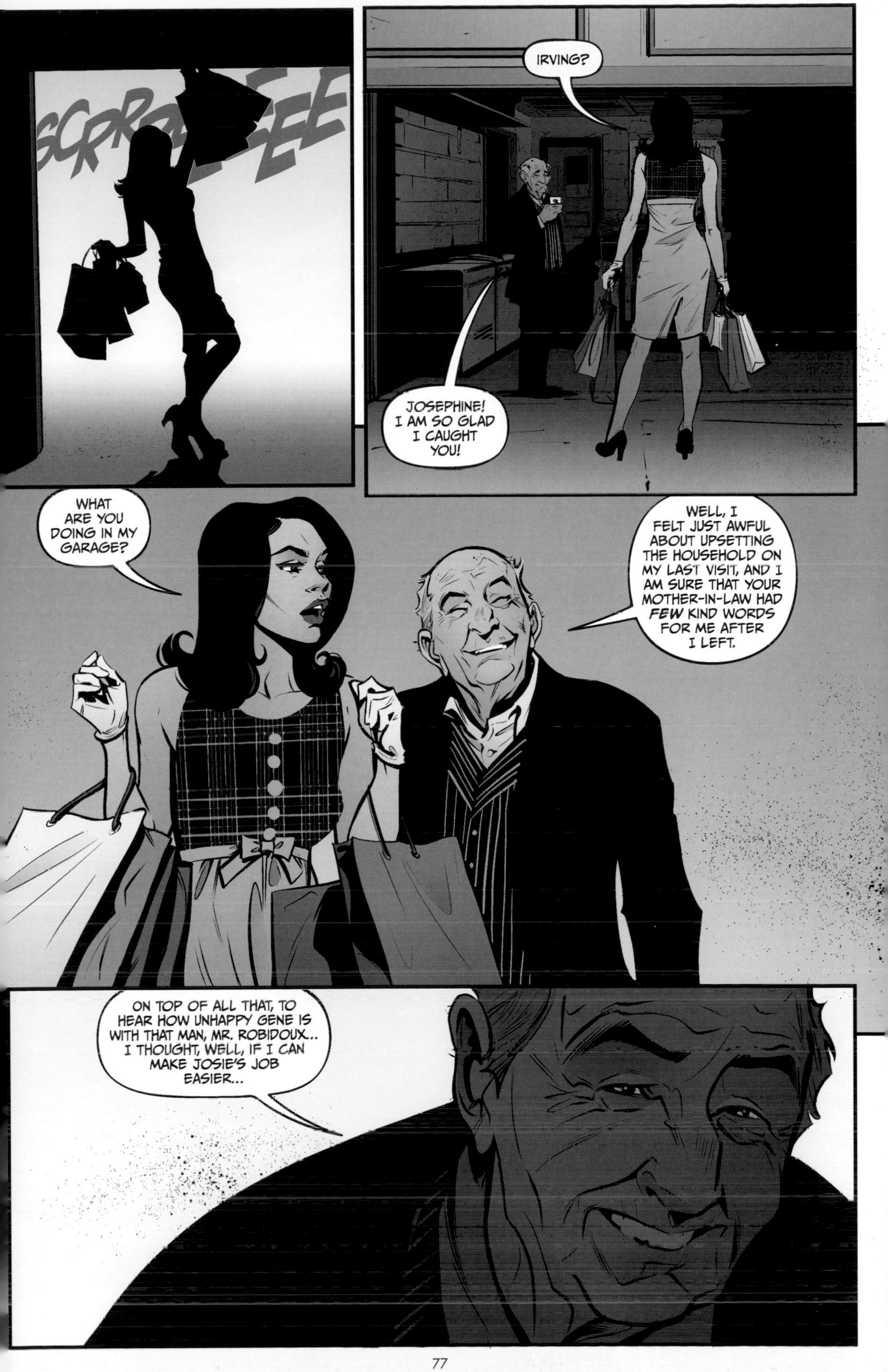
SCROEEEE
IRVING?
JOSEPHINE! I AM SO GLAD I CAUGHT YOU!
WHAT ARE YOU DOING IN MY GARAGE?
WELL, I FELT JUST AWFUL ABOUT UPSETTING THE HOUSEHOLD ON MY LAST VISIT, AND I AM SURE THAT YOUR MOTHER-IN-LAW HAD *FEW* KIND WORDS FOR ME AFTER I LEFT.
ON TOP OF ALL THAT, TO HEAR HOW UNHAPPY GENE IS WITH THAT MAN, MR. ROBIDOUX... I THOUGHT, WELL, IF I CAN MAKE JOSIE'S JOB EASIER...

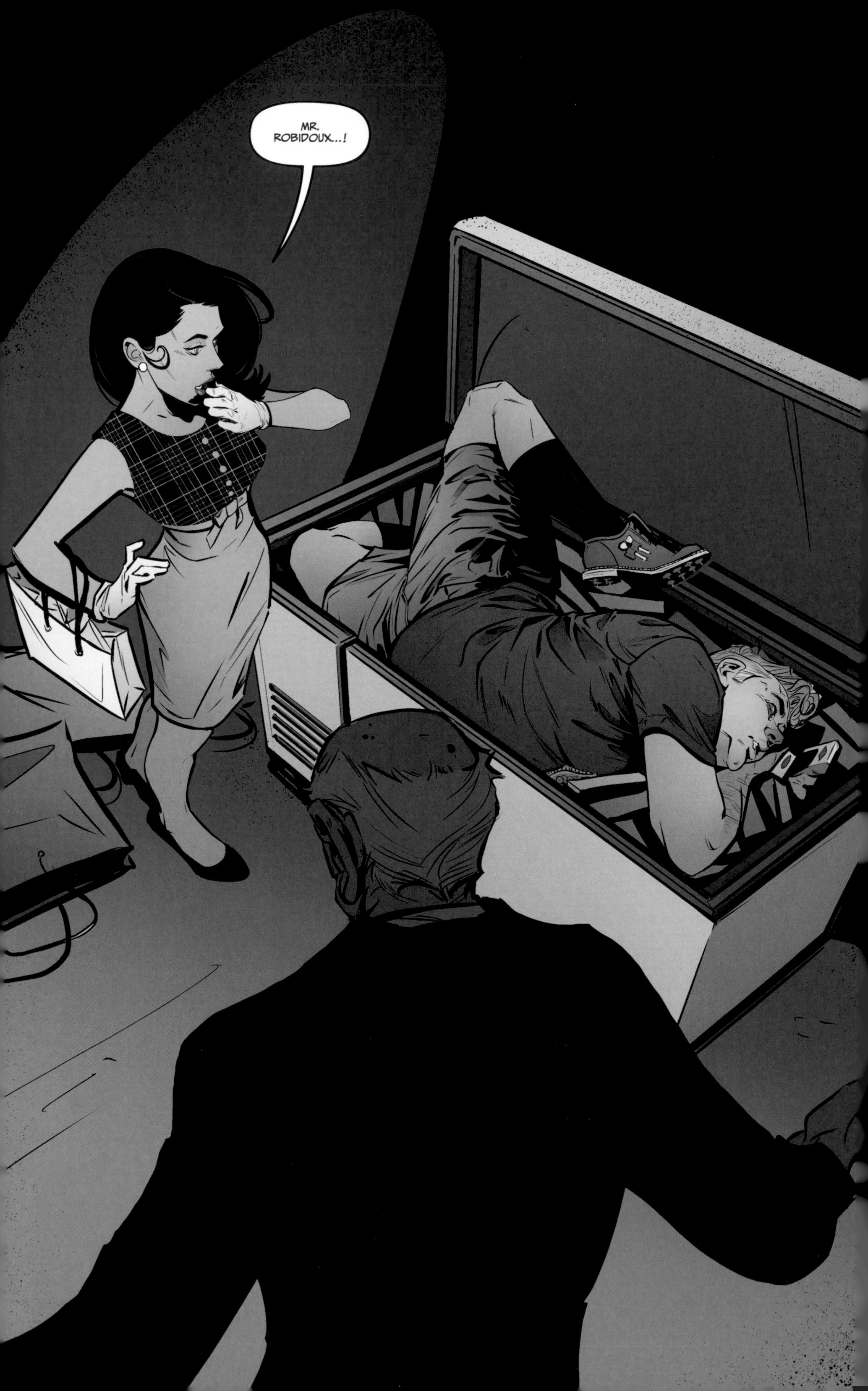
MR. ROBIDOUX...!

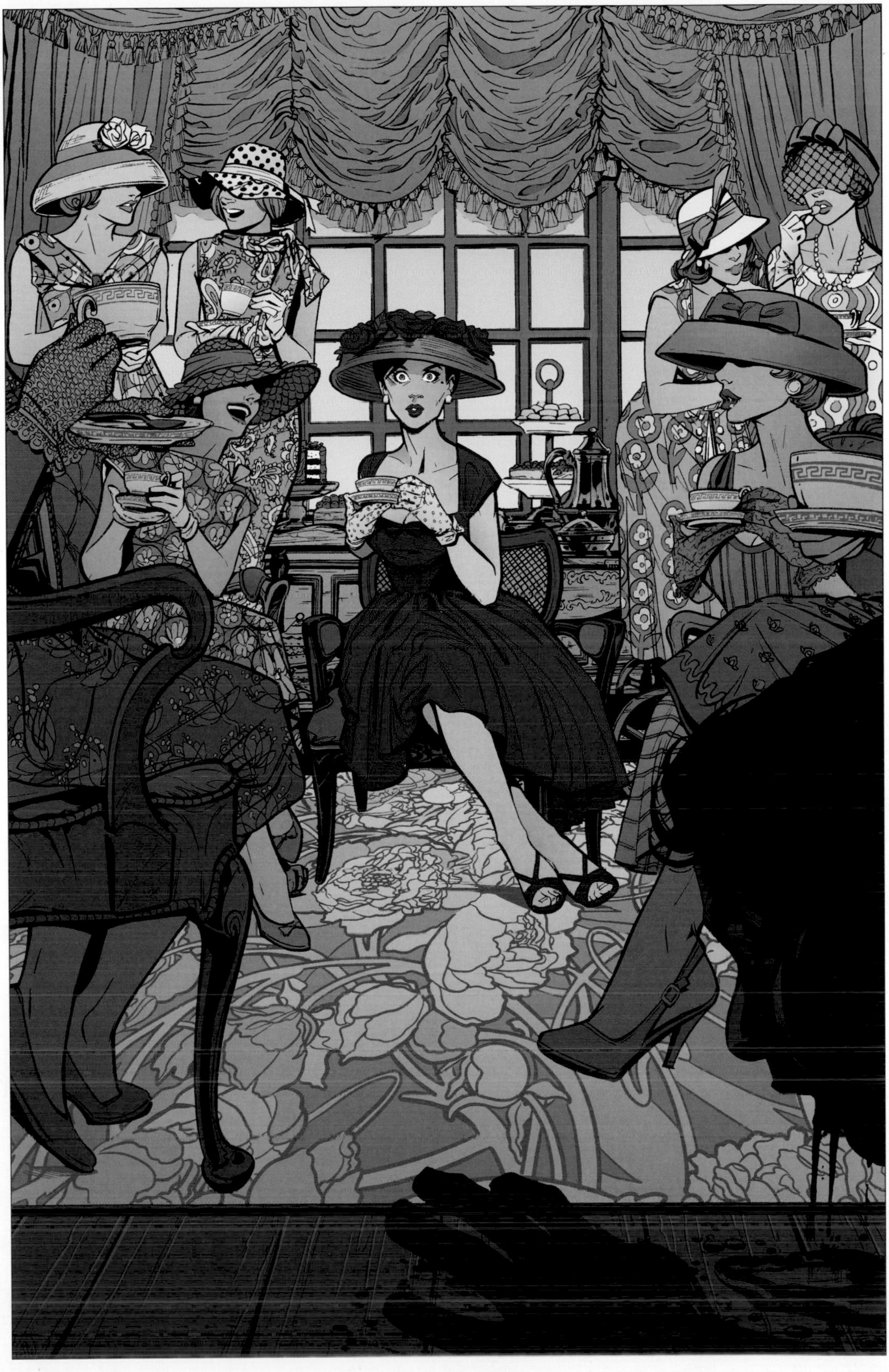

CHAPTER FOUR

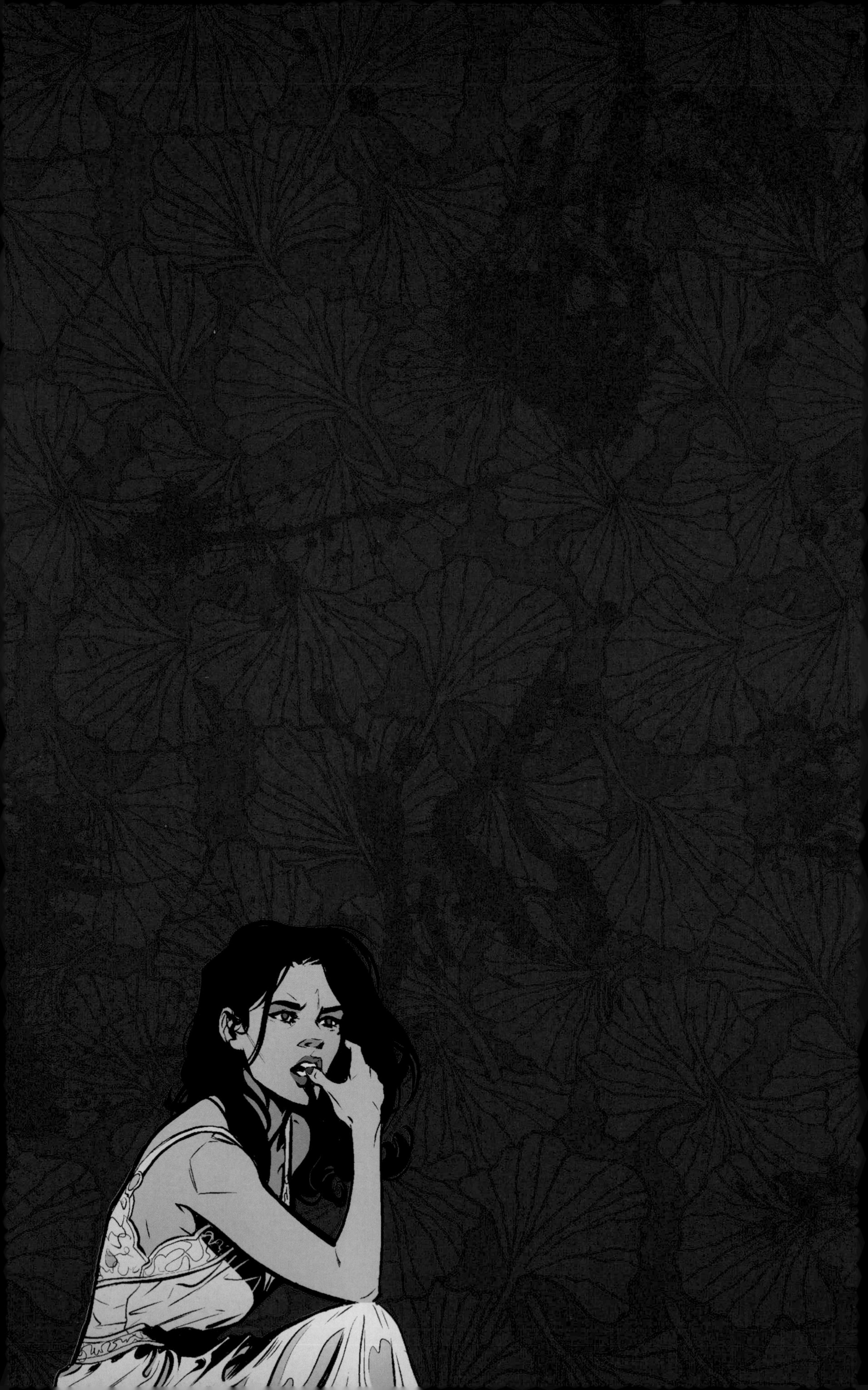

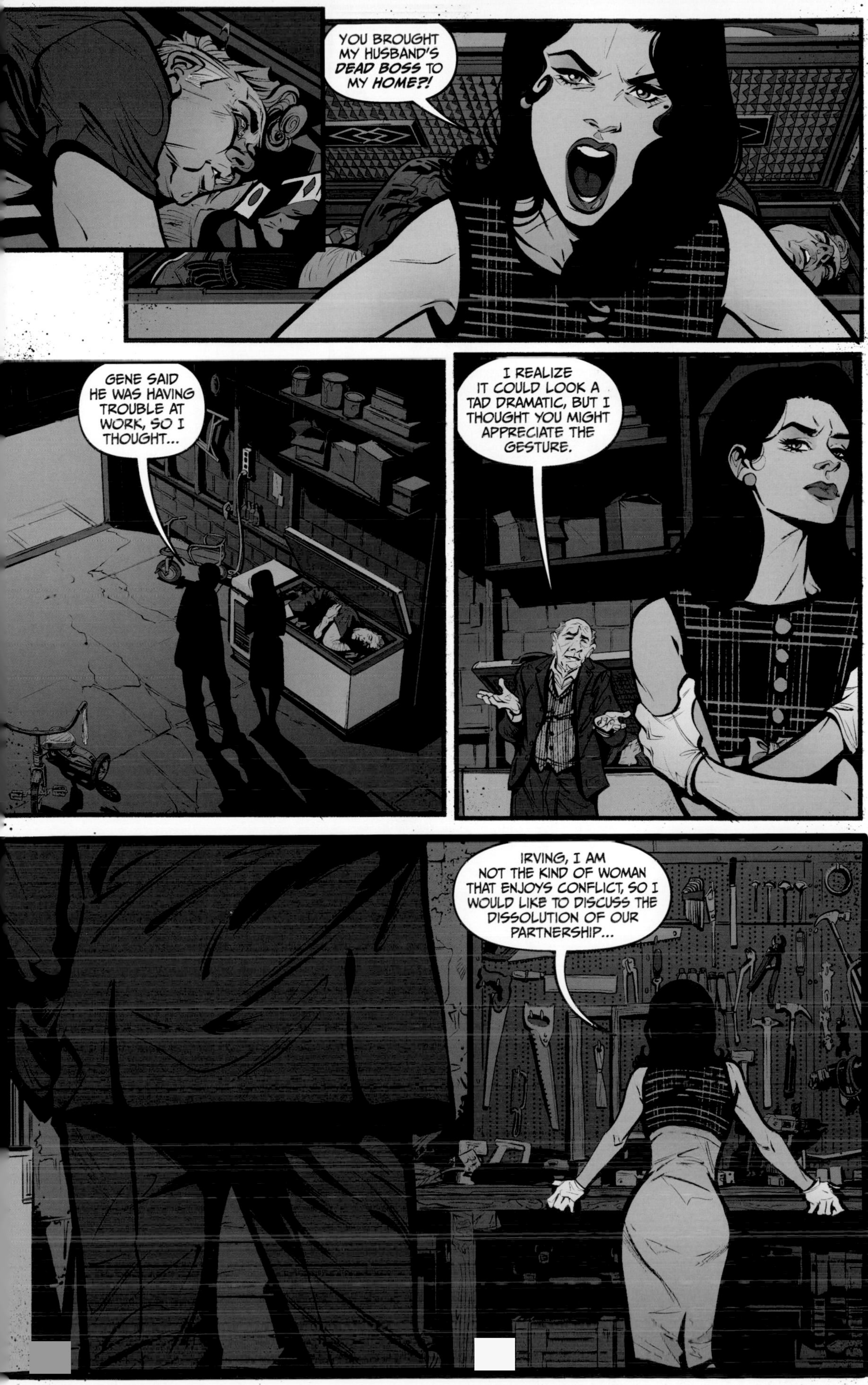

YOU BROUGHT MY HUSBAND'S *DEAD BOSS* TO MY *HOME?!*
GENE SAID HE WAS HAVING TROUBLE AT WORK, SO I THOUGHT...
I REALIZE IT COULD LOOK A TAD DRAMATIC, BUT I THOUGHT YOU MIGHT APPRECIATE THE GESTURE.
IRVING, I AM NOT THE KIND OF WOMAN THAT ENJOYS CONFLICT, SO I WOULD LIKE TO DISCUSS THE DISSOLUTION OF OUR PARTNERSHIP...

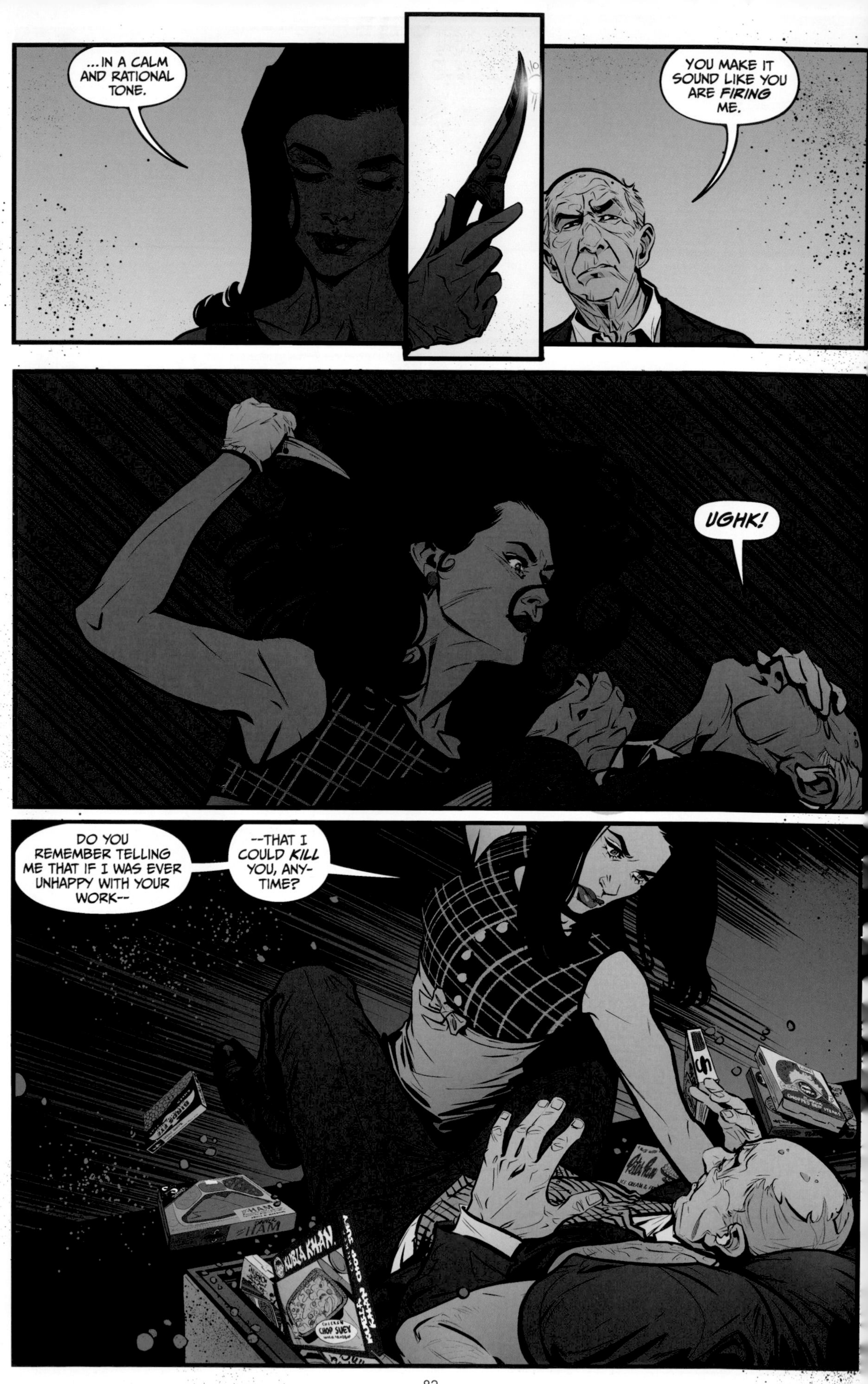
...IN A CALM AND RATIONAL TONE.
YOU MAKE IT SOUND LIKE YOU ARE FIRING ME.
UGHK!
DO YOU REMEMBER TELLING ME THAT IF I WAS EVER UNHAPPY WITH YOUR WORK--
--THAT I COULD KILL YOU, ANY-TIME?
KUBLA KHAN

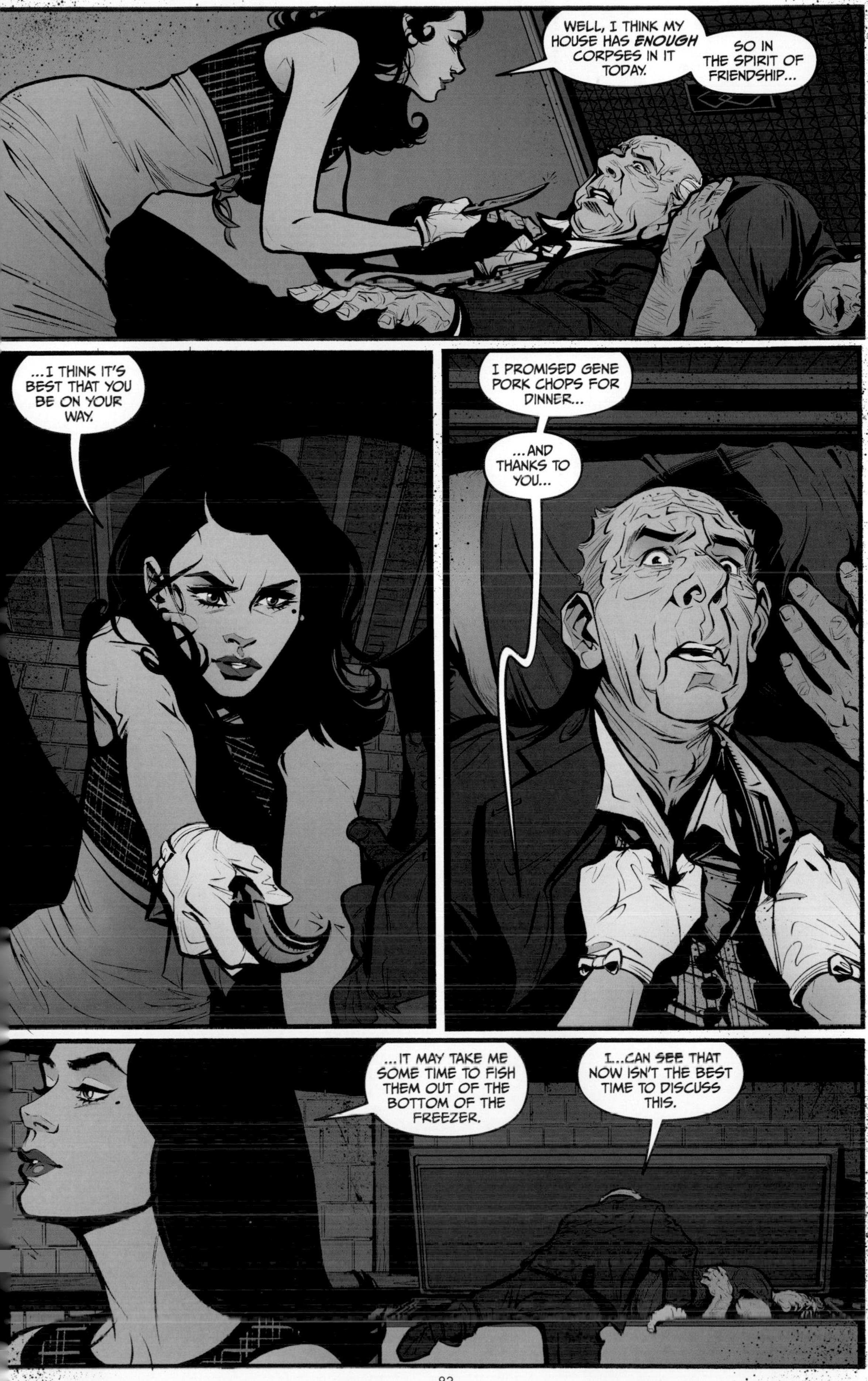
WELL, I THINK MY HOUSE HAS ENOUGH CORPSES IN IT TODAY.
SO IN THE SPIRIT OF FRIENDSHIP...
...I THINK IT'S BEST THAT YOU BE ON YOUR WAY.
I PROMISED GENE PORK CHOPS FOR DINNER...
...AND THANKS TO YOU...
...IT MAY TAKE ME SOME TIME TO FISH THEM OUT OF THE BOTTOM OF THE FREEZER.
I...CAN SEE THAT NOW ISN'T THE BEST TIME TO DISCUSS THIS.

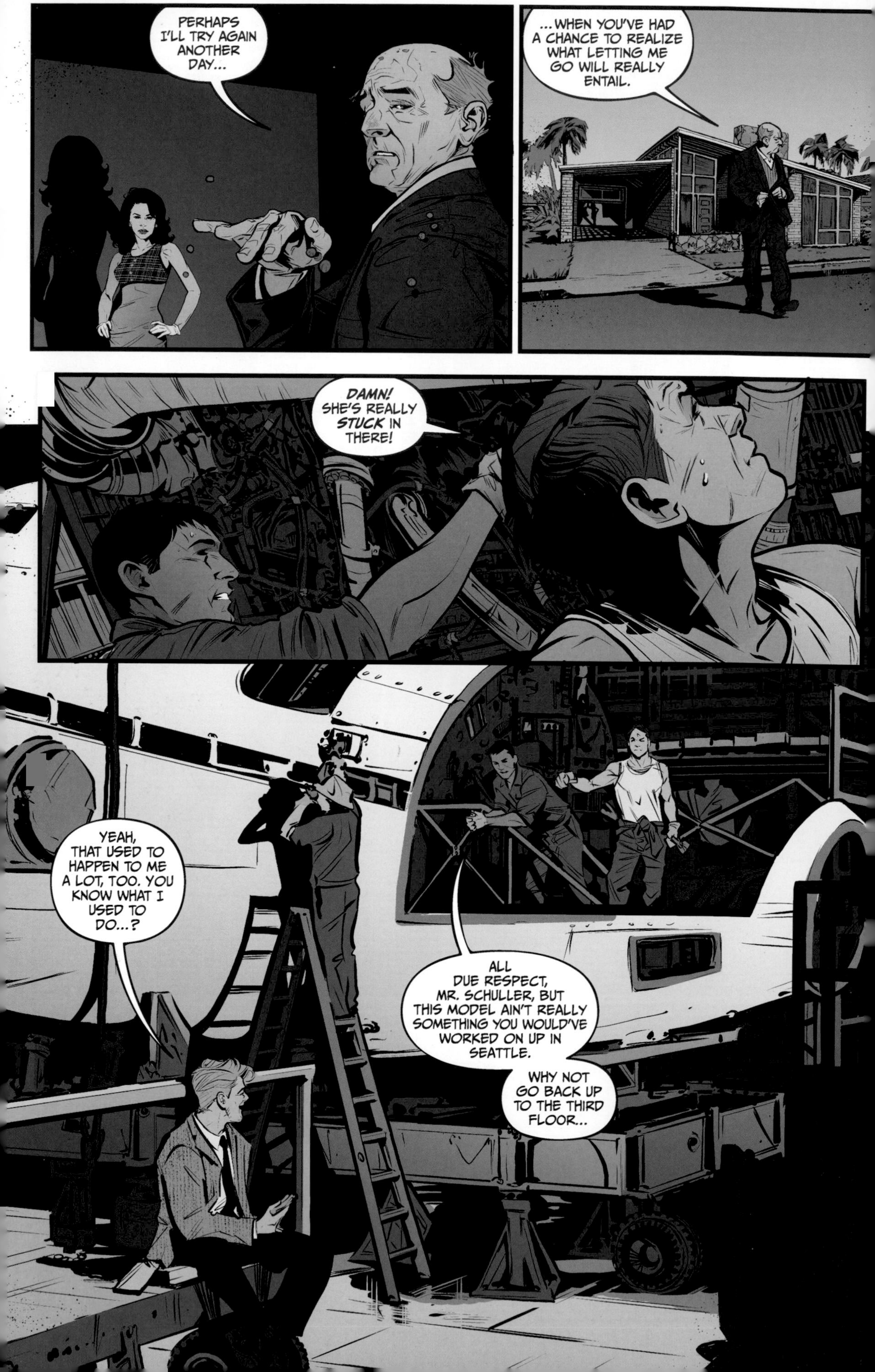
PERHAPS I'LL TRY AGAIN ANOTHER DAY...
...WHEN YOU'VE HAD A CHANCE TO REALIZE WHAT LETTING ME GO WILL REALLY ENTAIL.
DAMN! SHE'S REALLY STUCK IN THERE!
YEAH, THAT USED TO HAPPEN TO ME A LOT, TOO. YOU KNOW WHAT I USED TO DO...?
ALL DUE RESPECT, MR. SCHULLER, BUT THIS MODEL AIN'T REALLY SOMETHING YOU WOULD'VE WORKED ON UP IN SEATTLE.
WHY NOT GO BACK UP TO THE THIRD FLOOR...

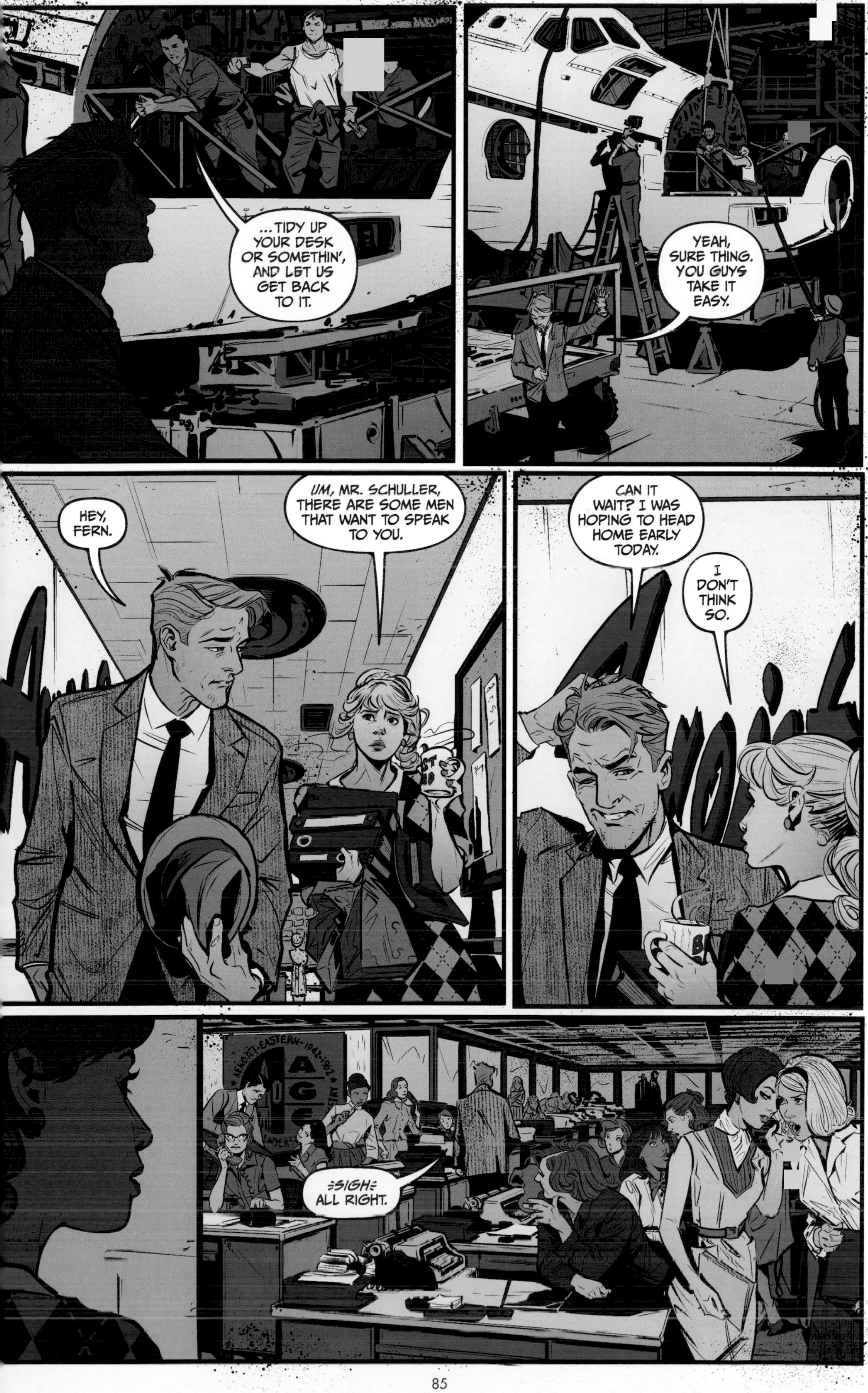
...TIDY UP YOUR DESK OR SOMETHIN', AND LET US GET BACK TO IT.
YEAH, SURE THING. YOU GUYS TAKE IT EASY.
HEY, FERN.
UM, MR. SCHULLER, THERE ARE SOME MEN THAT WANT TO SPEAK TO YOU.
CAN IT WAIT? I WAS HOPING TO HEAD HOME EARLY TODAY.
I DON'T THINK SO.
=SIGH= ALL RIGHT.

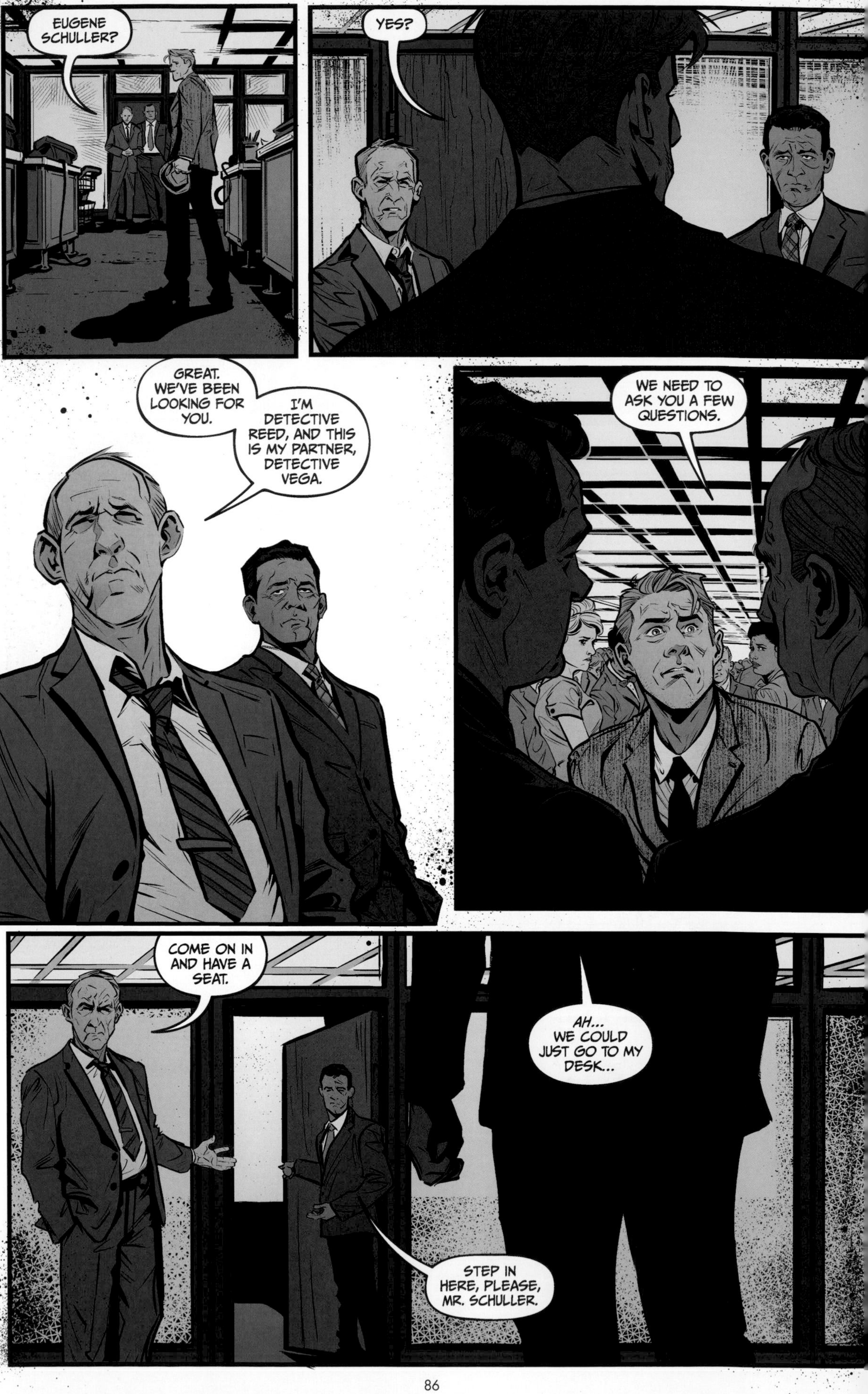
EUGENE SCHULLER?
YES?
GREAT. WE'VE BEEN LOOKING FOR YOU.
I'M DETECTIVE REED, AND THIS IS MY PARTNER, DETECTIVE VEGA.
WE NEED TO ASK YOU A FEW QUESTIONS.
COME ON IN AND HAVE A SEAT.
AH... WE COULD JUST GO TO MY DESK...
STEP IN HERE, PLEASE, MR. SCHULLER.

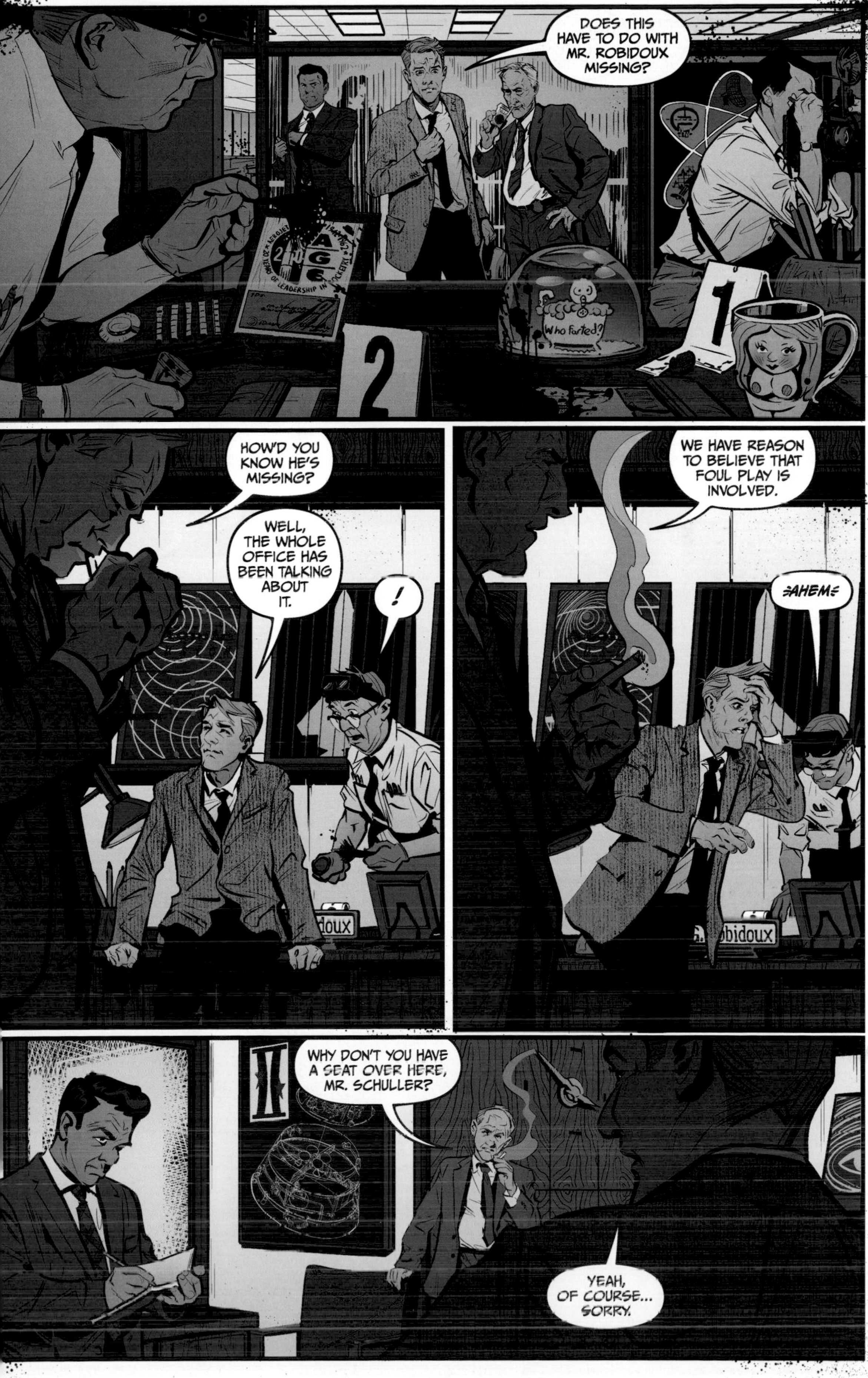
DOES THIS HAVE TO DO WITH MR. ROBIDOUX MISSING?
Who Farted?
1
2
HOW'D YOU KNOW HE'S MISSING?
WELL, THE WHOLE OFFICE HAS BEEN TALKING ABOUT IT.
!
WE HAVE REASON TO BELIEVE THAT FOUL PLAY IS INVOLVED.
AHEM
WHY DON'T YOU HAVE A SEAT OVER HERE, MR. SCHULLER?
YEAH, OF COURSE... SORRY.

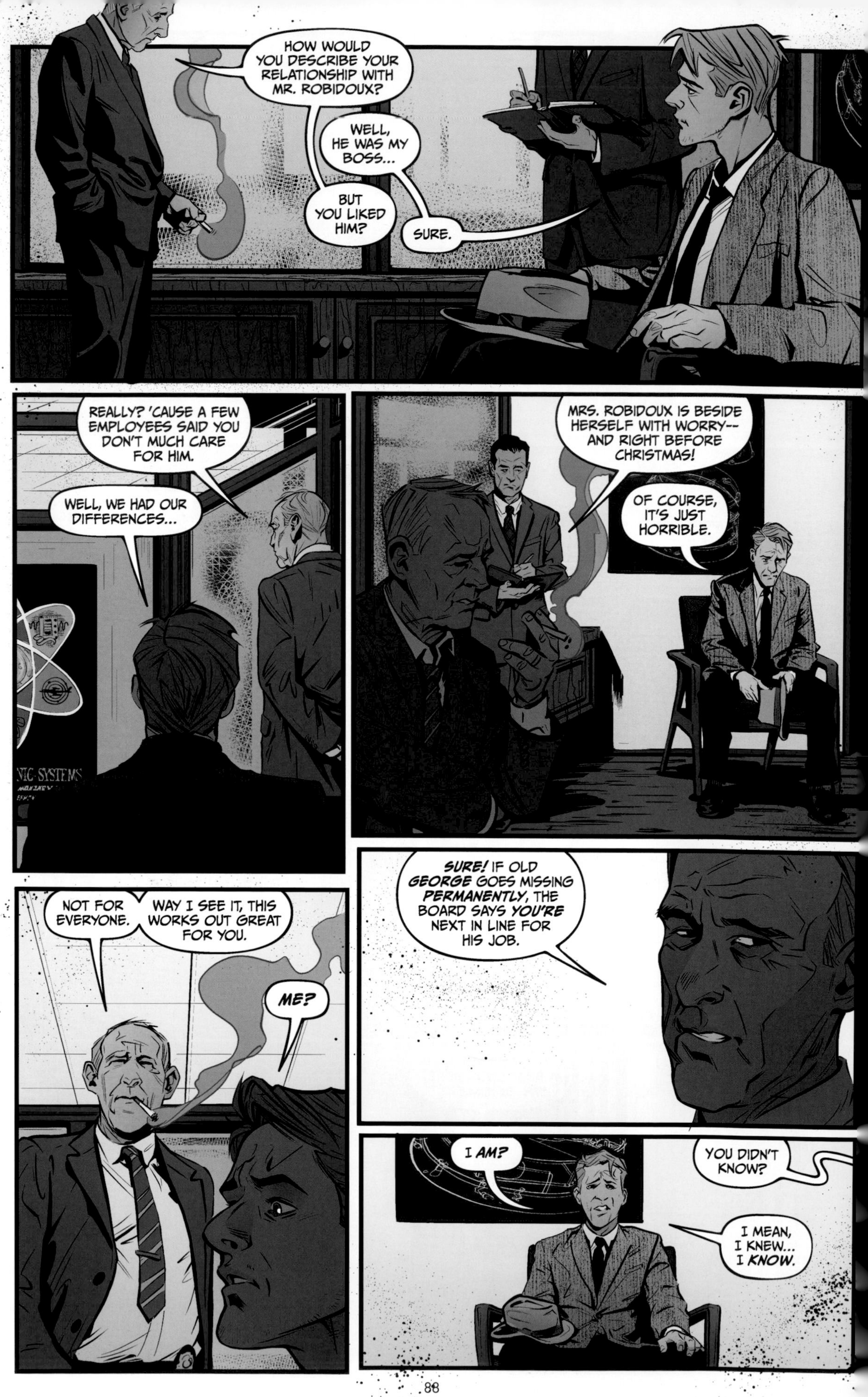
HOW WOULD YOU DESCRIBE YOUR RELATIONSHIP WITH MR. ROBIDOUX?
WELL, HE WAS MY BOSS...
BUT YOU LIKED HIM?
SURE.
REALLY? 'CAUSE A FEW EMPLOYEES SAID YOU DON'T MUCH CARE FOR HIM.
WELL, WE HAD OUR DIFFERENCES...
MRS. ROBIDOUX IS BESIDE HERSELF WITH WORRY-- AND RIGHT BEFORE CHRISTMAS!
OF COURSE, IT'S JUST HORRIBLE.
NOT FOR EVERYONE.
WAY I SEE IT, THIS WORKS OUT GREAT FOR YOU.
ME?
SURE! IF OLD GEORGE GOES MISSING PERMANENTLY, THE BOARD SAYS YOU'RE NEXT IN LINE FOR HIS JOB.
I AM?
YOU DIDN'T KNOW?
I MEAN, I KNEW... I KNOW.

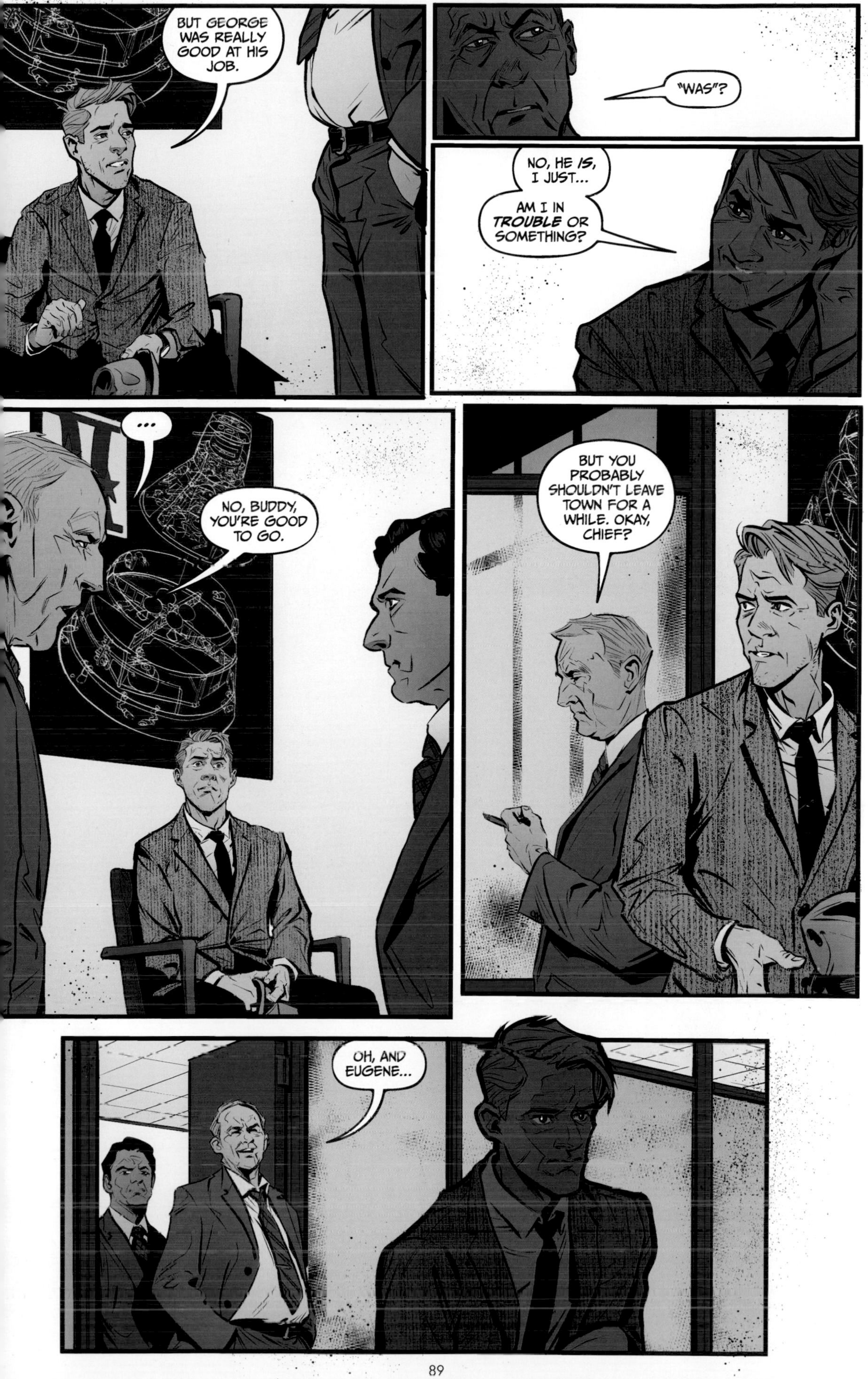
BUT GEORGE WAS REALLY GOOD AT HIS JOB.
"WAS"?
NO, HE *IS*, I JUST...
AM I IN ***TROUBLE*** OR SOMETHING?
...
NO, BUDDY, YOU'RE GOOD TO GO.
BUT YOU PROBABLY SHOULDN'T LEAVE TOWN FOR A WHILE. OKAY, CHIEF?
OH, AND EUGENE...

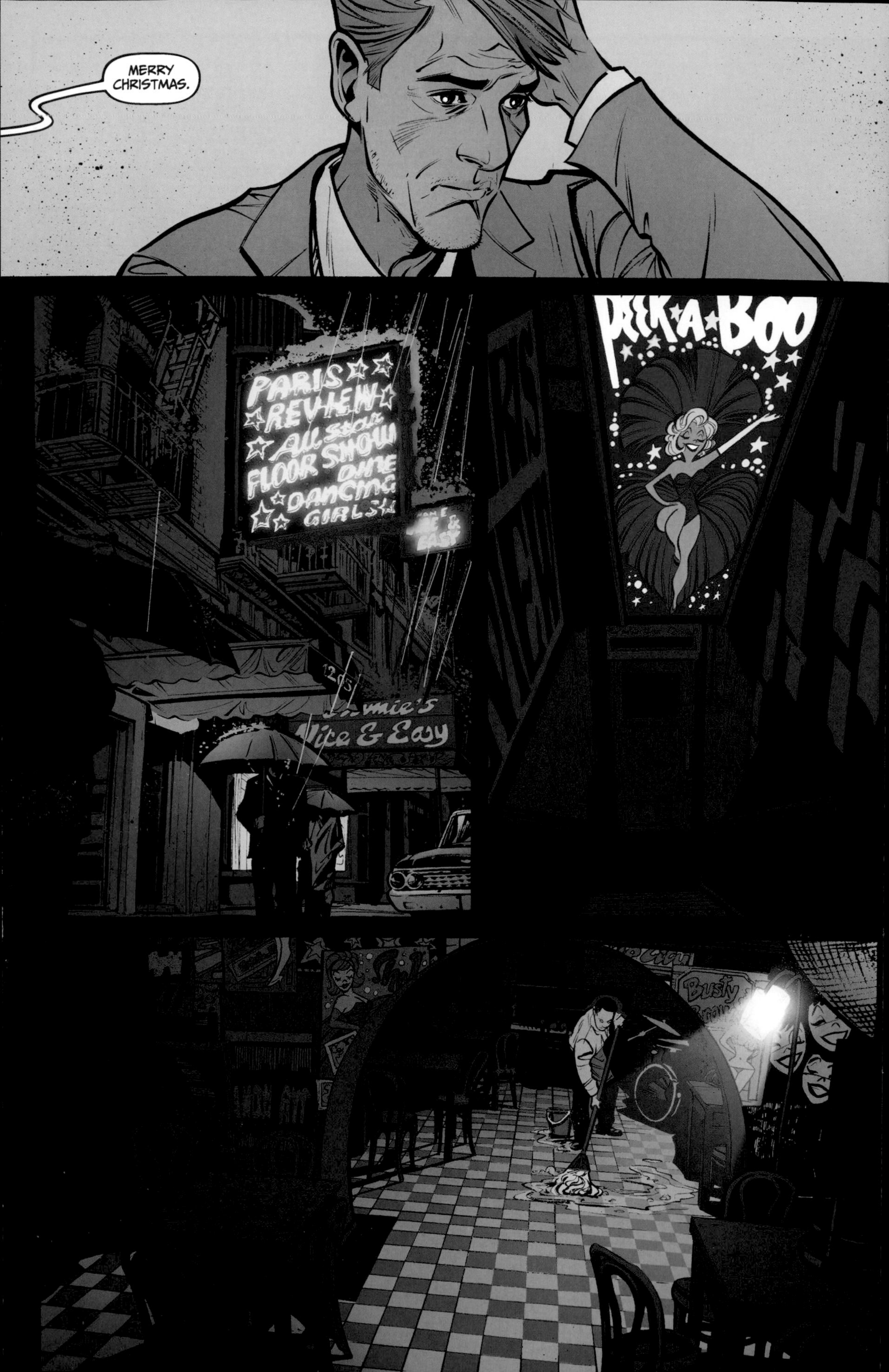
MERRY CHRISTMAS.
PARIS REVIEW
All Star
FLOOR SHOW
DINE
DANCING
GIRLS
PEEK-A-BOO
Busty

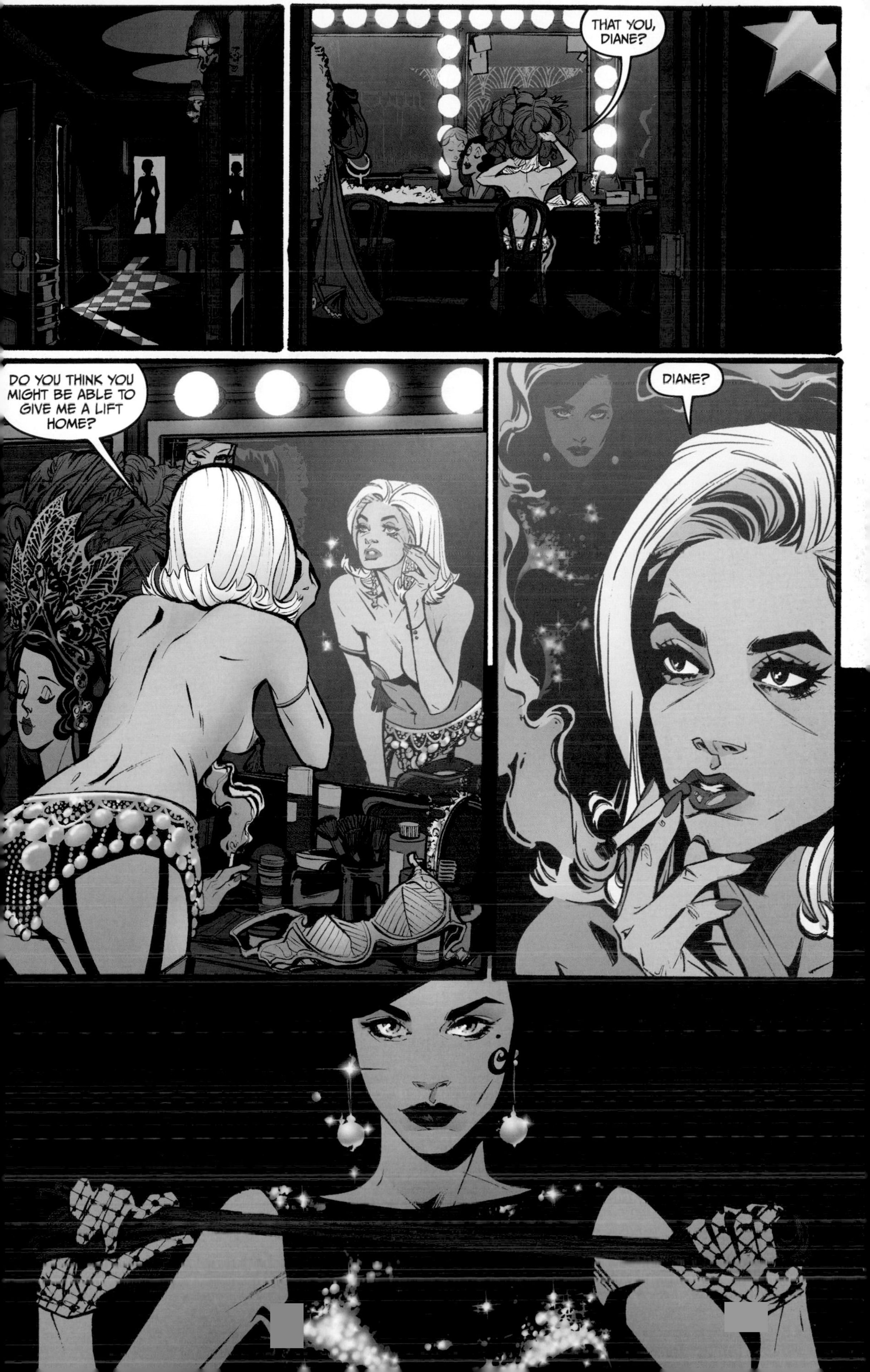
THAT YOU, DIANE?
DO YOU THINK YOU MIGHT BE ABLE TO GIVE ME A LIFT HOME?
DIANE?

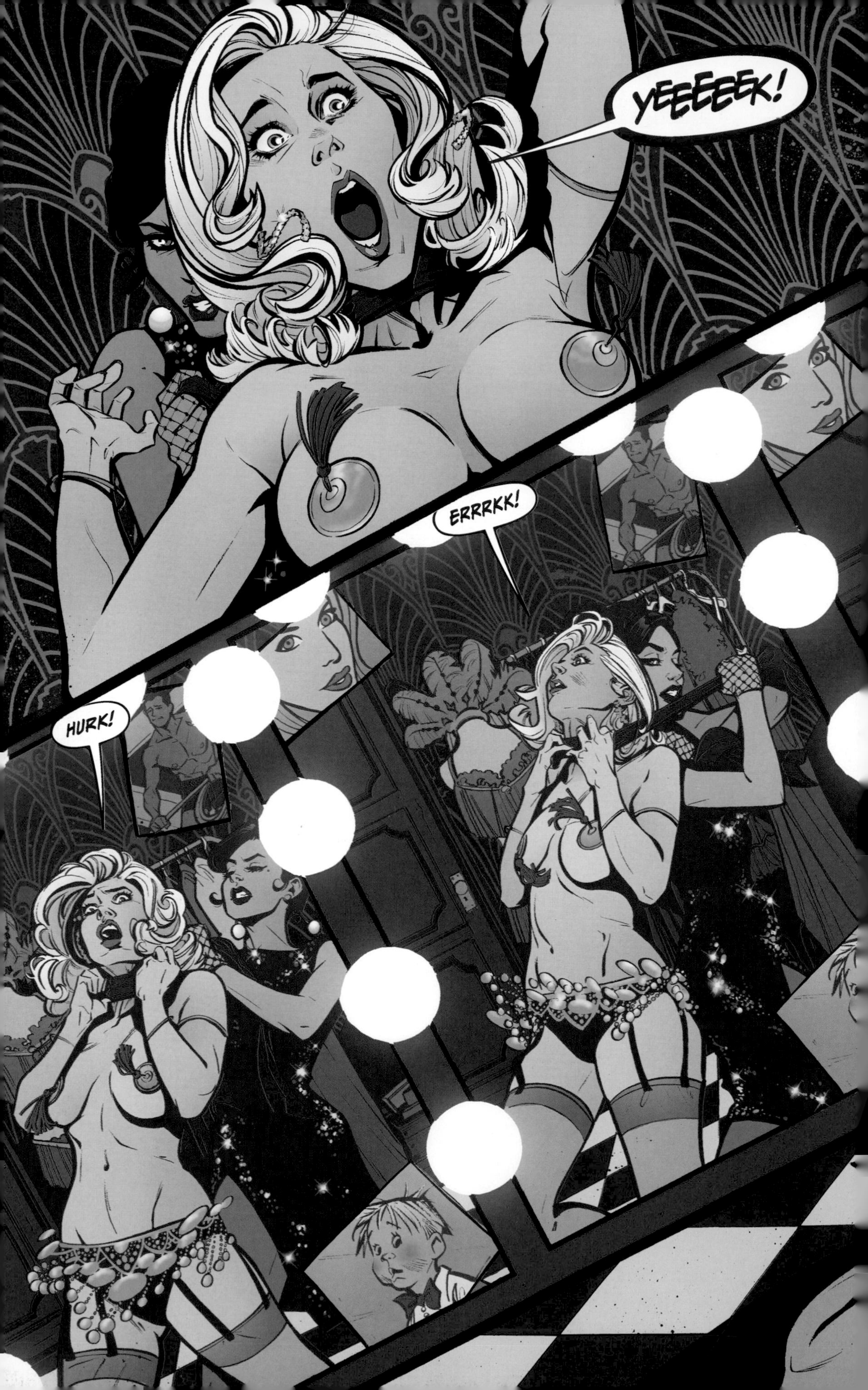
YEEEEEK!
ERRRKK!
HURK!

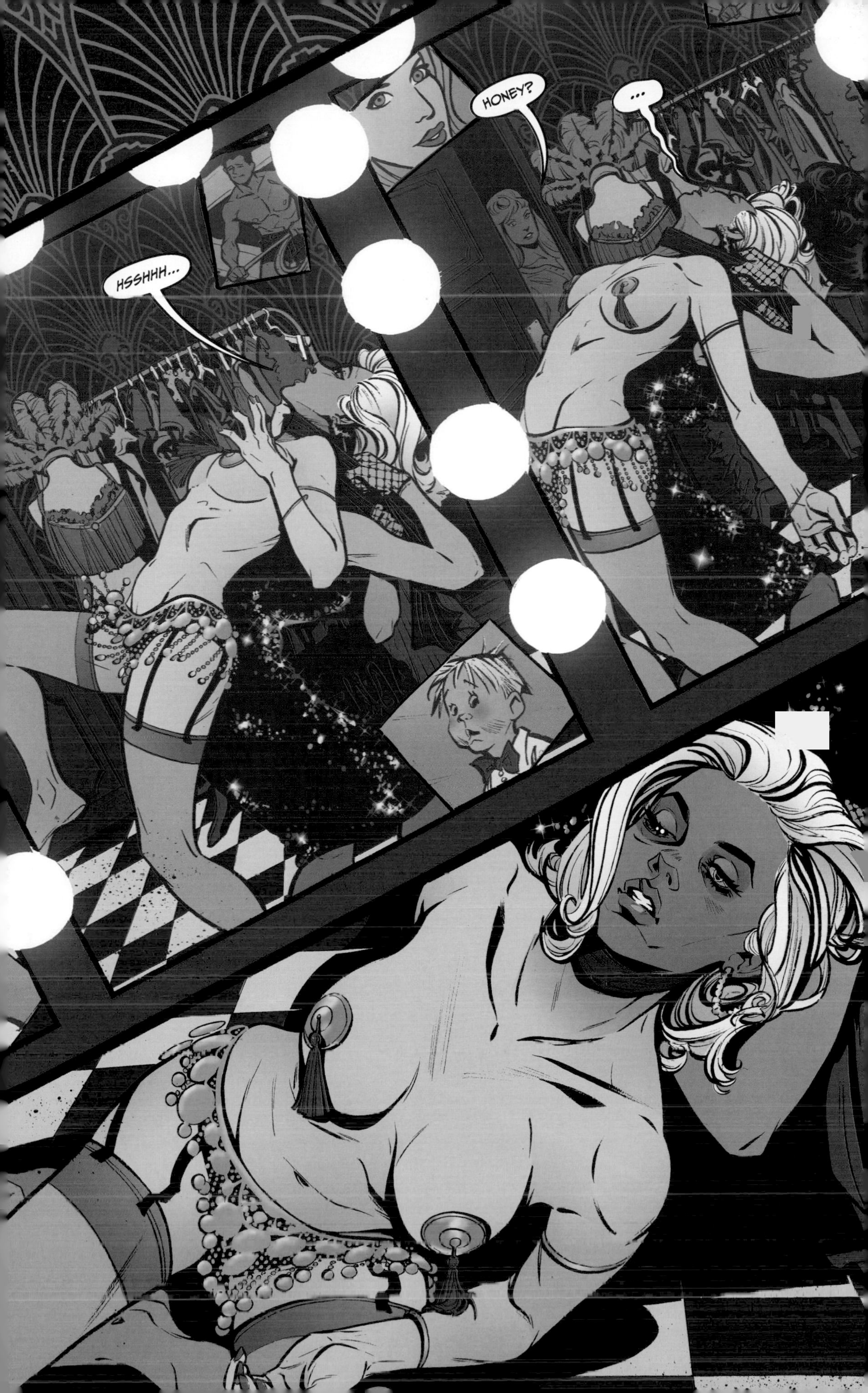
HSSHHH...
HONEY?
...

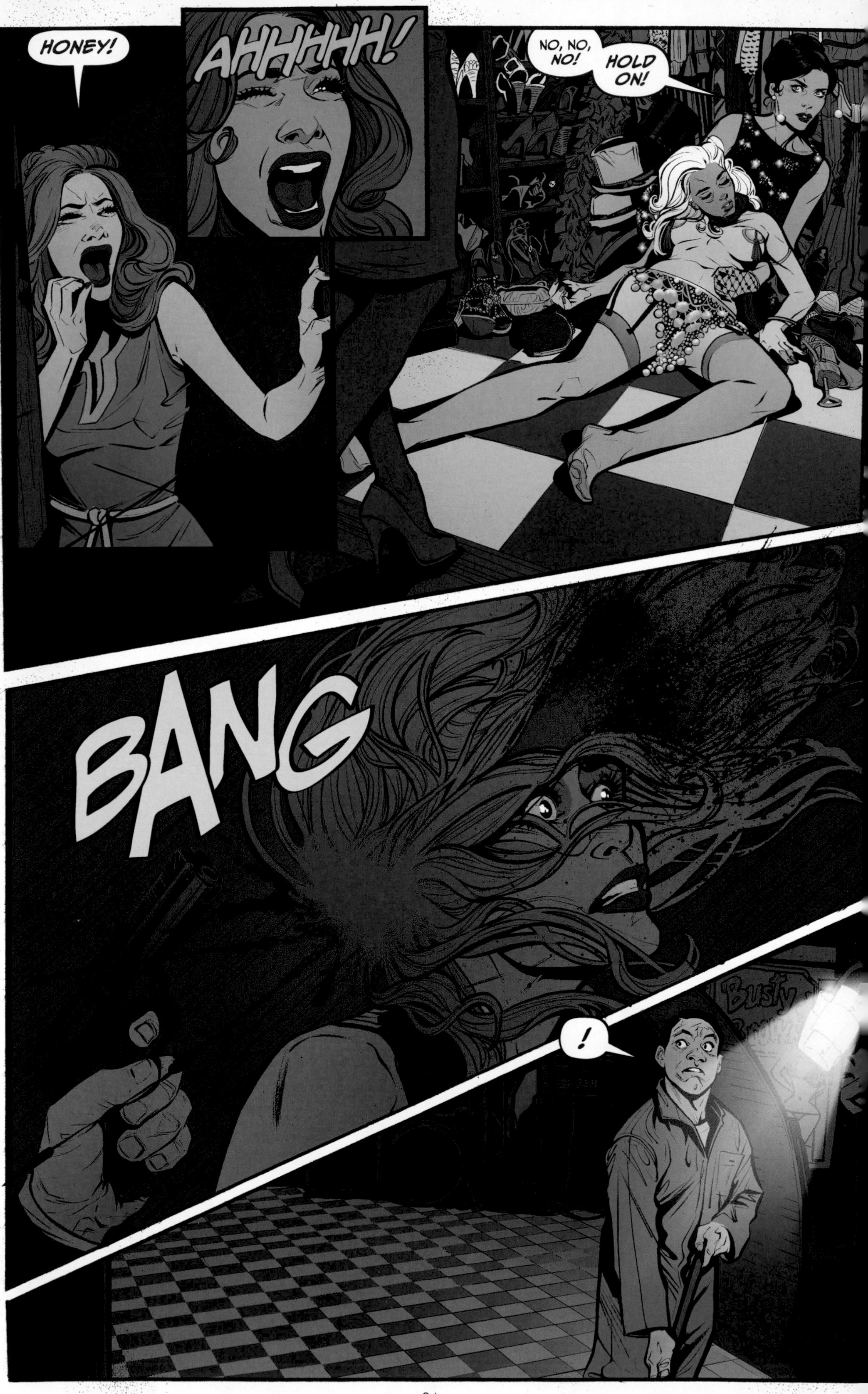
HONEY!
AHHHHH!
NO, NO, NO!
HOLD ON!
BANG
!

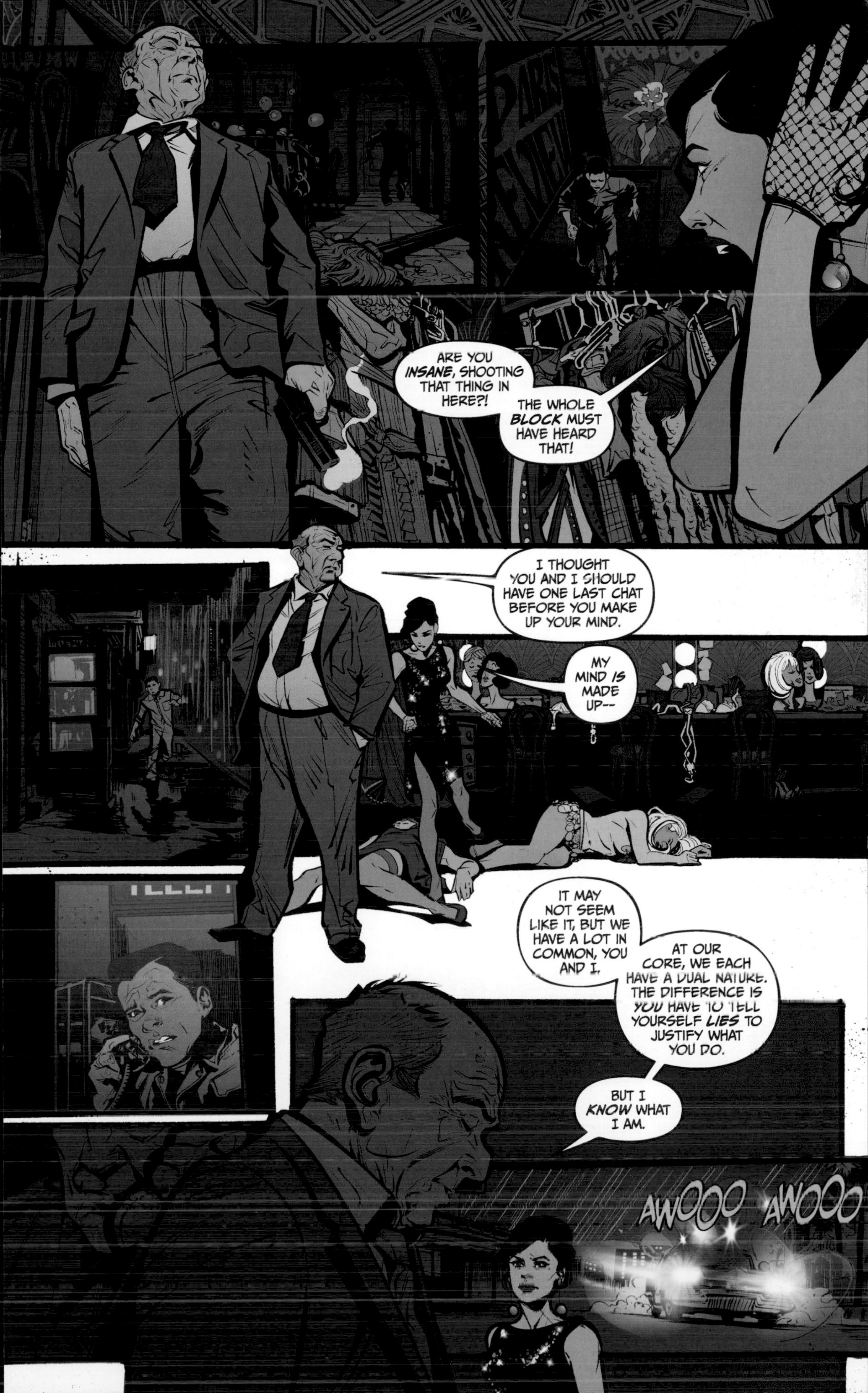
ARE YOU INSANE, SHOOTING THAT THING IN HERE?!
THE WHOLE BLOCK MUST HAVE HEARD THAT!
I THOUGHT YOU AND I SHOULD HAVE ONE LAST CHAT BEFORE YOU MAKE UP YOUR MIND.
MY MIND IS MADE UP--
IT MAY NOT SEEM LIKE IT, BUT WE HAVE A LOT IN COMMON, YOU AND I.
AT OUR CORE, WE EACH HAVE A DUAL NATURE. THE DIFFERENCE IS YOU HAVE TO TELL YOURSELF LIES TO JUSTIFY WHAT YOU DO.
BUT I KNOW WHAT I AM.
AWOOO AWOOO

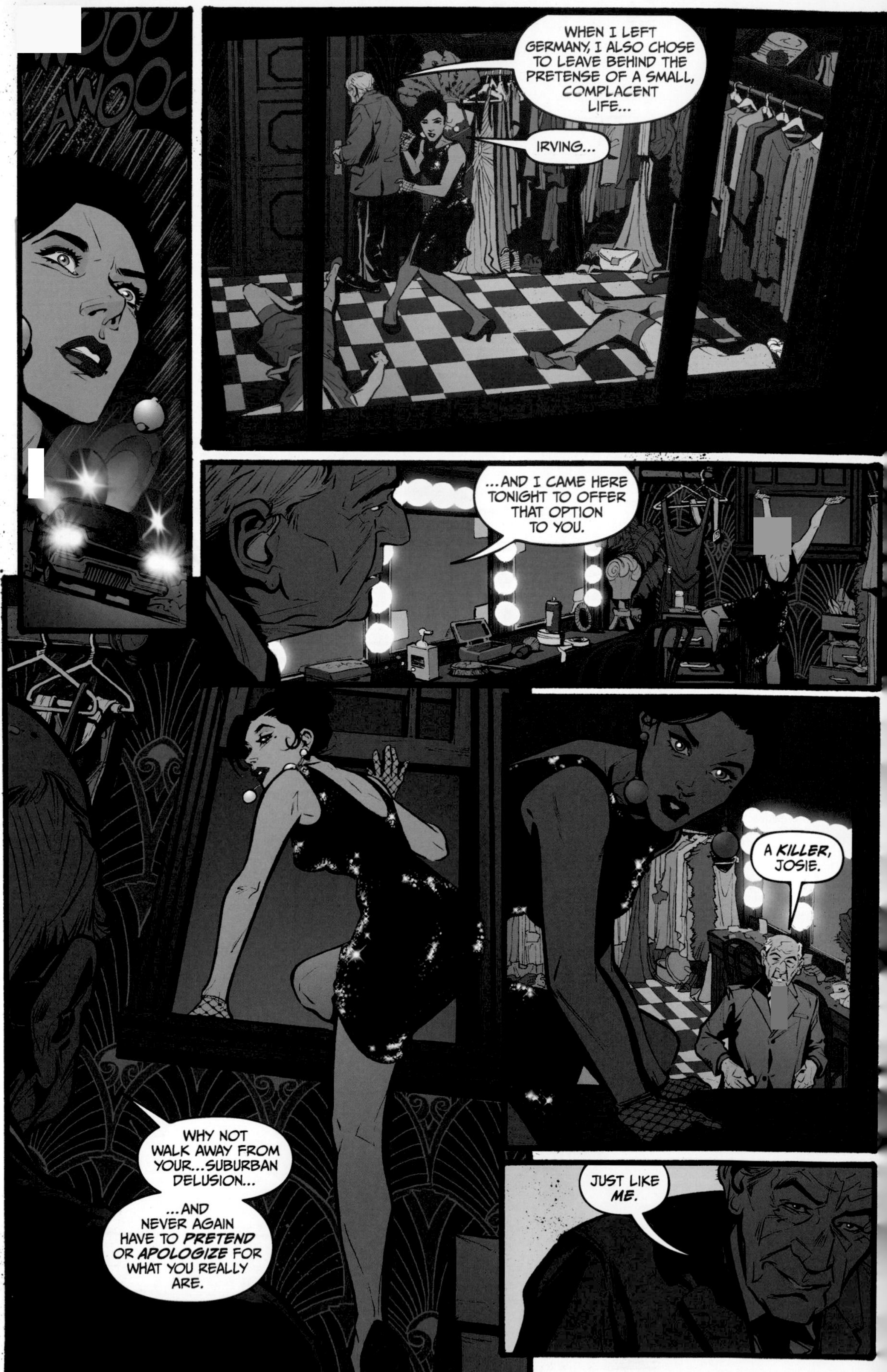
WHEN I LEFT GERMANY, I ALSO CHOSE TO LEAVE BEHIND THE PRETENSE OF A SMALL, COMPLACENT LIFE...
IRVING...
...AND I CAME HERE TONIGHT TO OFFER THAT OPTION TO YOU.
WHY NOT WALK AWAY FROM YOUR...SUBURBAN DELUSION...
...AND NEVER AGAIN HAVE TO PRETEND OR APOLOGIZE FOR WHAT YOU REALLY ARE.
A KILLER, JOSIE.
JUST LIKE ME.

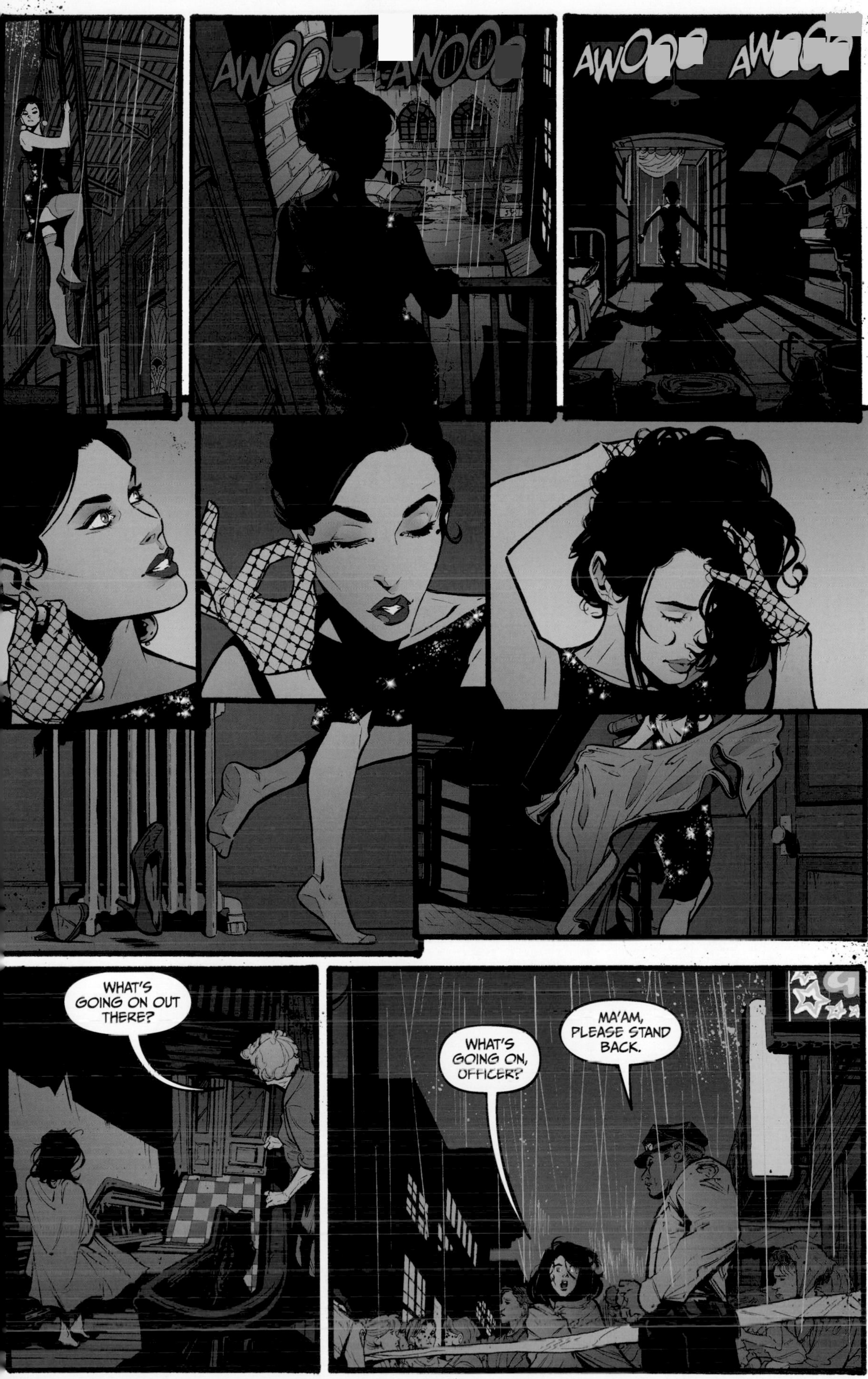
AWOO
AWOO
AWO
AW
WHAT'S GOING ON OUT THERE?
WHAT'S GOING ON, OFFICER?
MA'AM, PLEASE STAND BACK.

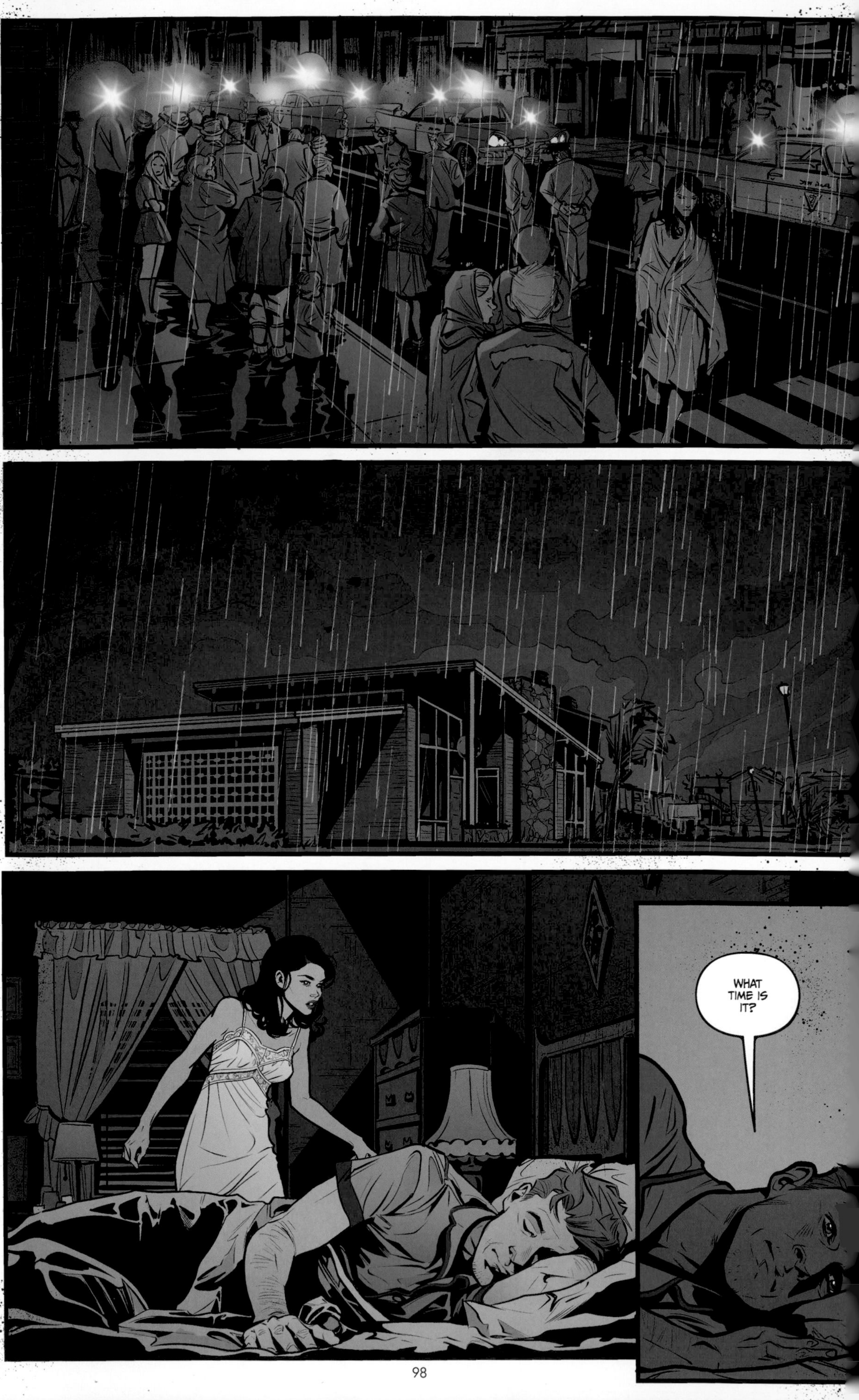
WHAT TIME IS IT?

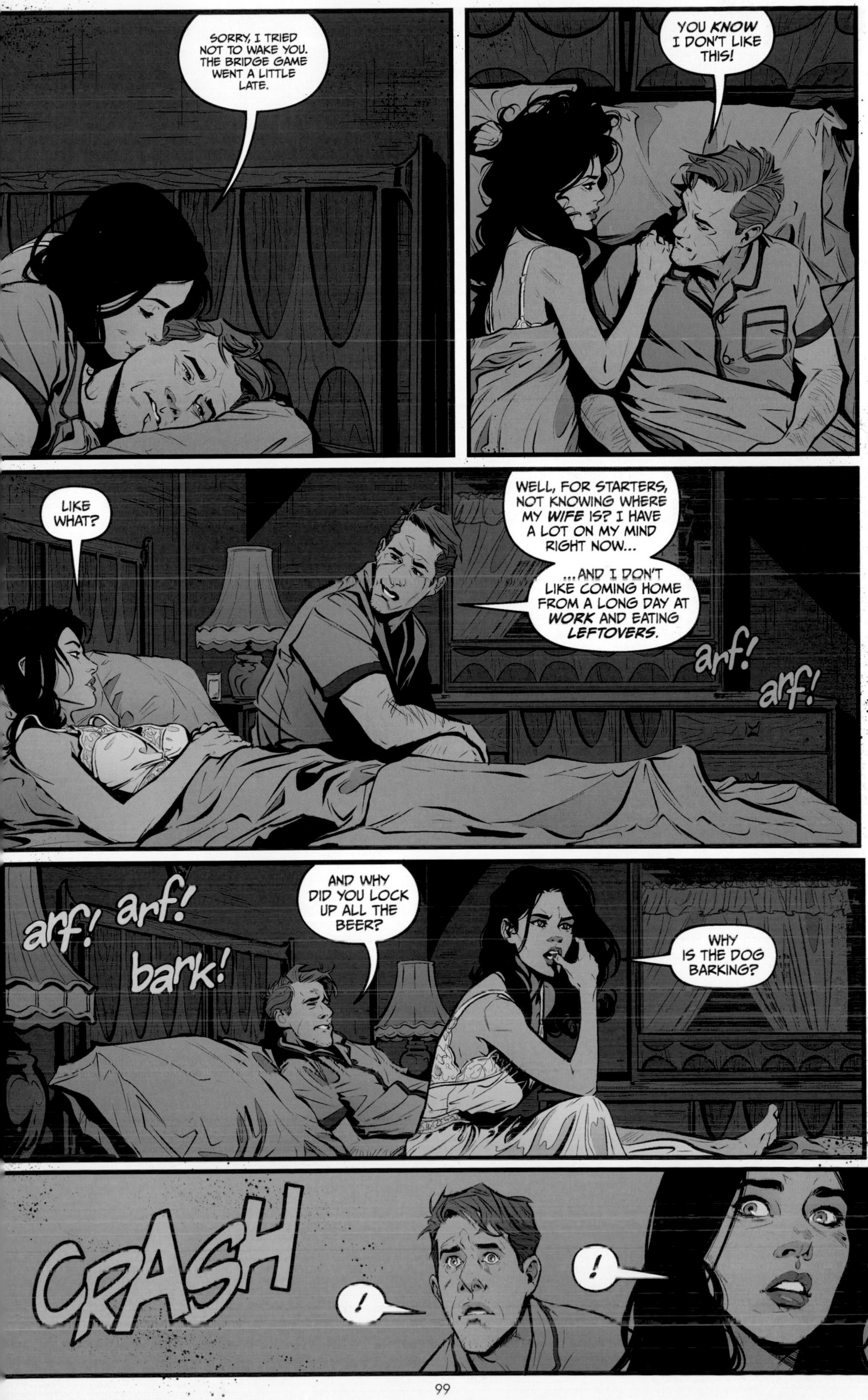
SORRY, I TRIED NOT TO WAKE YOU. THE BRIDGE GAME WENT A LITTLE LATE.
YOU KNOW I DON'T LIKE THIS!
LIKE WHAT?
WELL, FOR STARTERS, NOT KNOWING WHERE MY WIFE IS? I HAVE A LOT ON MY MIND RIGHT NOW...
...AND I DON'T LIKE COMING HOME FROM A LONG DAY AT WORK AND EATING LEFTOVERS.
arf! arf!
arf! arf!
bark!
AND WHY DID YOU LOCK UP ALL THE BEER?
WHY IS THE DOG BARKING?
CRASH
!
!

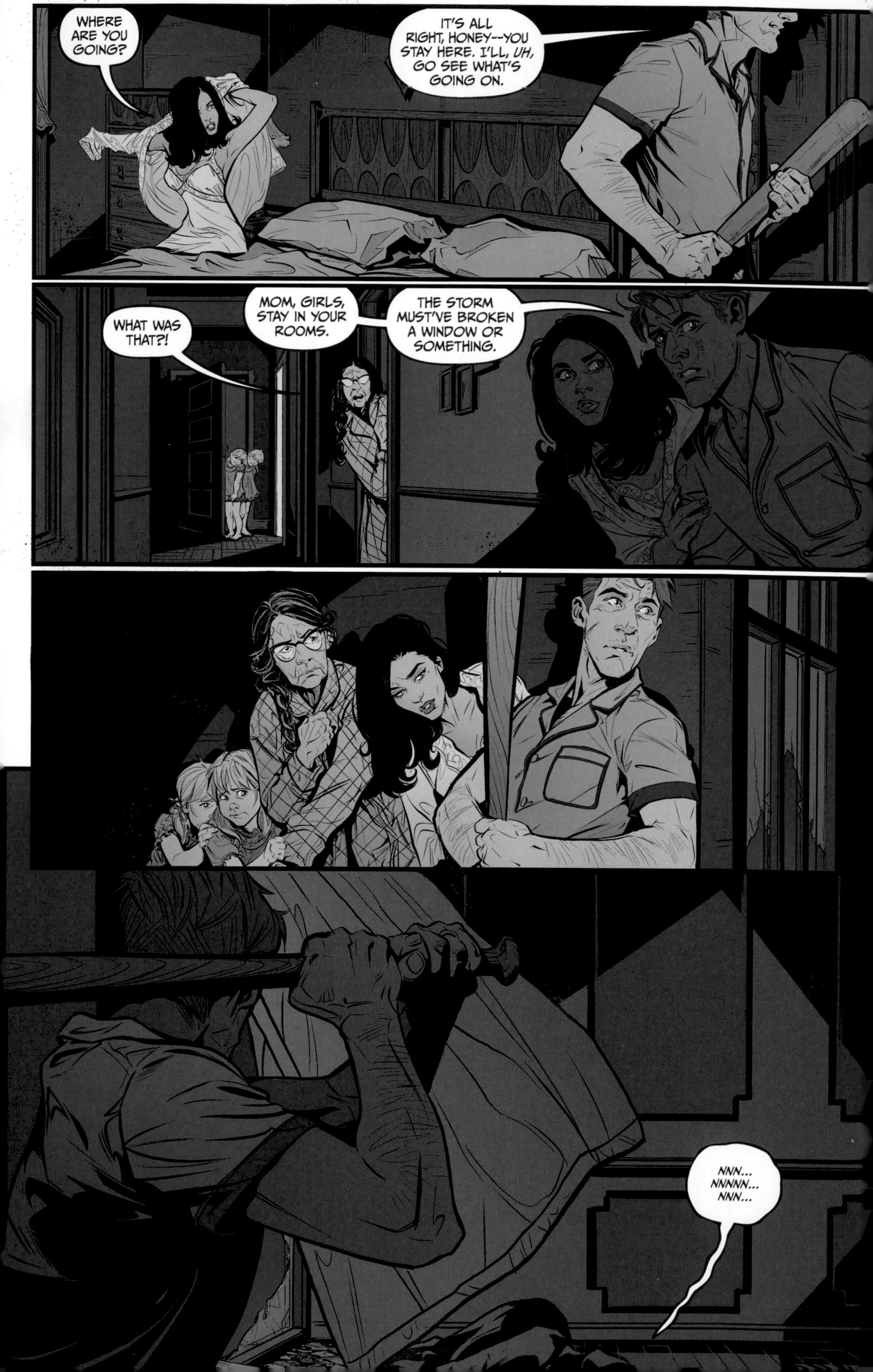
WHERE ARE YOU GOING?
IT'S ALL RIGHT, HONEY--YOU STAY HERE. I'LL, *UH*, GO SEE WHAT'S GOING ON.
WHAT WAS THAT?!
MOM, GIRLS, STAY IN YOUR ROOMS.
THE STORM MUST'VE BROKEN A WINDOW OR SOMETHING.
NNN... NNNNN... NNN...

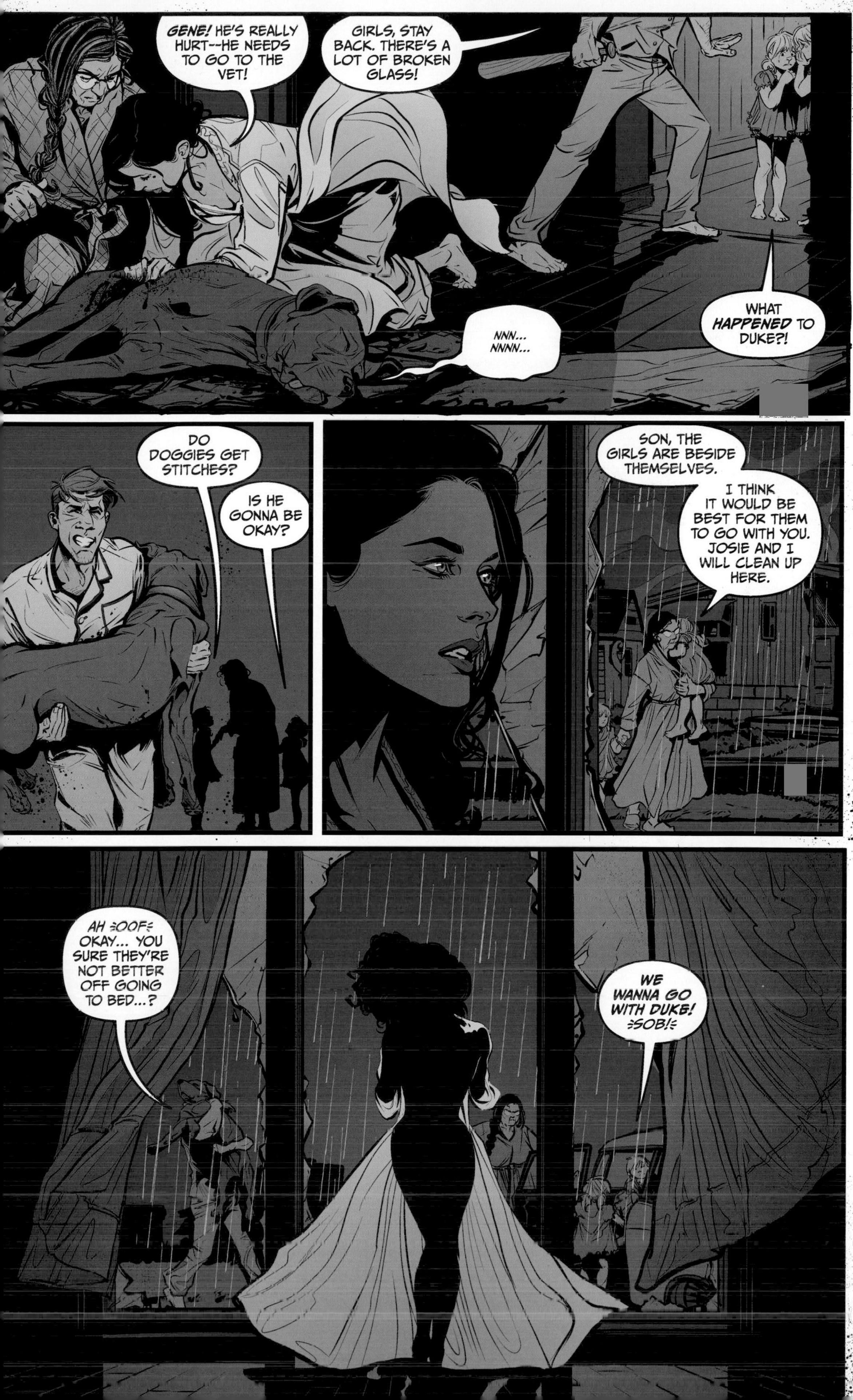
GENE! HE'S REALLY HURT--HE NEEDS TO GO TO THE VET!
GIRLS, STAY BACK. THERE'S A LOT OF BROKEN GLASS!
NNN... NNNN...
WHAT HAPPENED TO DUKE?!
DO DOGGIES GET STITCHES?
IS HE GONNA BE OKAY?
SON, THE GIRLS ARE BESIDE THEMSELVES.
I THINK IT WOULD BE BEST FOR THEM TO GO WITH YOU. JOSIE AND I WILL CLEAN UP HERE.
AH ≈OOF≈ OKAY... YOU SURE THEY'RE NOT BETTER OFF GOING TO BED...?
WE WANNA GO WITH DUKE! ≈SOB!≈

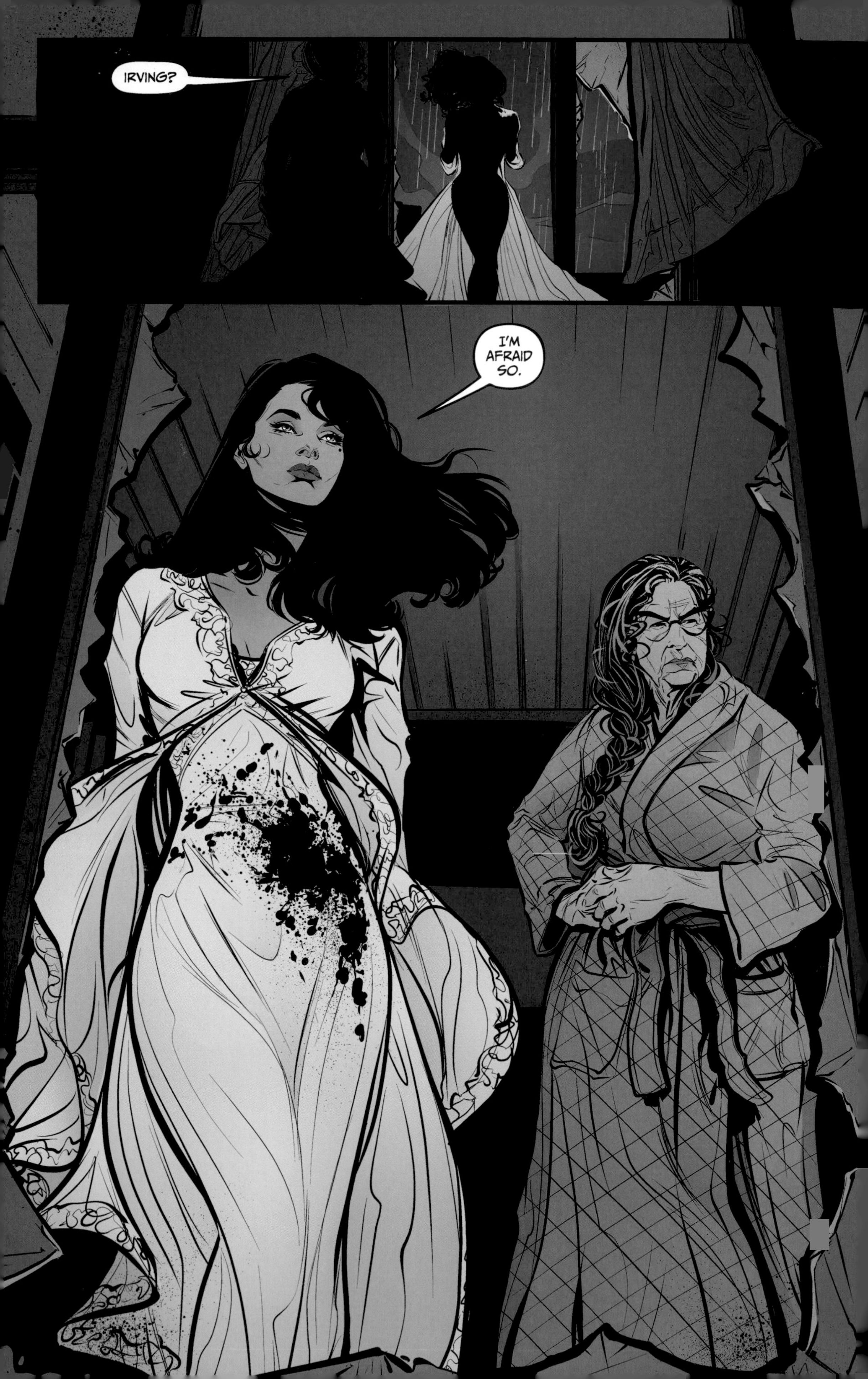
IRVING?
I'M AFRAID SO.

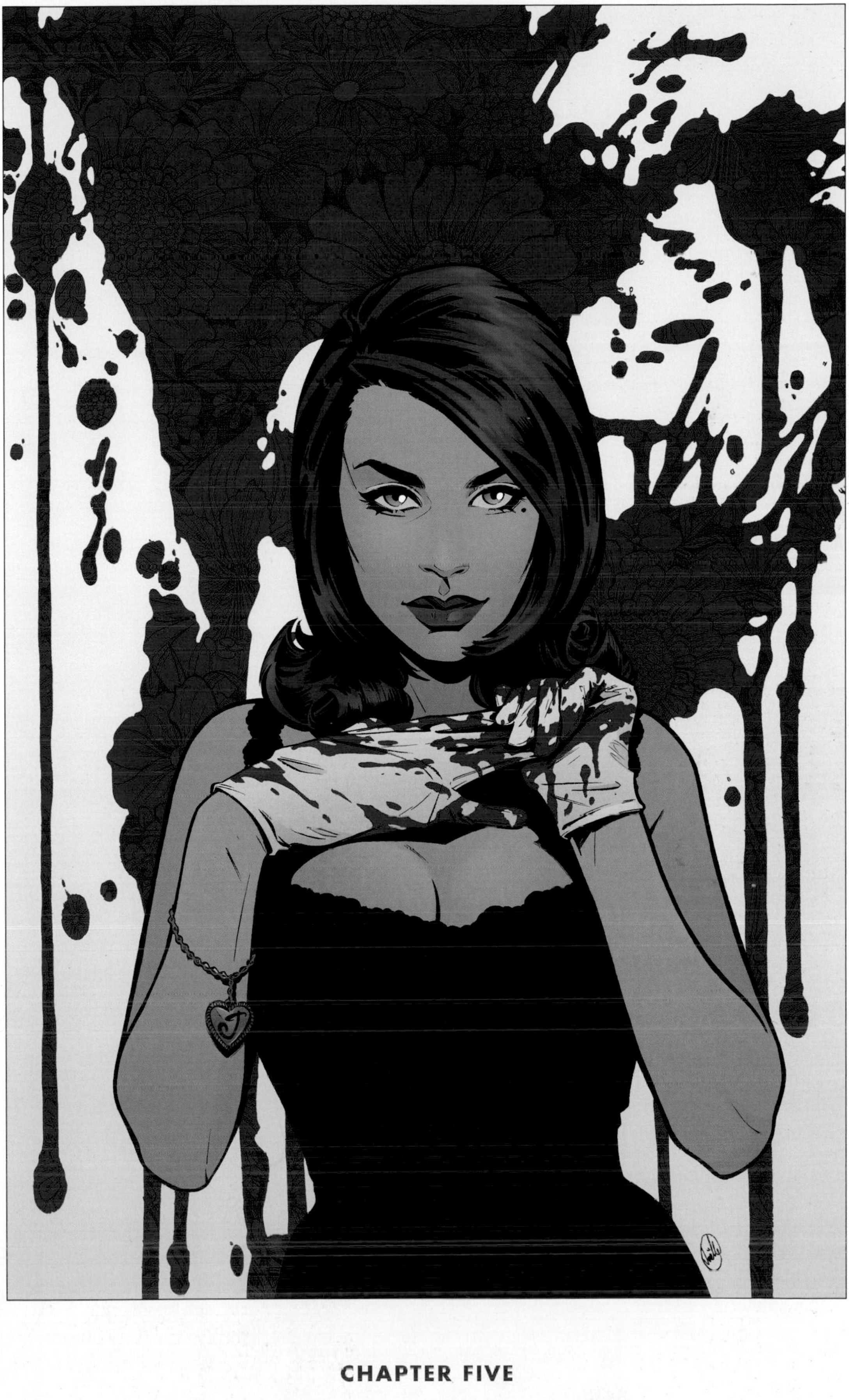

CHAPTER FIVE

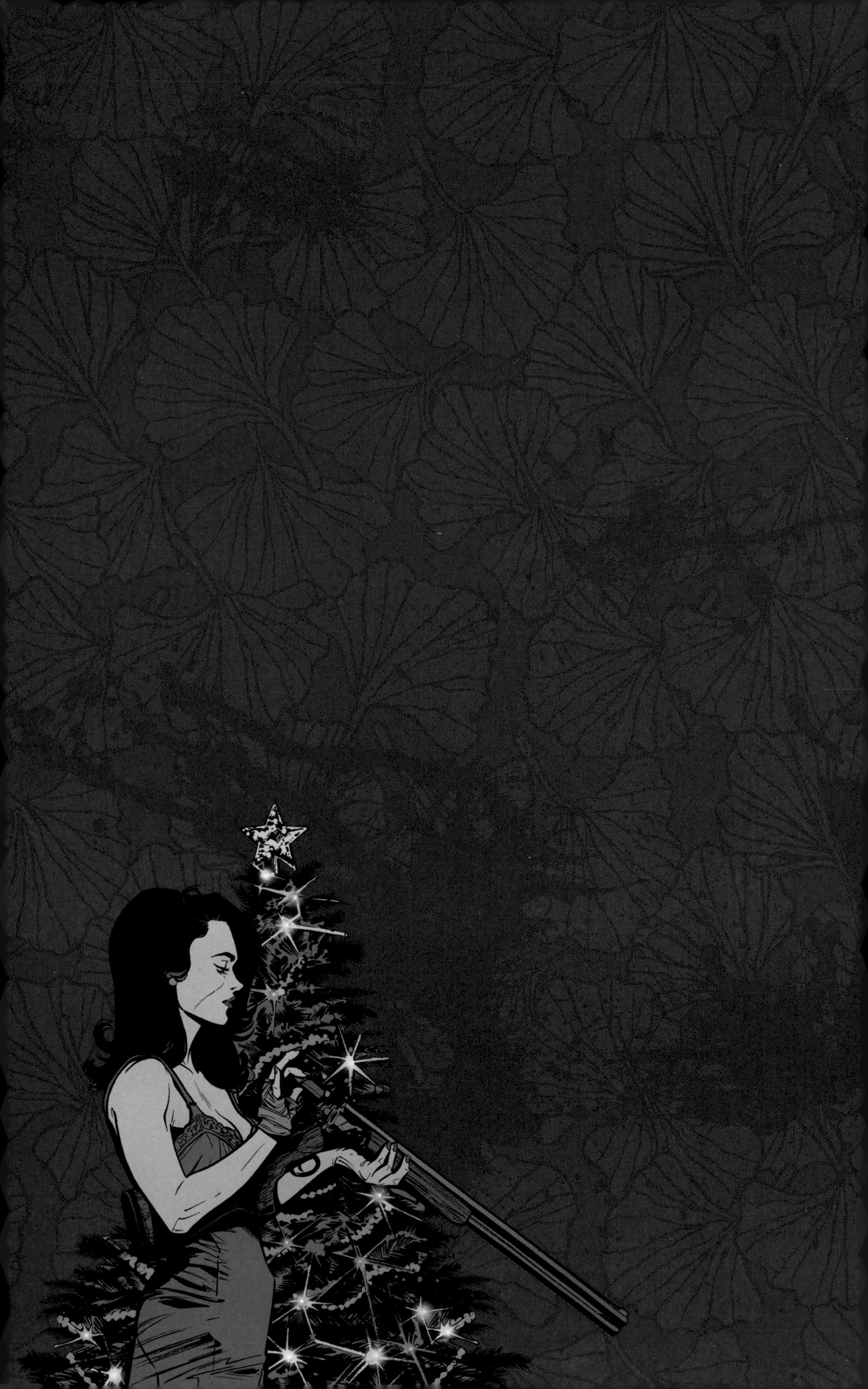

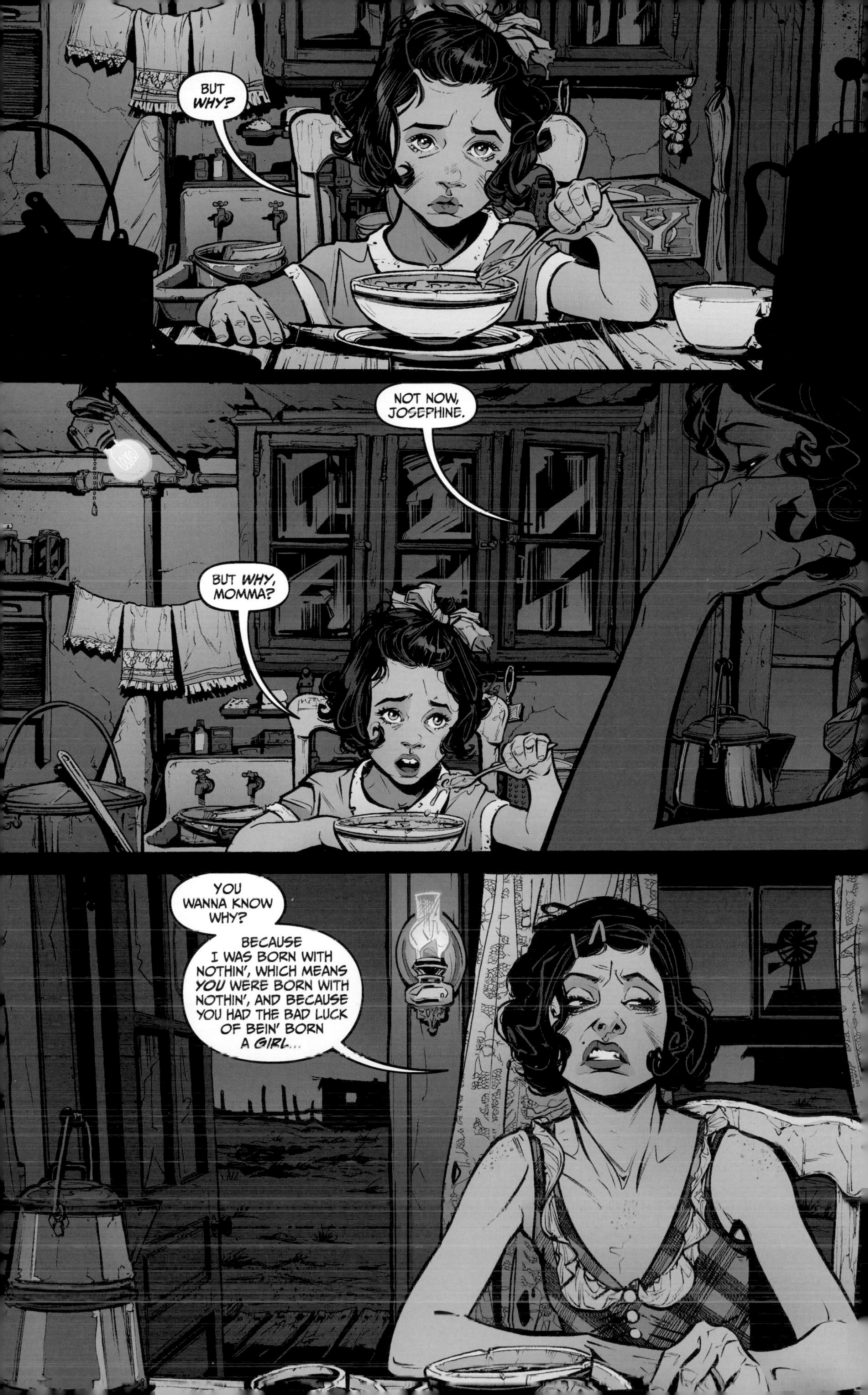
BUT WHY?
NOT NOW, JOSEPHINE.
BUT WHY, MOMMA?
YOU WANNA KNOW WHY?
BECAUSE I WAS BORN WITH NOTHIN', WHICH MEANS YOU WERE BORN WITH NOTHIN', AND BECAUSE YOU HAD THE BAD LUCK OF BEIN' BORN A GIRL...

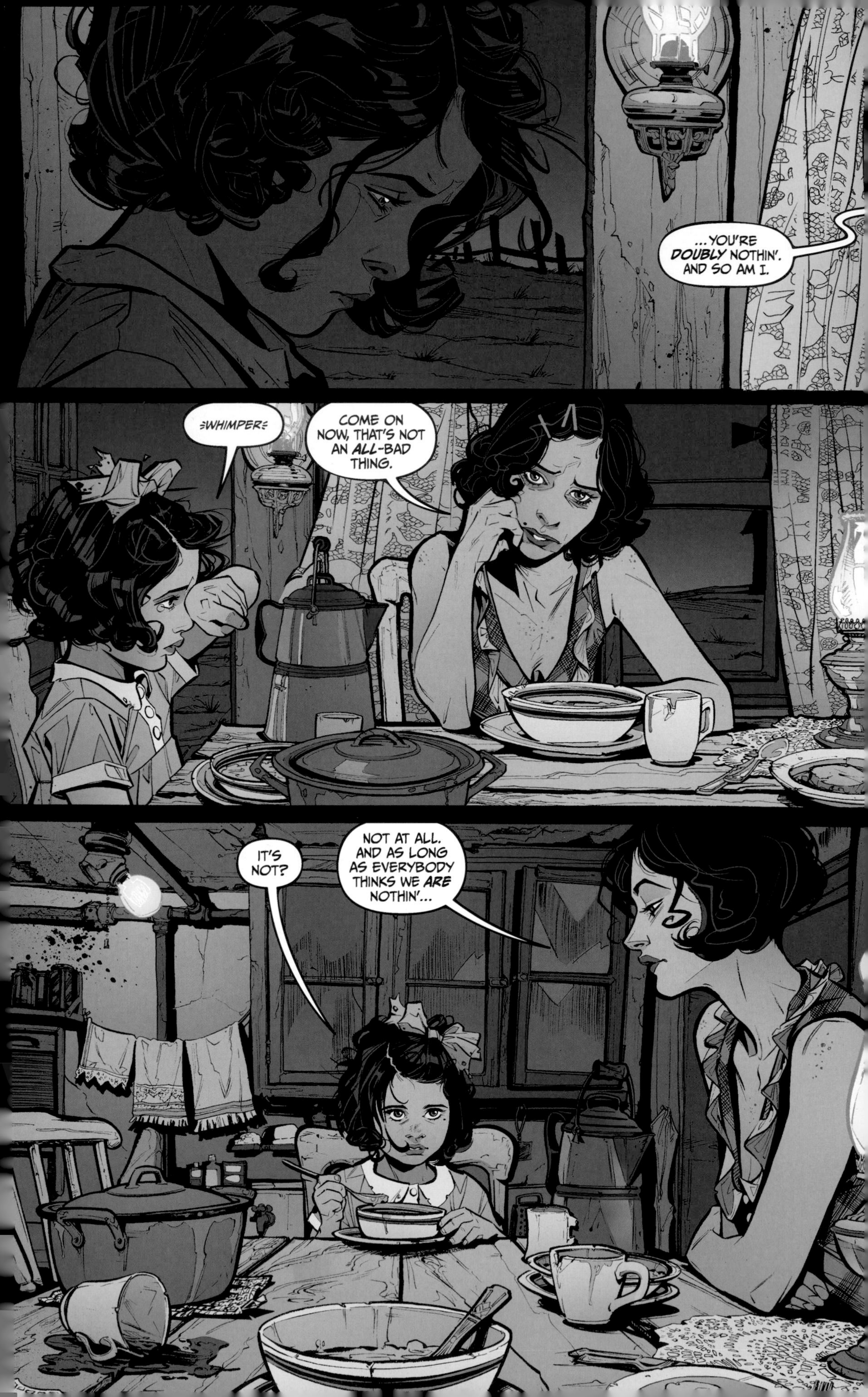
...YOU'RE DOUBLY NOTHIN'. AND SO AM I.
=WHIMPER=
COME ON NOW, THAT'S NOT AN ALL-BAD THING.
IT'S NOT?
NOT AT ALL. AND AS LONG AS EVERYBODY THINKS WE ARE NOTHIN'...

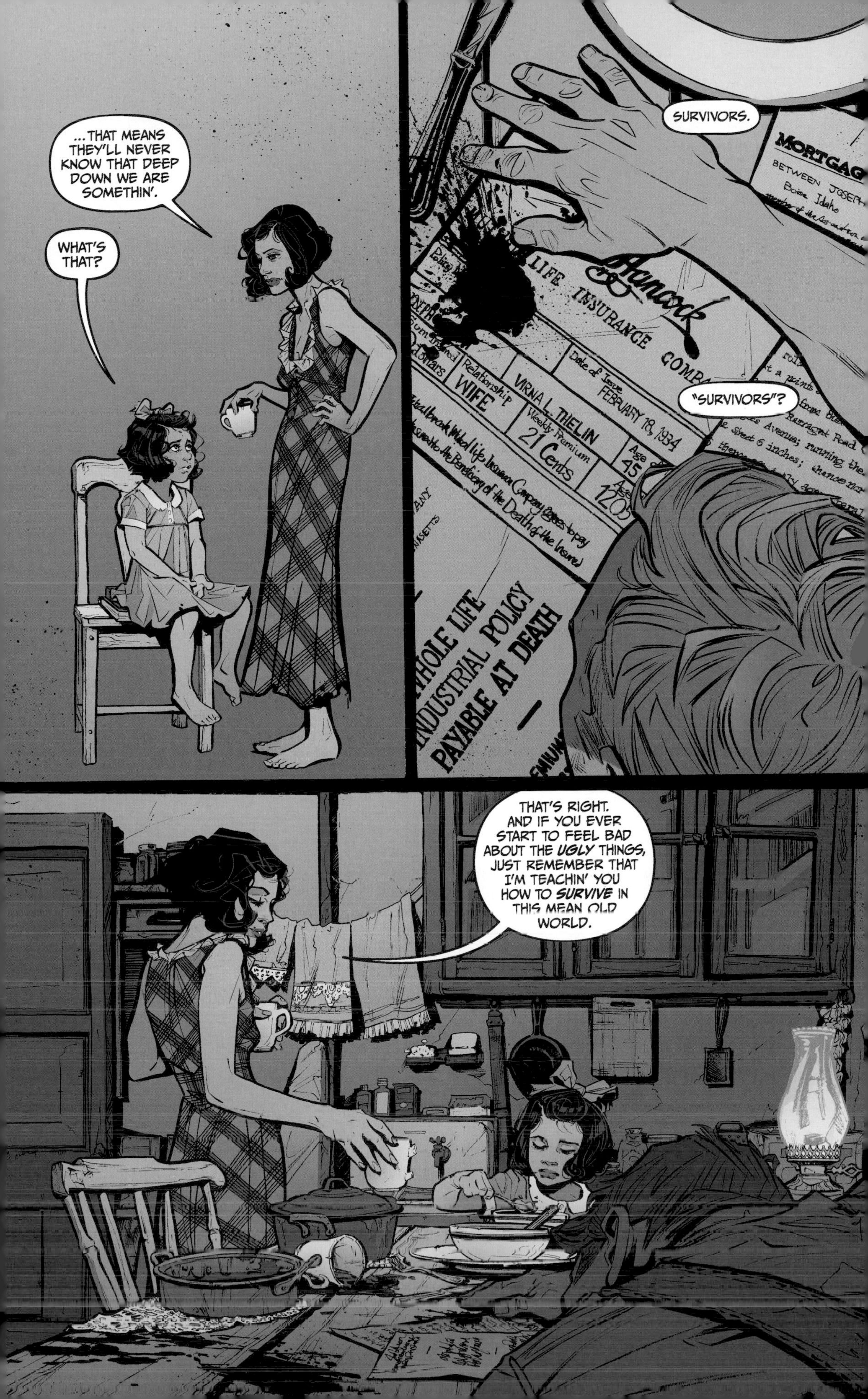
...THAT MEANS THEY'LL NEVER KNOW THAT DEEP DOWN WE ARE SOMETHIN'.
WHAT'S THAT?
SURVIVORS.
"SURVIVORS"?
LIFE INSURANCE
VIRNA L. THELIN
FEBRUARY 18, 1934
WIFE
21 Cents
INDUSTRIAL POLICY
PAYABLE AT DEATH
THAT'S RIGHT. AND IF YOU EVER START TO FEEL BAD ABOUT THE *UGLY* THINGS, JUST REMEMBER THAT I'M TEACHIN' YOU HOW TO *SURVIVE* IN THIS MEAN OLD WORLD.

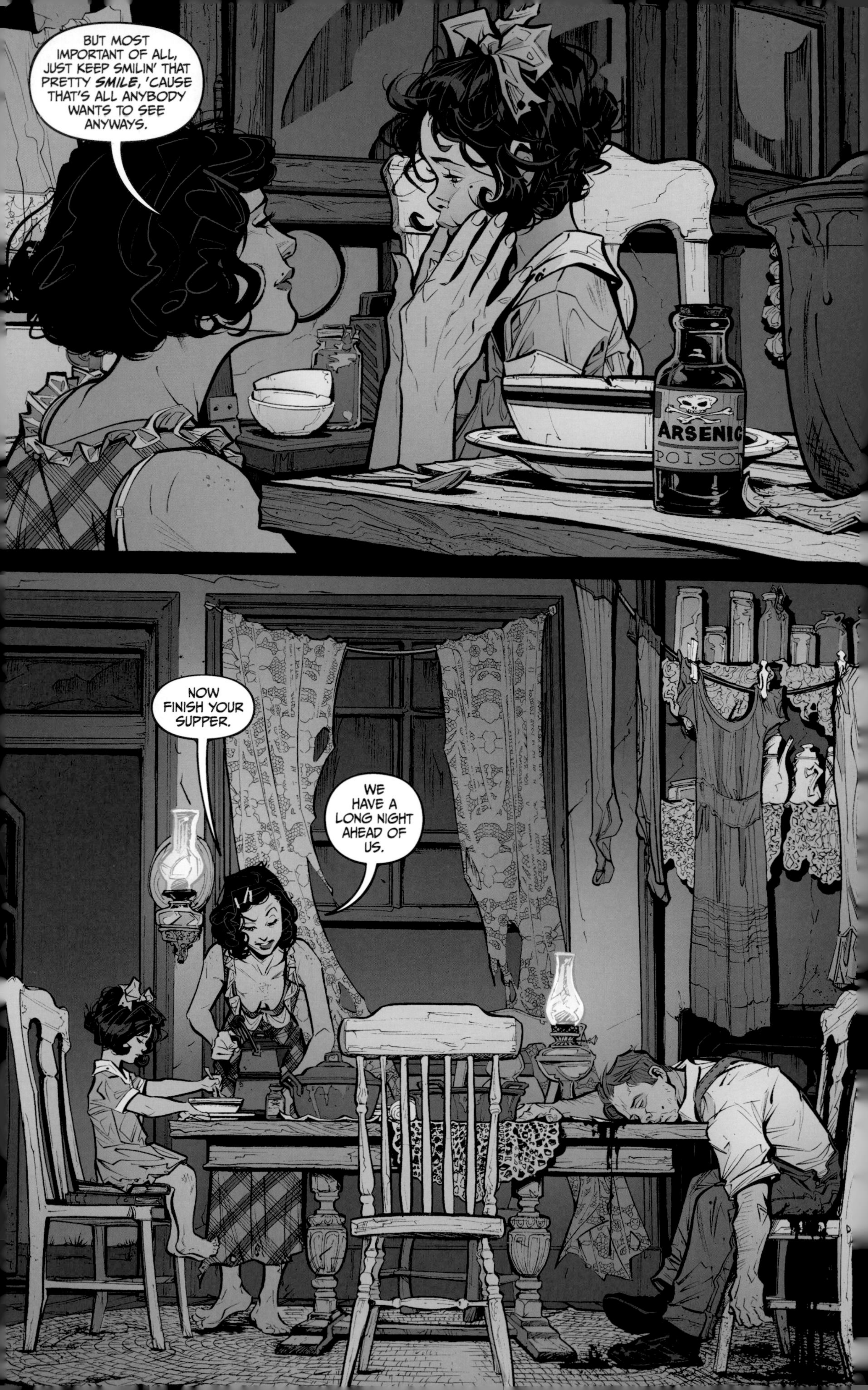
BUT MOST IMPORTANT OF ALL, JUST KEEP SMILIN' THAT PRETTY SMILE, 'CAUSE THAT'S ALL ANYBODY WANTS TO SEE ANYWAYS.
ARSENIC
POISON
NOW FINISH YOUR SUPPER.
WE HAVE A LONG NIGHT AHEAD OF US.

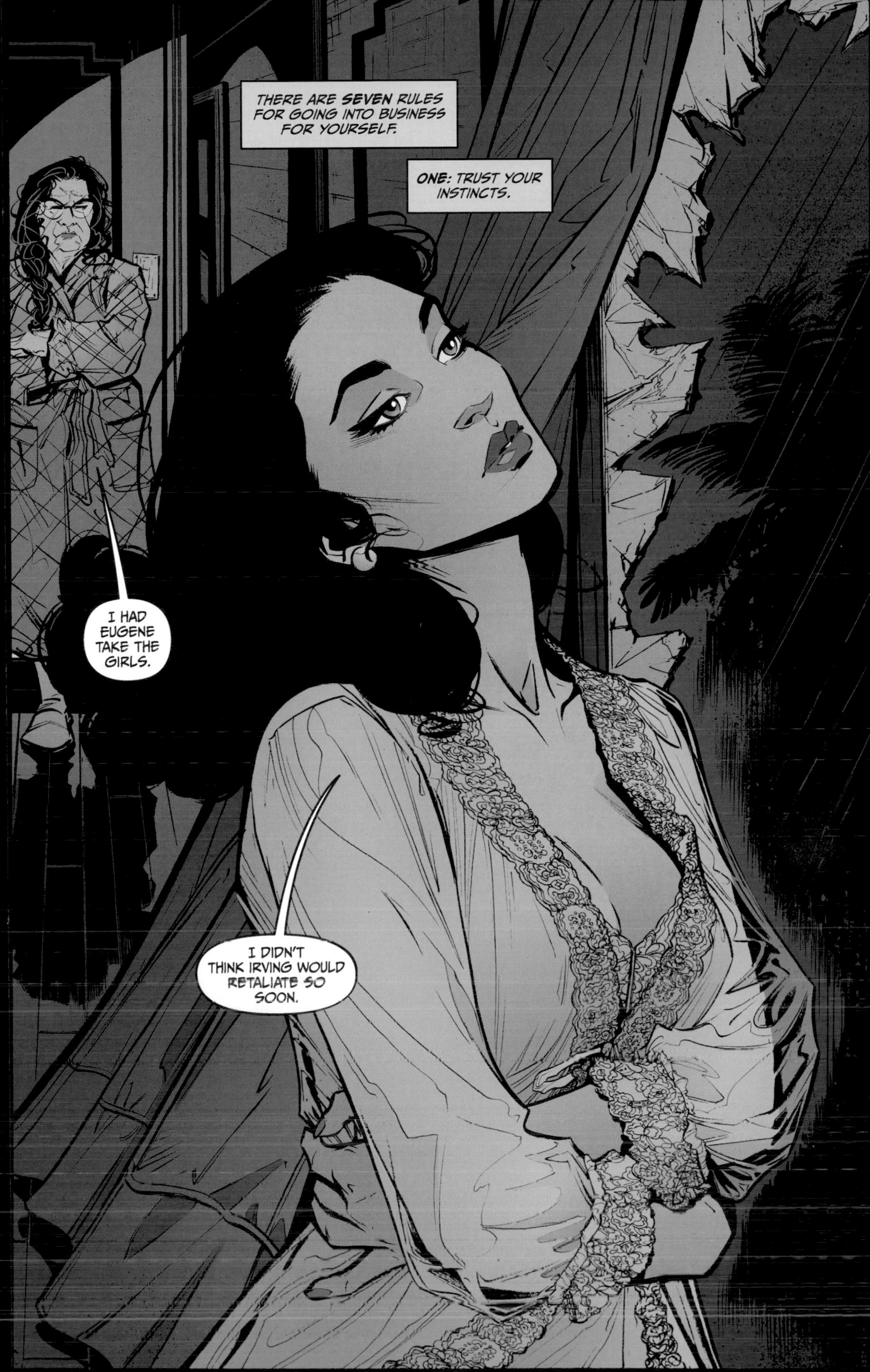
THERE ARE SEVEN RULES FOR GOING INTO BUSINESS FOR YOURSELF.
ONE: TRUST YOUR INSTINCTS.
I HAD EUGENE TAKE THE GIRLS.
I DIDN'T THINK IRVING WOULD RETALIATE SO SOON.

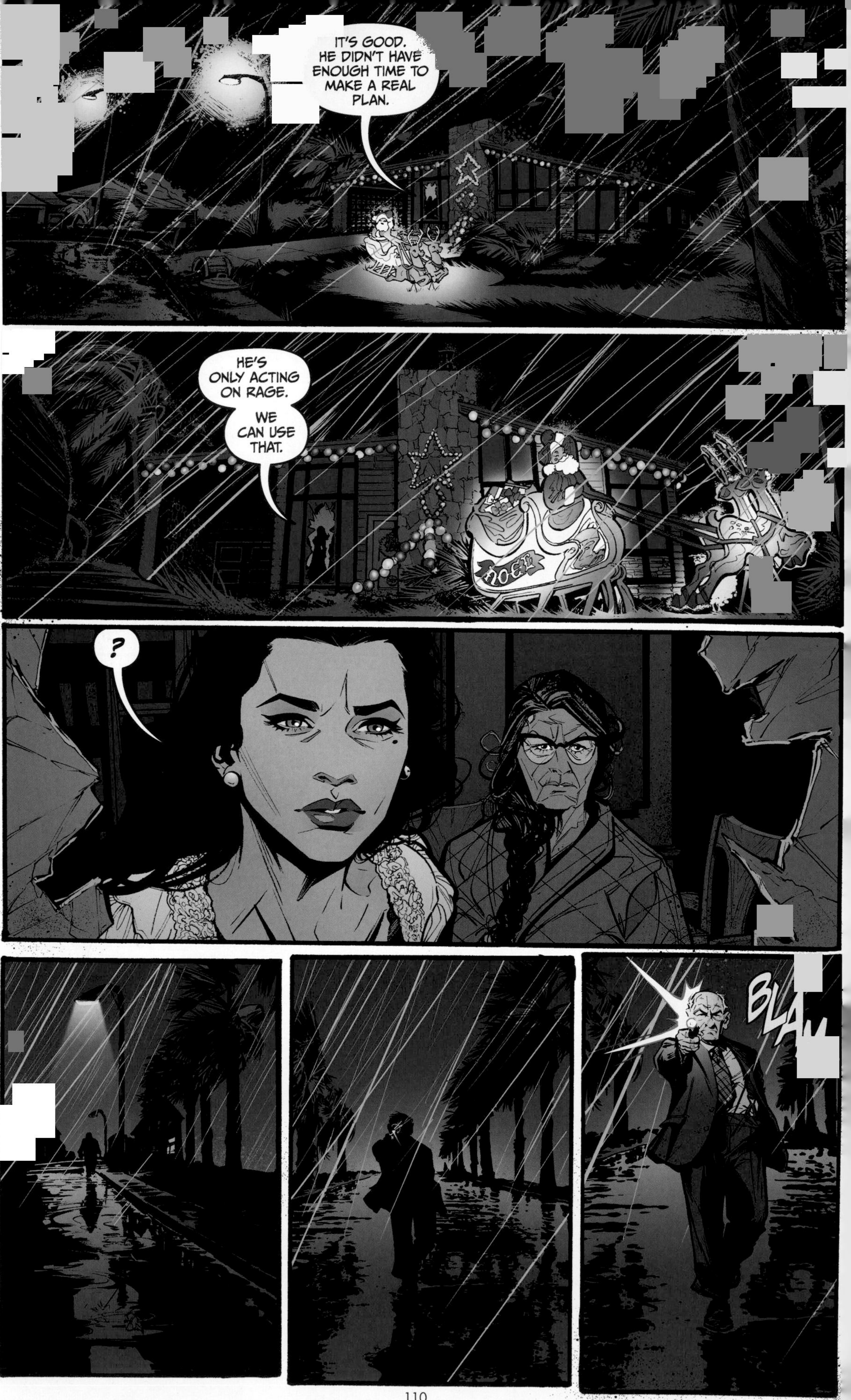
IT'S GOOD. HE DIDN'T HAVE ENOUGH TIME TO MAKE A REAL PLAN.
HE'S ONLY ACTING ON RAGE.
WE CAN USE THAT.
NOEL
?
BLA

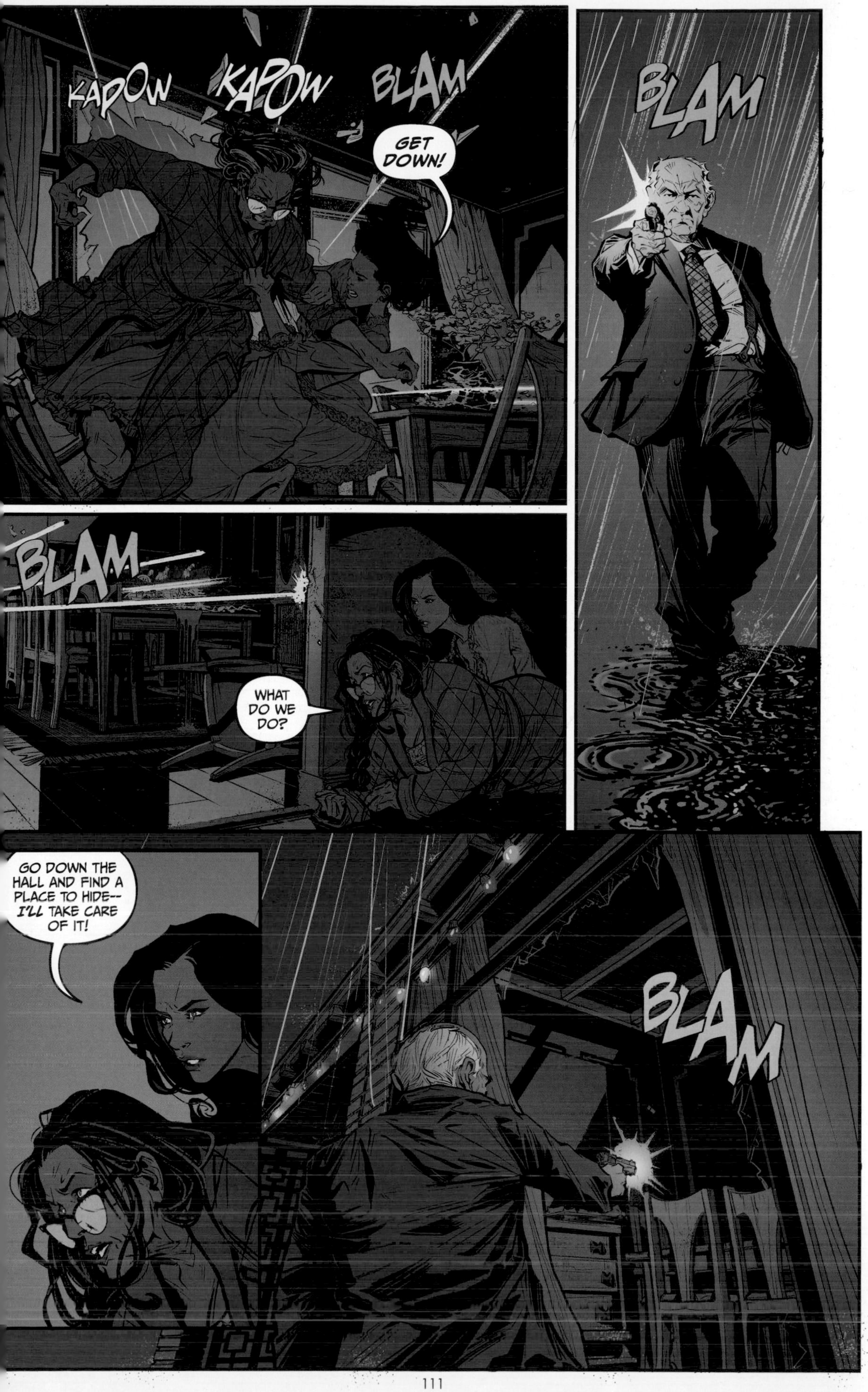
KAPOW
KAPOW
BLAM
GET DOWN!
BLAM
BLAM
WHAT DO WE DO?
GO DOWN THE HALL AND FIND A PLACE TO HIDE-- I'LL TAKE CARE OF IT!
BLAM

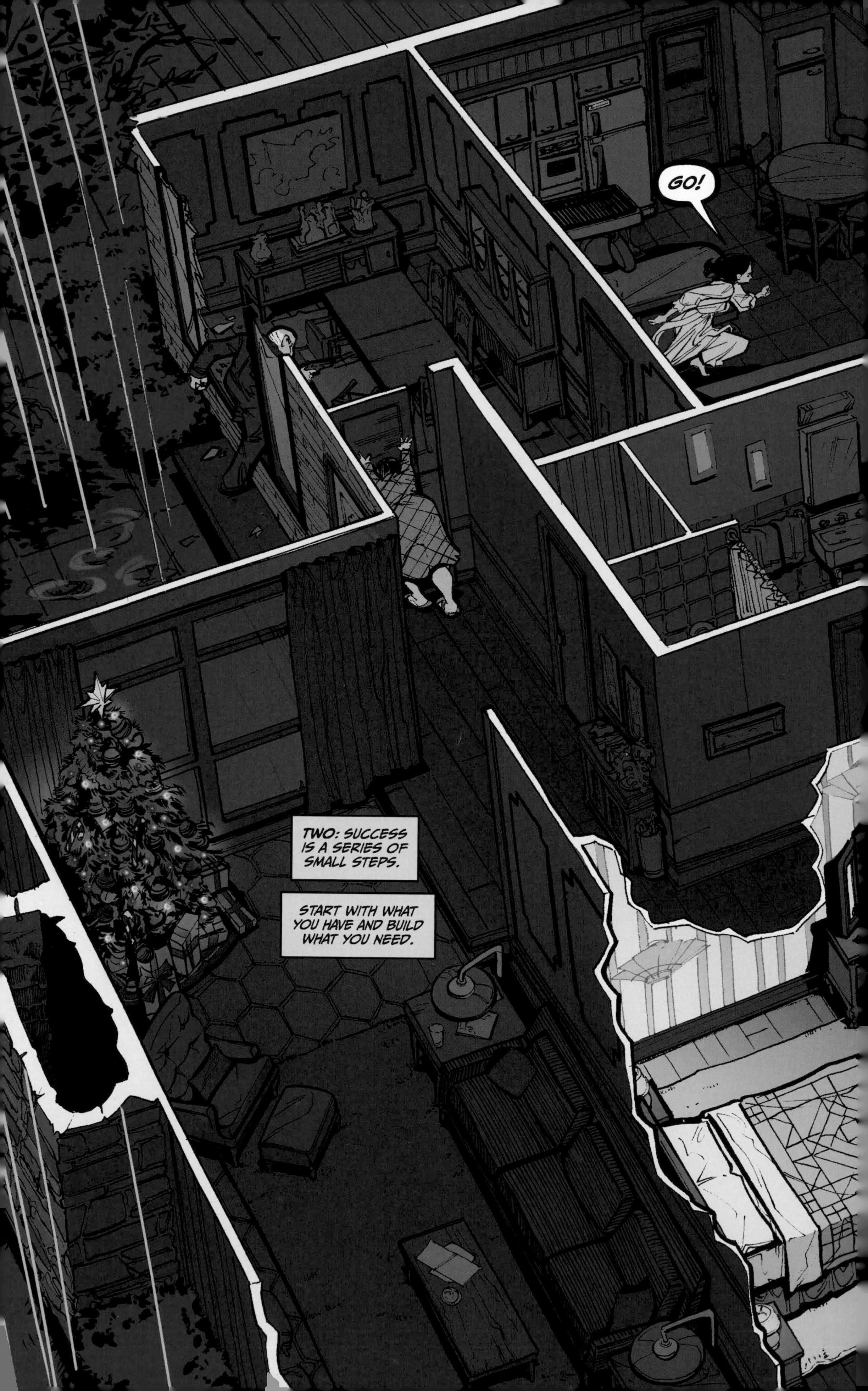
GO!
TWO: SUCCESS IS A SERIES OF SMALL STEPS.
START WITH WHAT YOU HAVE AND BUILD WHAT YOU NEED.

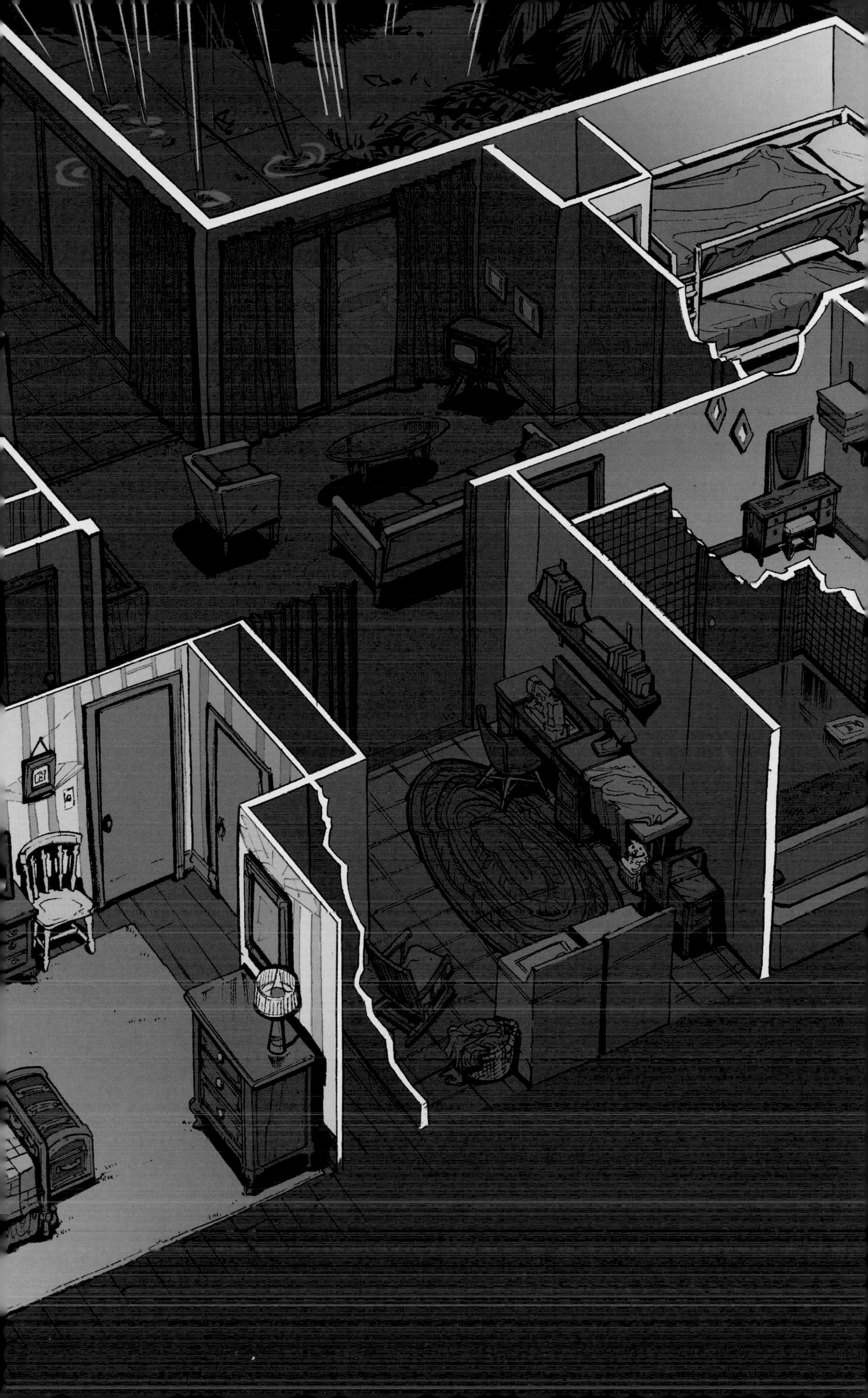

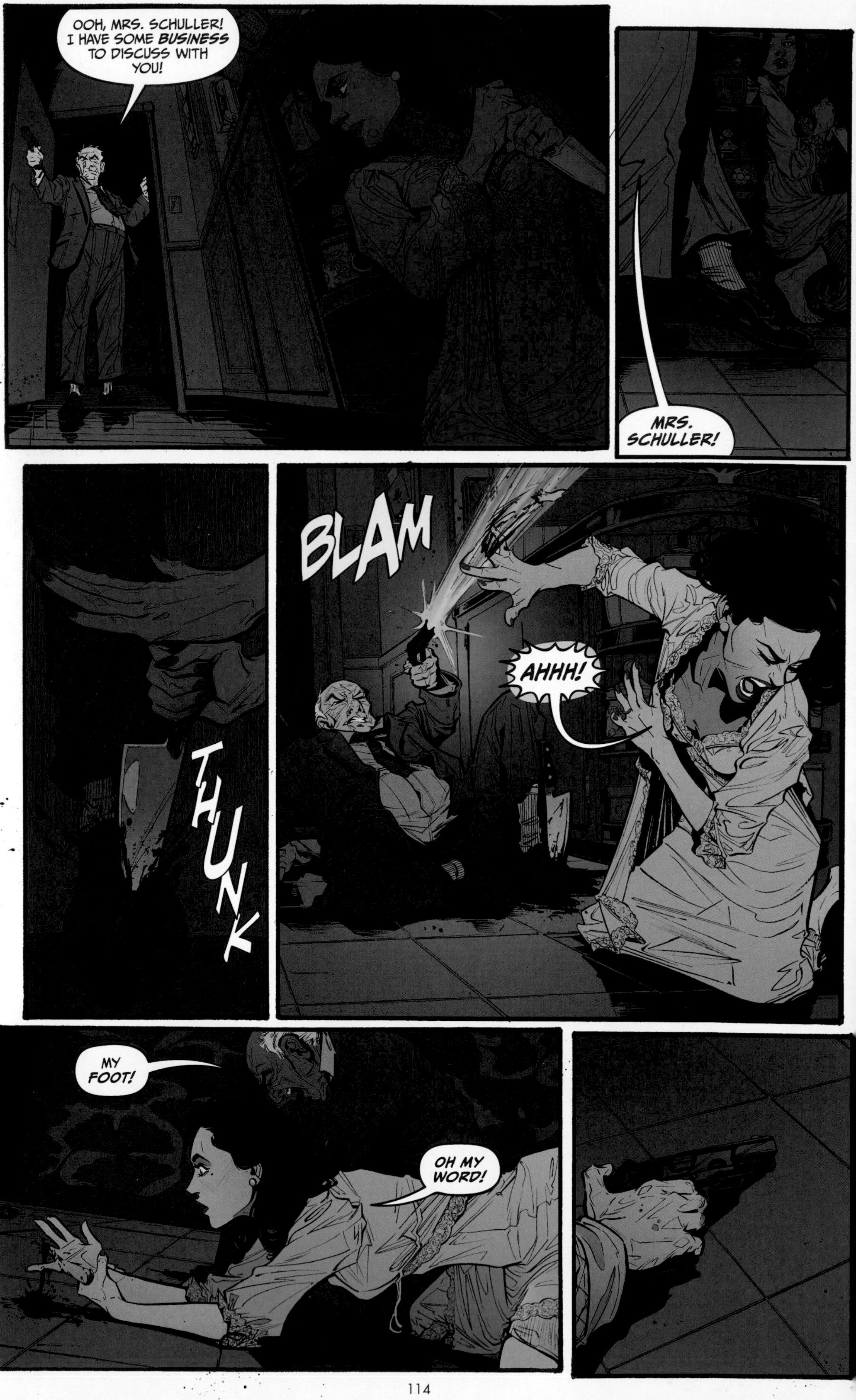
OOH, MRS. SCHULLER! I HAVE SOME BUSINESS TO DISCUSS WITH YOU!
MRS. SCHULLER!
THUNK
BLAM
AHHH!
MY FOOT!
OH MY WORD!

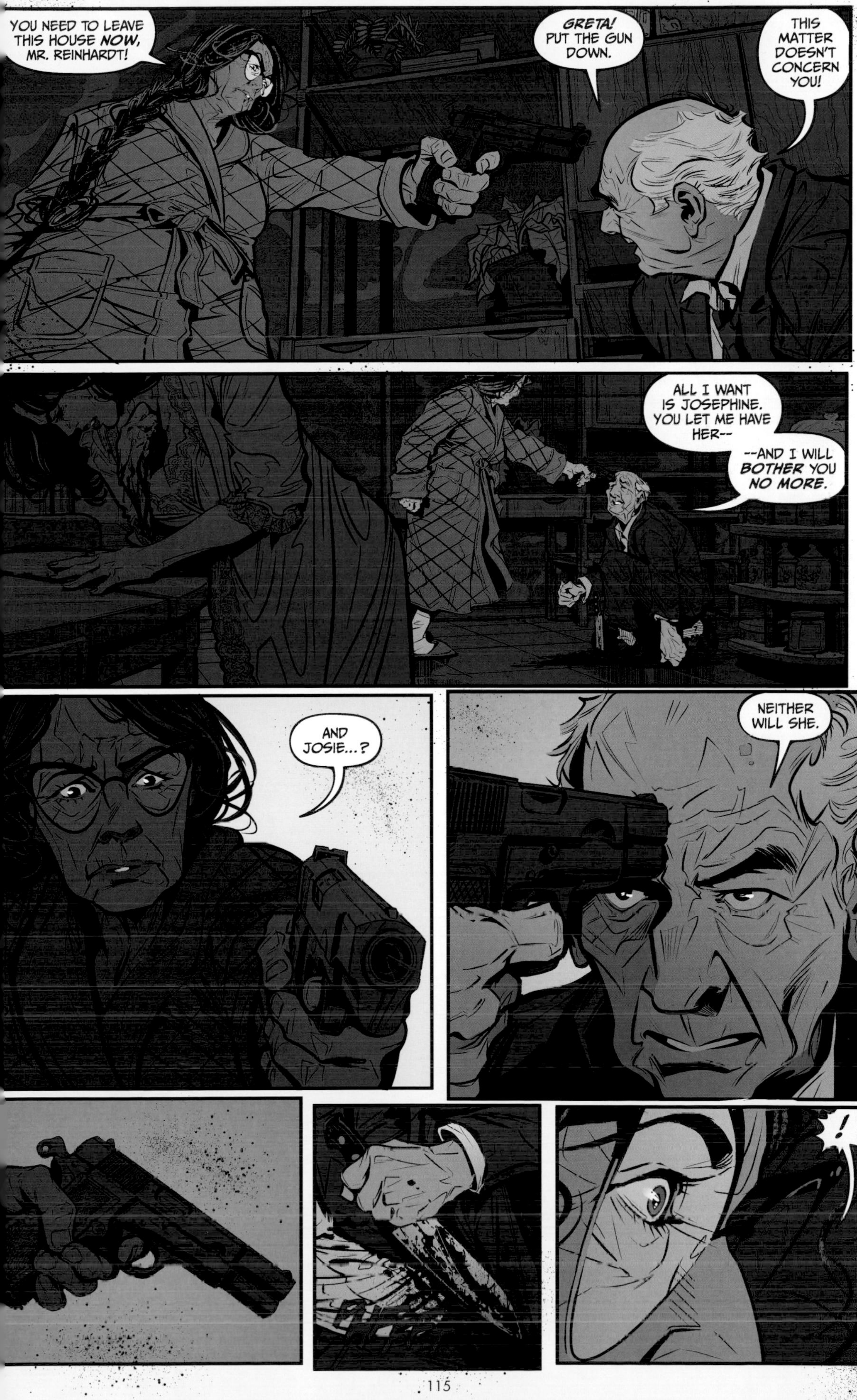
YOU NEED TO LEAVE THIS HOUSE NOW, MR. REINHARDT!
GRETA! PUT THE GUN DOWN.
THIS MATTER DOESN'T CONCERN YOU!
ALL I WANT IS JOSEPHINE. YOU LET ME HAVE HER--
--AND I WILL BOTHER YOU NO MORE.
AND JOSIE...?
NEITHER WILL SHE.
!

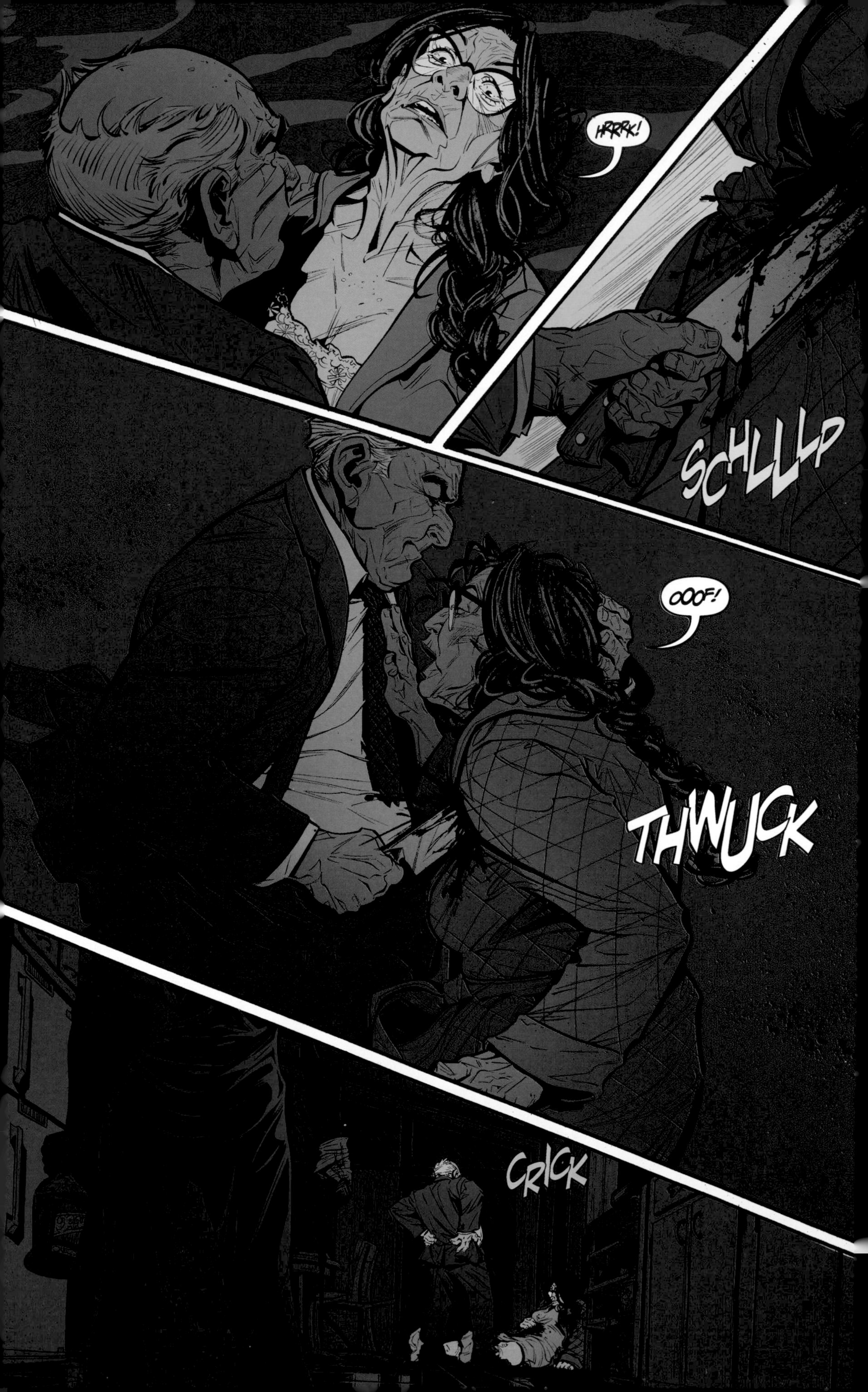
HRRRK!
SCHLLLP
OOOF!
THWUCK
CRICK

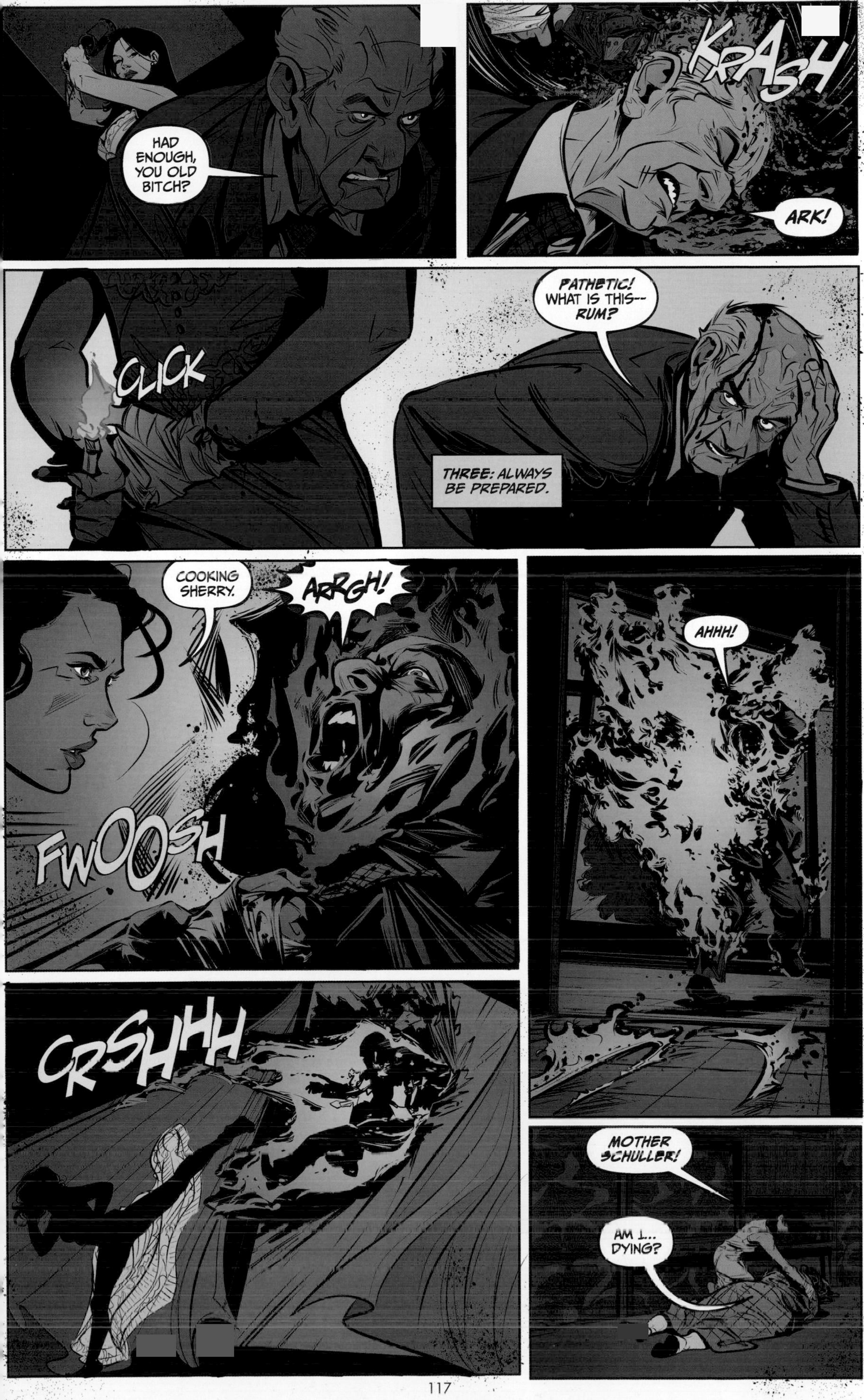
HAD ENOUGH, YOU OLD BITCH?
KRASH
ARK!
CLICK
PATHETIC! WHAT IS THIS-- RUM?
THREE: ALWAYS BE PREPARED.
COOKING SHERRY.
ARRGH!
FWOOSH
AHHH!
CRSHHH
MOTHER SCHULLER!
AM I... DYING?

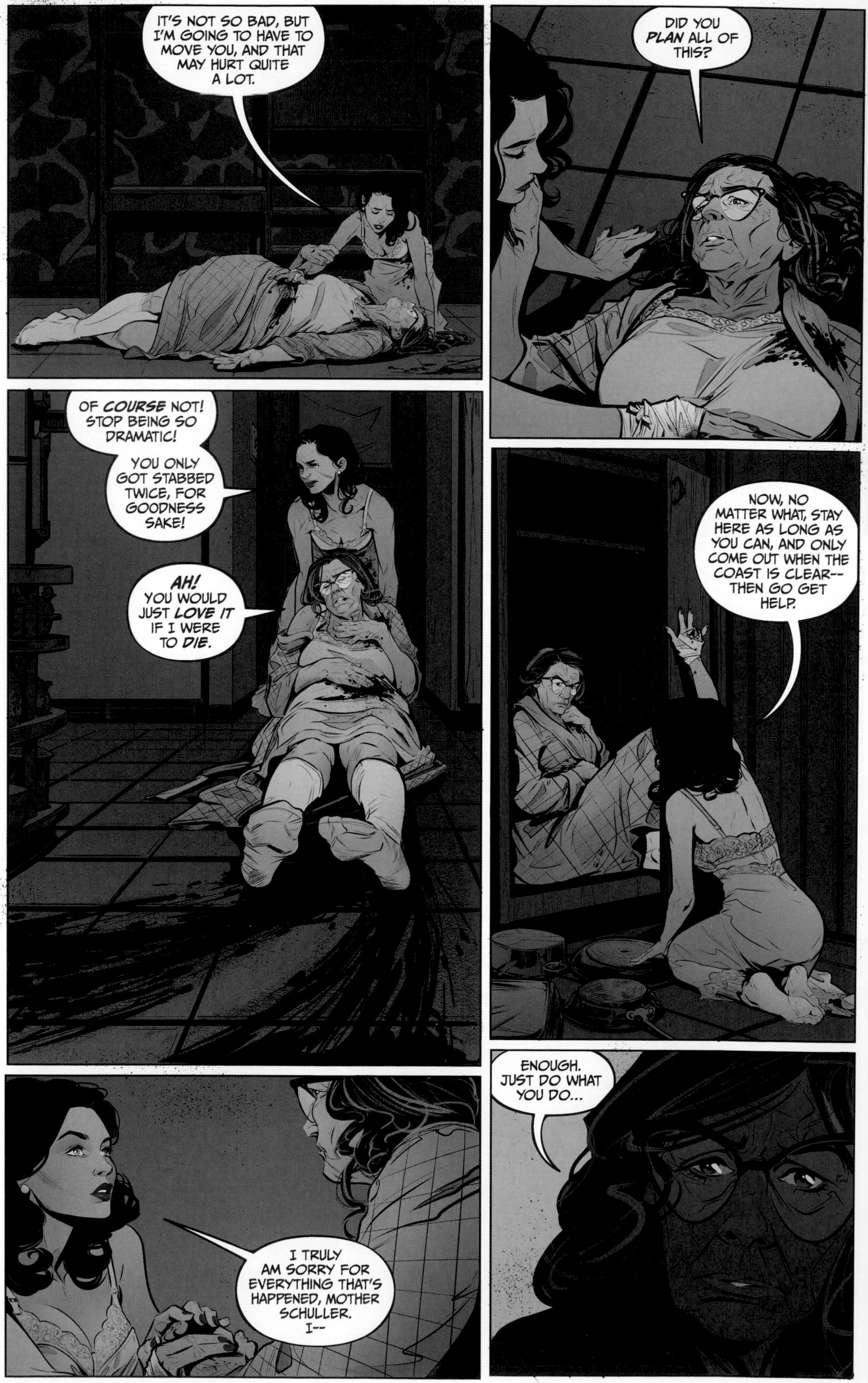
IT'S NOT SO BAD, BUT I'M GOING TO HAVE TO MOVE YOU, AND THAT MAY HURT QUITE A LOT.
DID YOU PLAN ALL OF THIS?
OF COURSE NOT! STOP BEING SO DRAMATIC!
YOU ONLY GOT STABBED TWICE, FOR GOODNESS SAKE!
AH! YOU WOULD JUST LOVE IT IF I WERE TO DIE.
NOW, NO MATTER WHAT, STAY HERE AS LONG AS YOU CAN, AND ONLY COME OUT WHEN THE COAST IS CLEAR-- THEN GO GET HELP.
I TRULY AM SORRY FOR EVERYTHING THAT'S HAPPENED, MOTHER SCHULLER. I--
ENOUGH. JUST DO WHAT YOU DO...

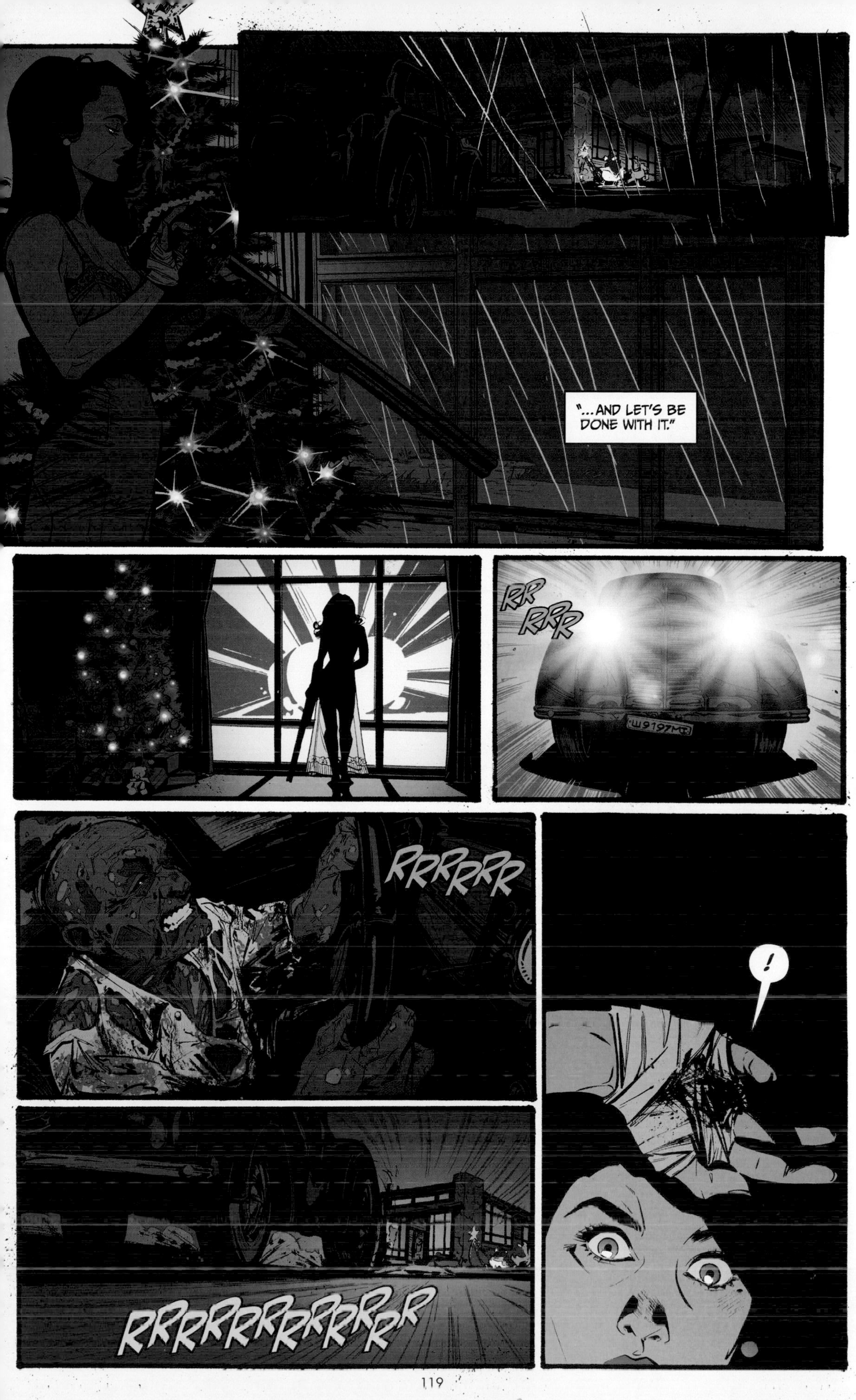
"...AND LET'S BE DONE WITH IT."
RR RRR
RRRRRR
!
RRRRRRRRRRRRRR

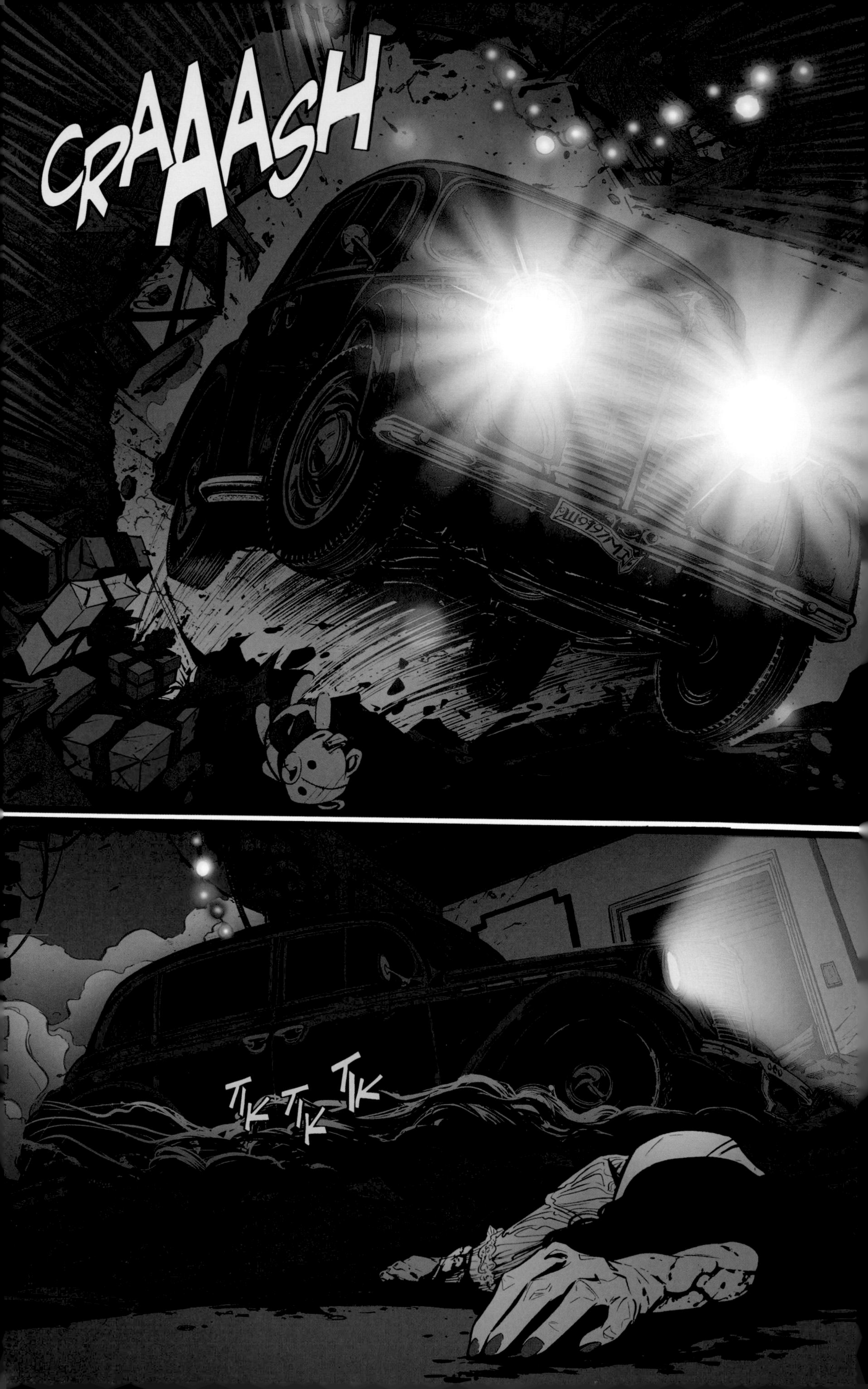
CRAAASH
TIK TIK TIK

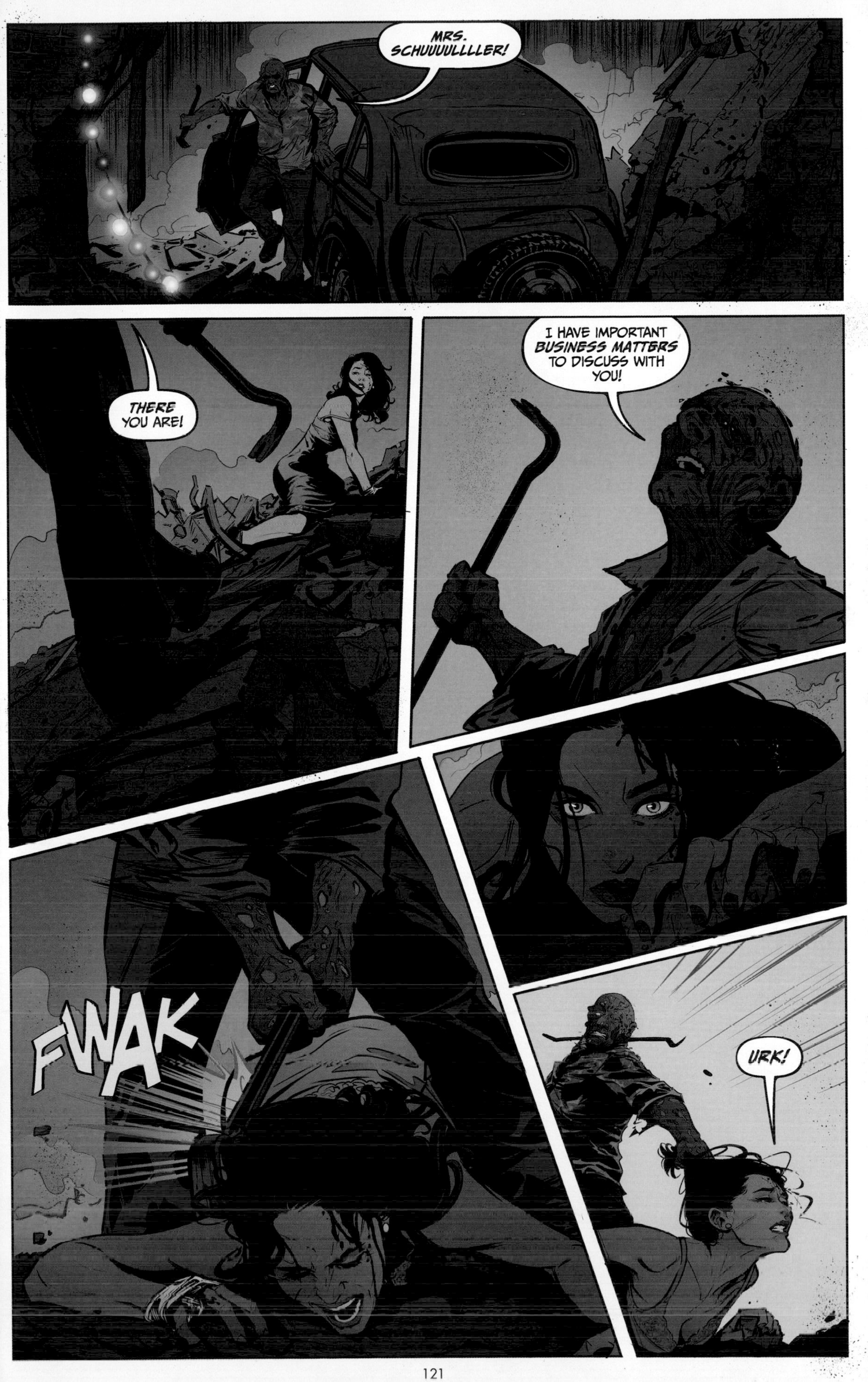
MRS. SCHUUUULLLLER!
THERE YOU ARE!
I HAVE IMPORTANT BUSINESS MATTERS TO DISCUSS WITH YOU!
FWAK
URK!

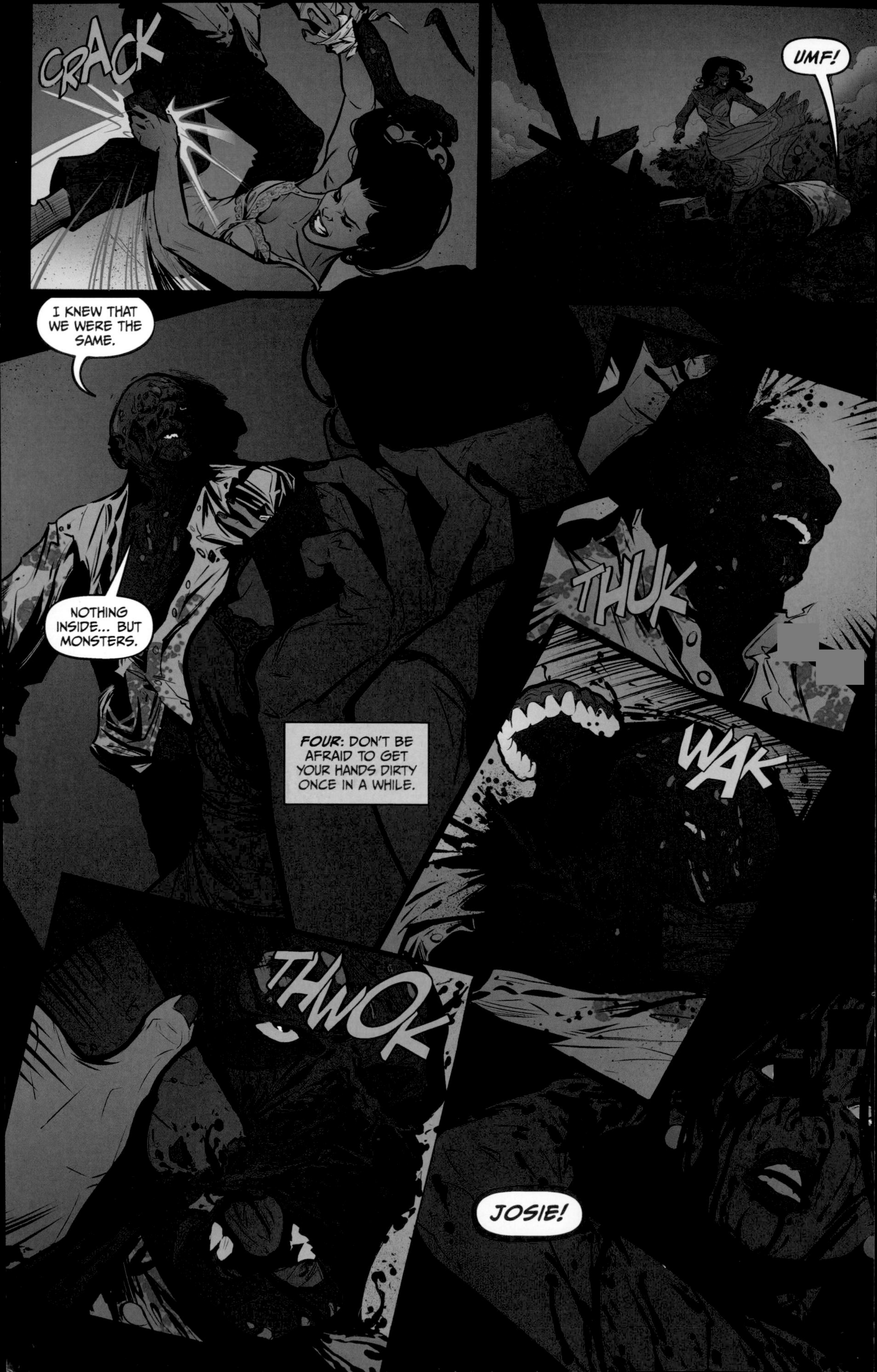
CRACK
UMF!
I KNEW THAT WE WERE THE SAME.
NOTHING INSIDE... BUT MONSTERS.
FOUR: DON'T BE AFRAID TO GET YOUR HANDS DIRTY ONCE IN A WHILE.
THUK
WAK
THWOK
JOSIE!

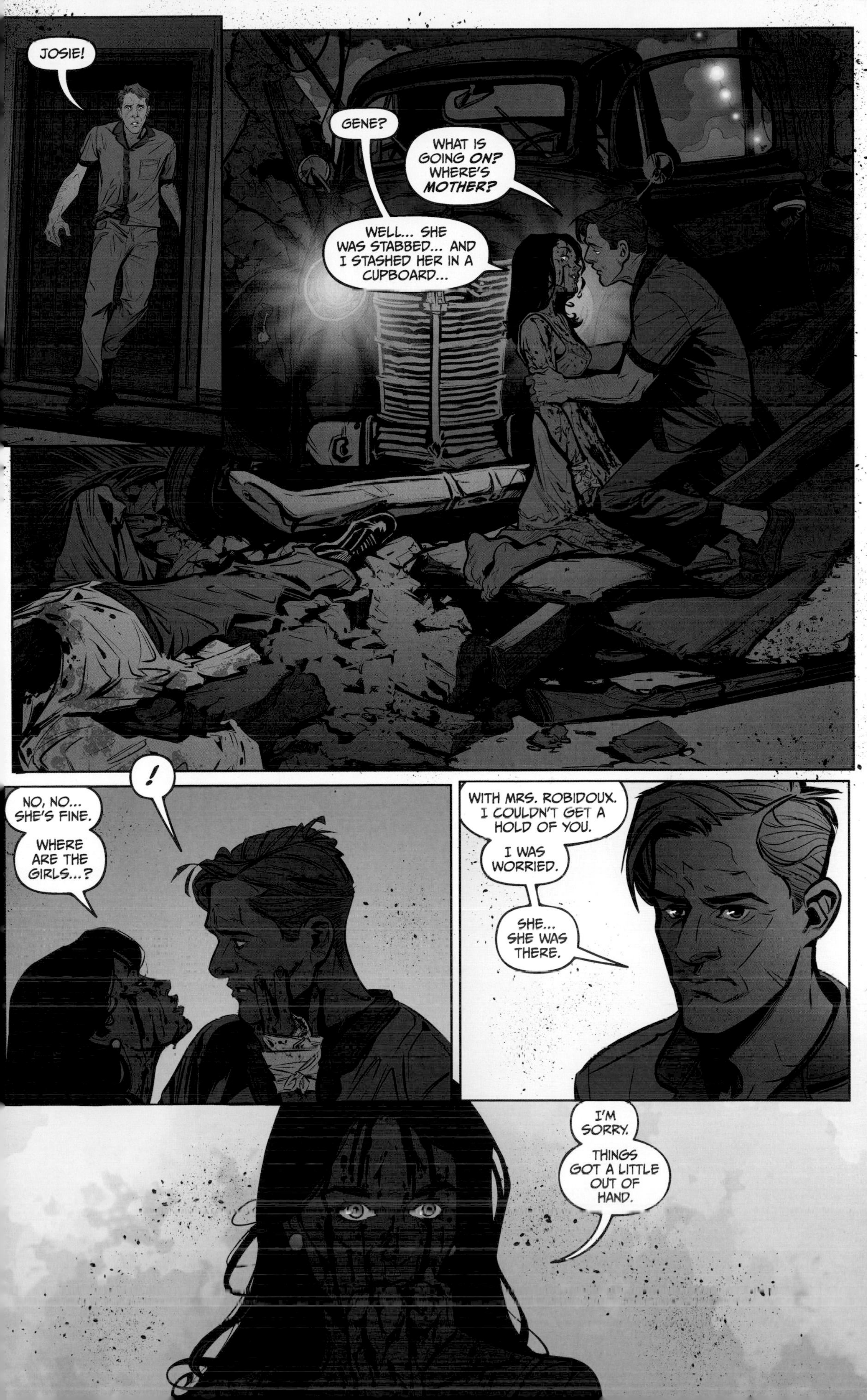
JOSIE!
GENE?
WHAT IS GOING ON? WHERE'S MOTHER?
WELL... SHE WAS STABBED... AND I STASHED HER IN A CUPBOARD...
!
NO, NO... SHE'S FINE.
WHERE ARE THE GIRLS...?
WITH MRS. ROBIDOUX. I COULDN'T GET A HOLD OF YOU.
I WAS WORRIED.
SHE... SHE WAS THERE.
I'M SORRY.
THINGS GOT A LITTLE OUT OF HAND.

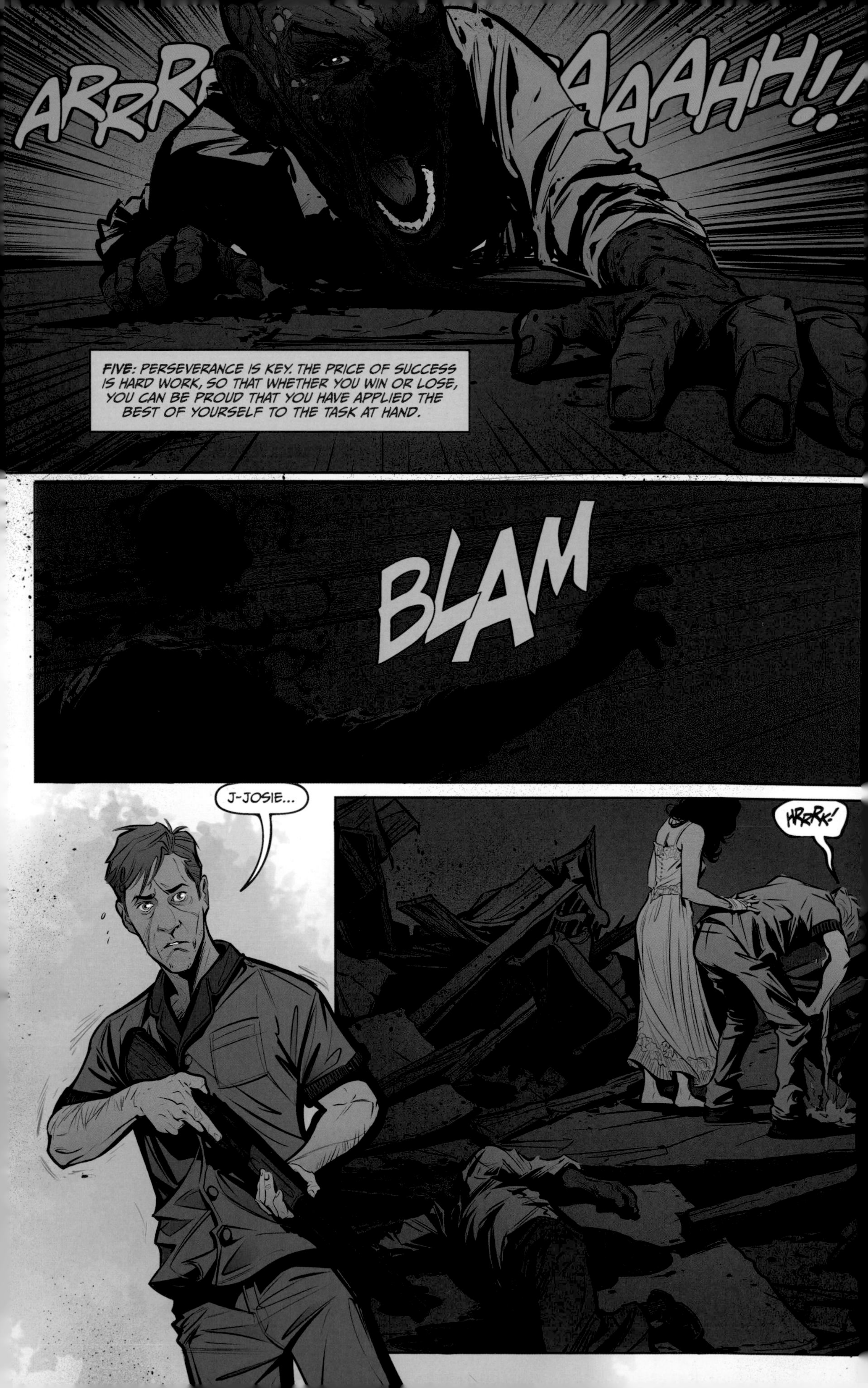
ARRRRAAAAHH!!
FIVE: PERSEVERANCE IS KEY. THE PRICE OF SUCCESS IS HARD WORK, SO THAT WHETHER YOU WIN OR LOSE, YOU CAN BE PROUD THAT YOU HAVE APPLIED THE BEST OF YOURSELF TO THE TASK AT HAND.
BLAM
J-JOSIE...
HRRRK!

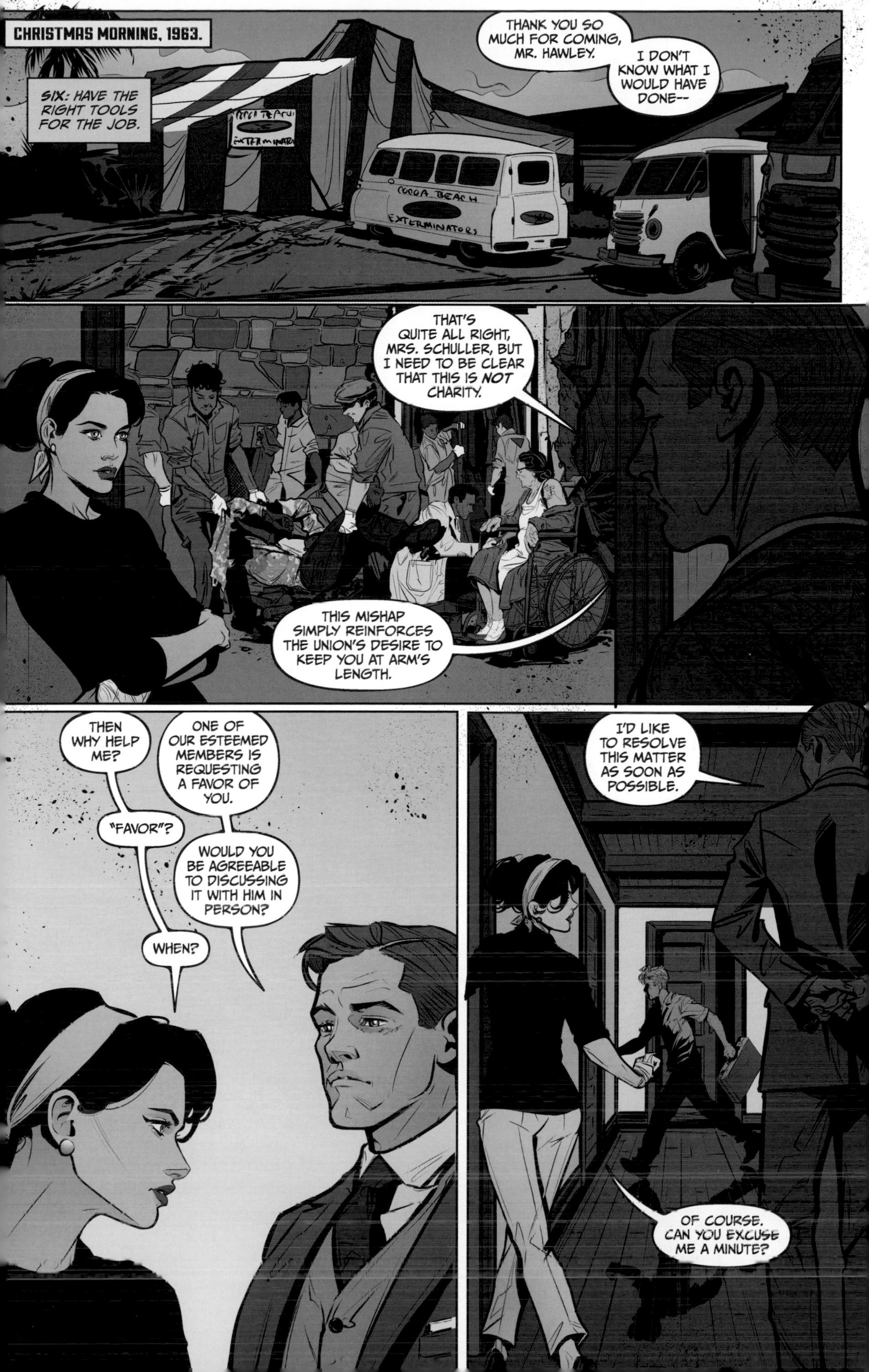

CHRISTMAS MORNING, 1963.
SIX: HAVE THE RIGHT TOOLS FOR THE JOB.
THANK YOU SO MUCH FOR COMING, MR. HAWLEY.
I DON'T KNOW WHAT I WOULD HAVE DONE--
EXTERMINATORS
THAT'S QUITE ALL RIGHT, MRS. SCHULLER, BUT I NEED TO BE CLEAR THAT THIS IS NOT CHARITY.
THIS MISHAP SIMPLY REINFORCES THE UNION'S DESIRE TO KEEP YOU AT ARM'S LENGTH.
THEN WHY HELP ME?
ONE OF OUR ESTEEMED MEMBERS IS REQUESTING A FAVOR OF YOU.
"FAVOR"?
WOULD YOU BE AGREEABLE TO DISCUSSING IT WITH HIM IN PERSON?
WHEN?
I'D LIKE TO RESOLVE THIS MATTER AS SOON AS POSSIBLE.
OF COURSE. CAN YOU EXCUSE ME A MINUTE?

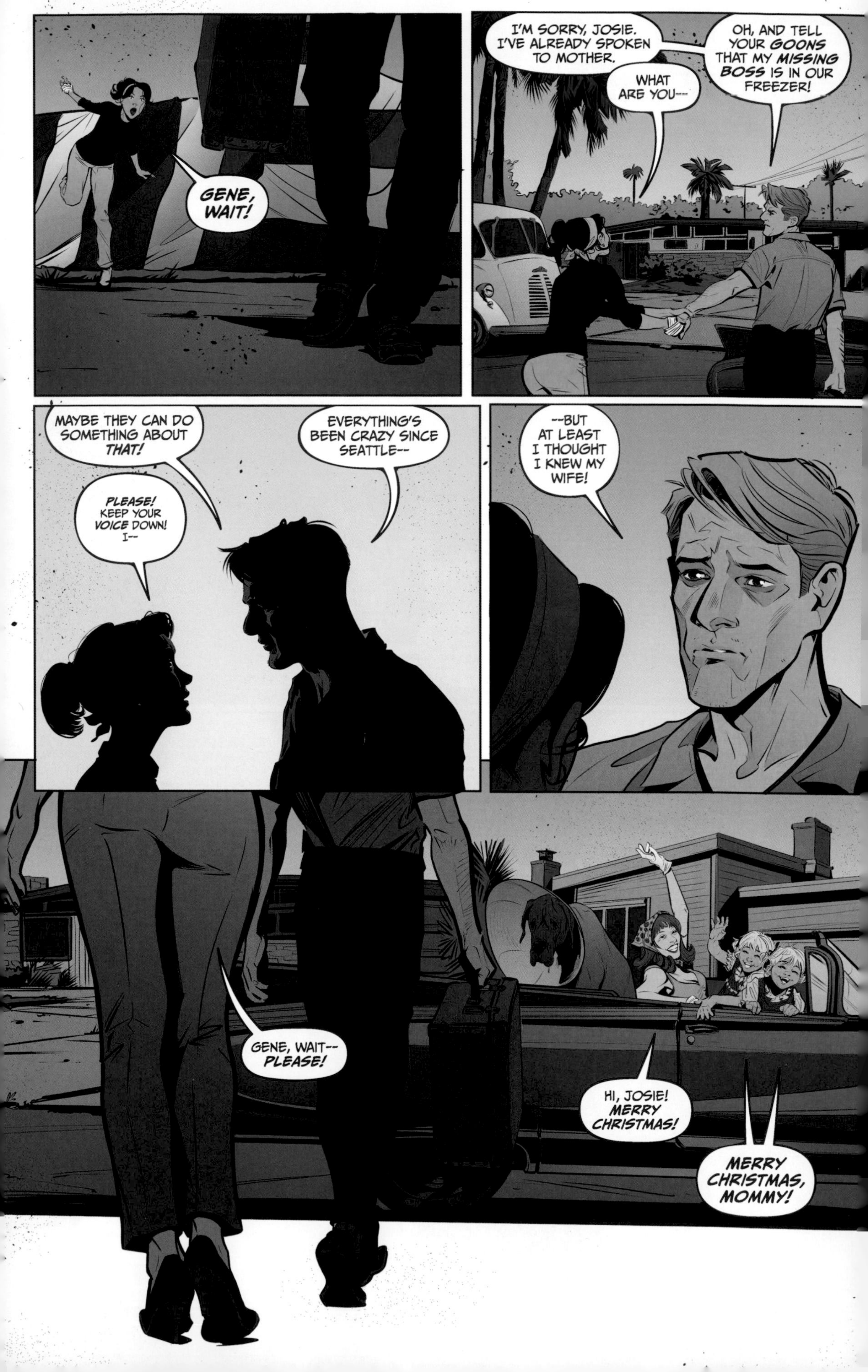
GENE, WAIT!
I'M SORRY, JOSIE. I'VE ALREADY SPOKEN TO MOTHER.
WHAT ARE YOU--
OH, AND TELL YOUR GOONS THAT MY MISSING BOSS IS IN OUR FREEZER!
MAYBE THEY CAN DO SOMETHING ABOUT THAT!
PLEASE! KEEP YOUR VOICE DOWN! I--
EVERYTHING'S BEEN CRAZY SINCE SEATTLE--
--BUT AT LEAST I THOUGHT I KNEW MY WIFE!
GENE, WAIT-- PLEASE!
HI, JOSIE! MERRY CHRISTMAS!
MERRY CHRISTMAS, MOMMY!

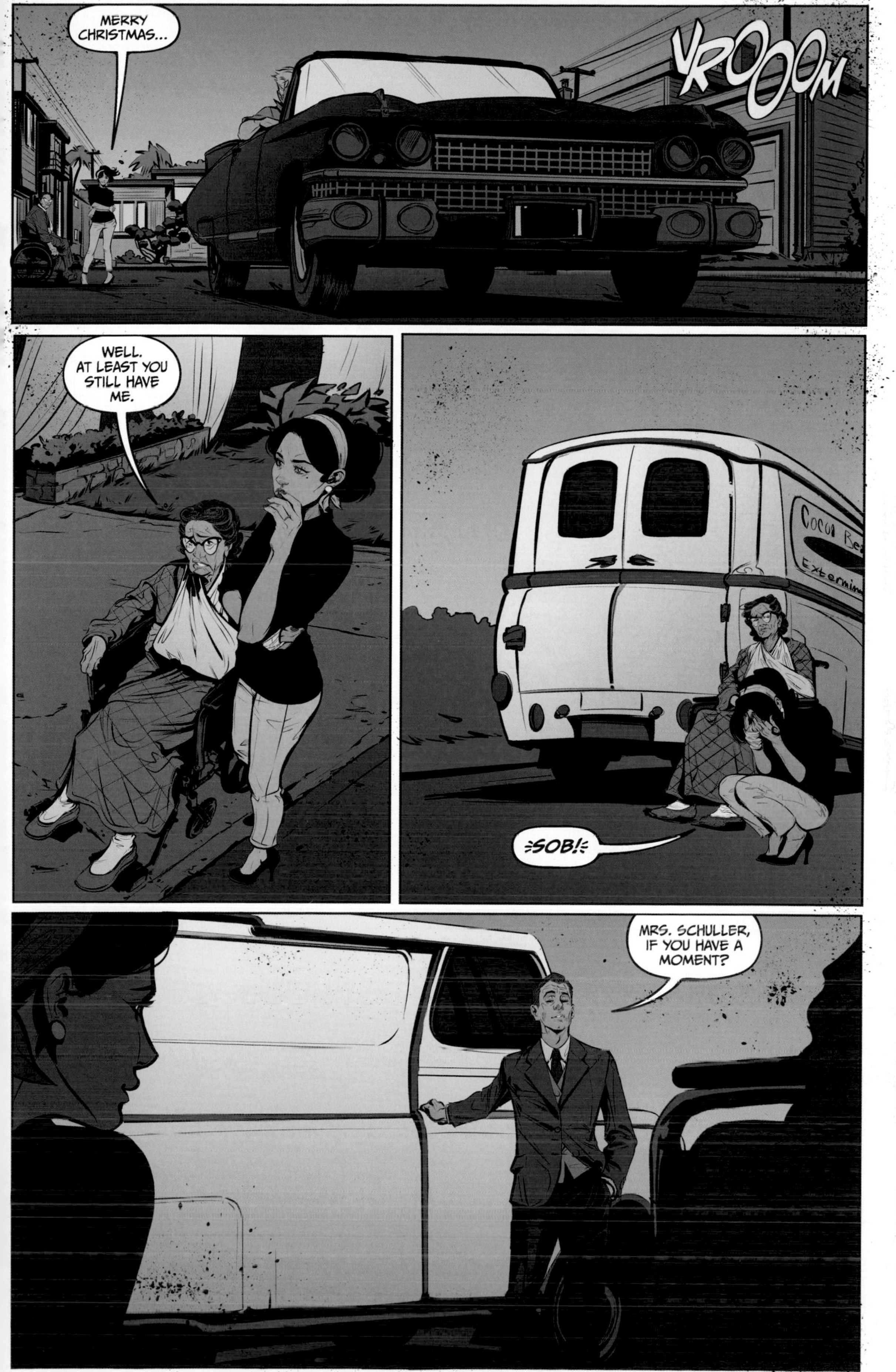
MERRY CHRISTMAS...
VROOOM
WELL. AT LEAST YOU STILL HAVE ME.
SOB!
MRS. SCHULLER, IF YOU HAVE A MOMENT?

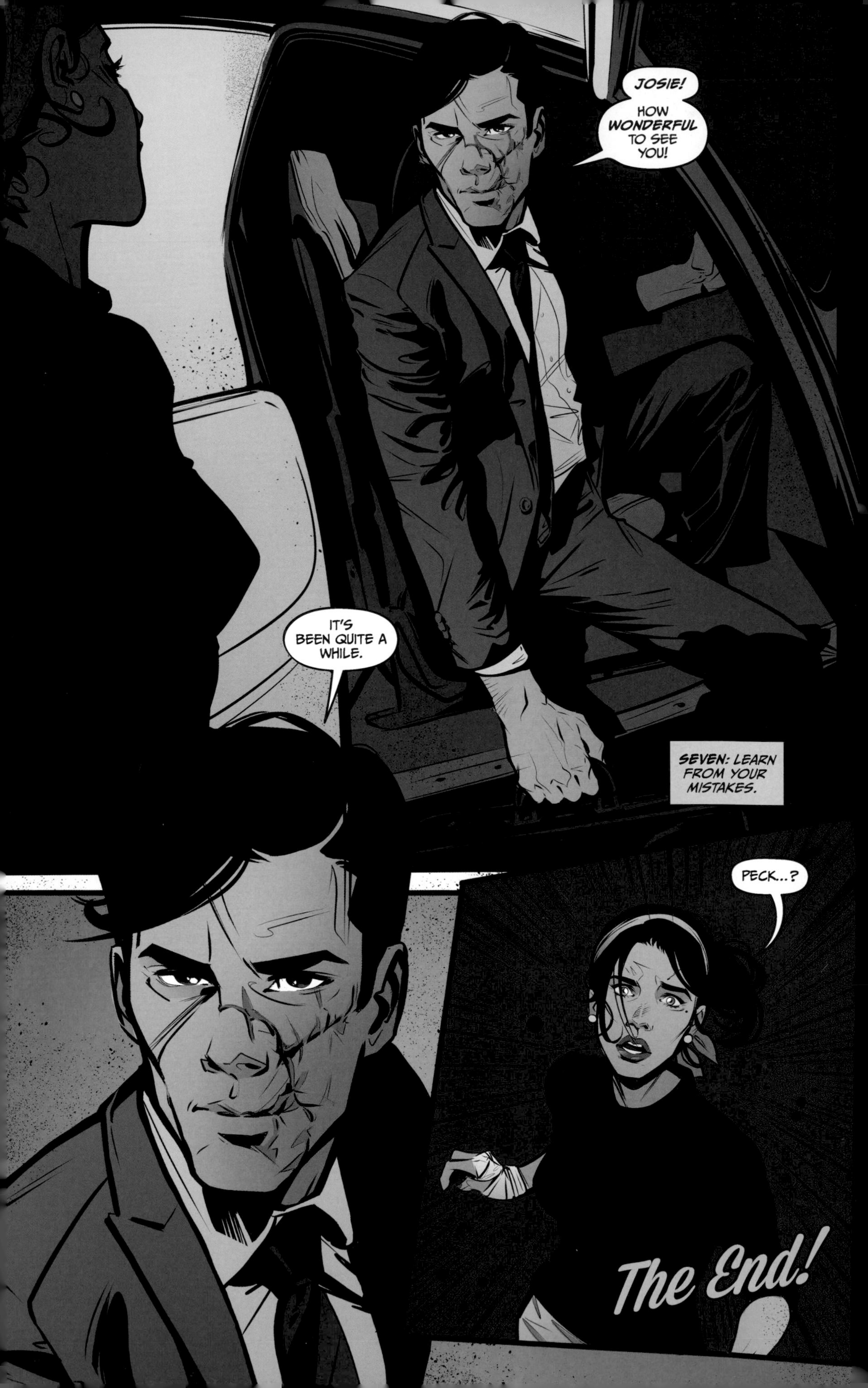
JOSIE! HOW WONDERFUL TO SEE YOU!
IT'S BEEN QUITE A WHILE.
SEVEN: LEARN FROM YOUR MISTAKES.
PECK...?
The End!

Lady Killer™
SKETCHBOOK

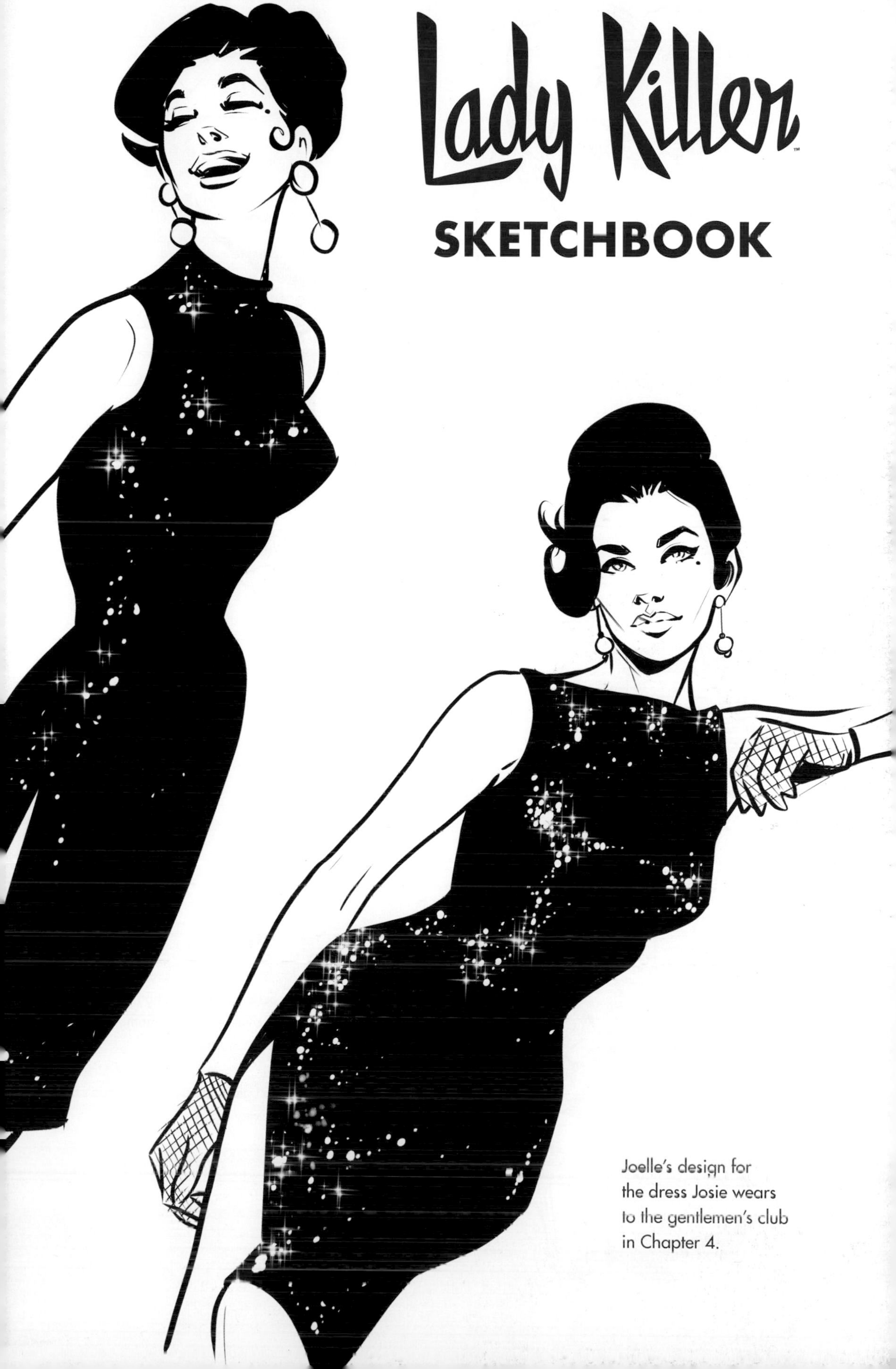

Joelle's design for
the dress Josie wears
to the gentlemen's club
in Chapter 4.

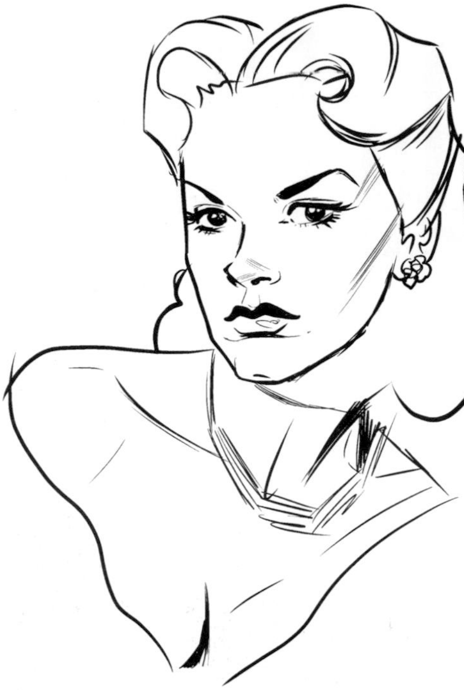

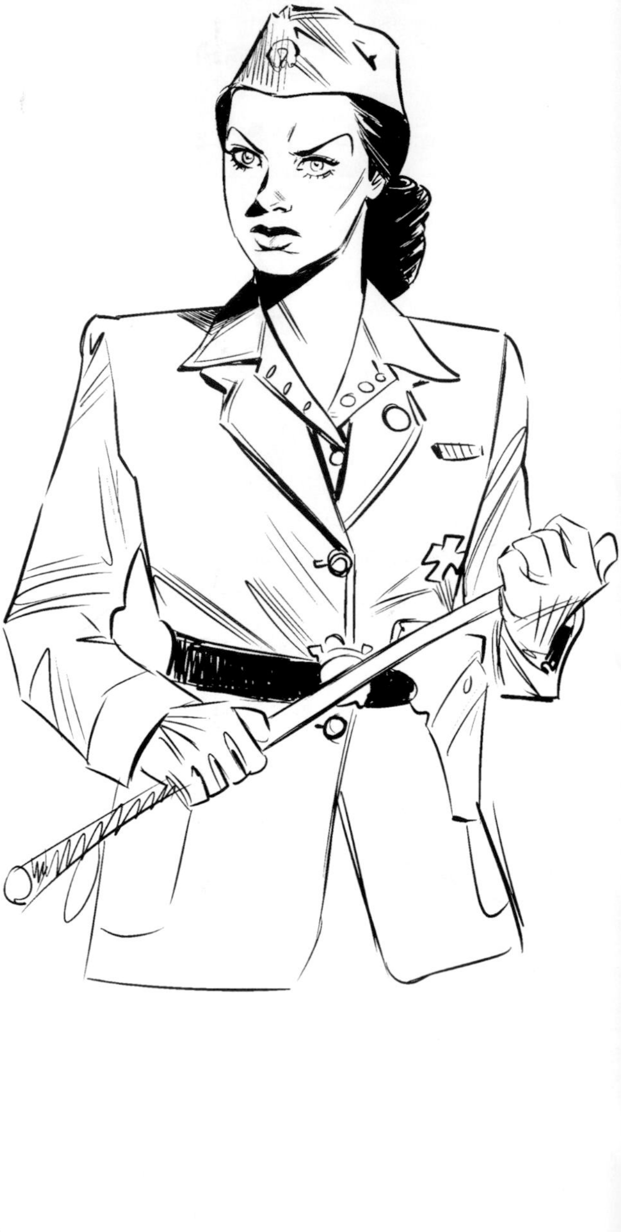

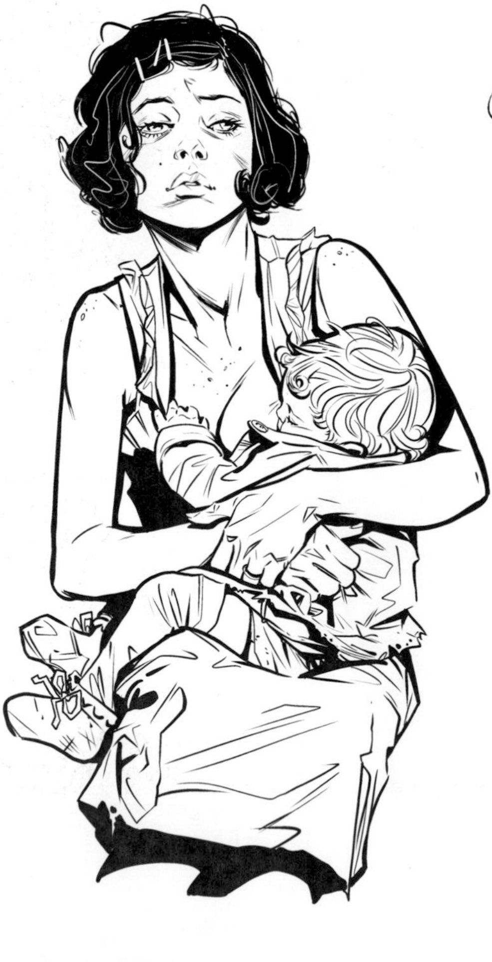

TWO MOMS: Joelle developed a great character in the young Mother Schuller for her lengthy flashback in Chapter 3. Josie's own less exotic mother was a last-minute addition to Chapter 5.

FACING: The stained glass window from Josie's first meeting with Mr. Hawley in Chapter 2.

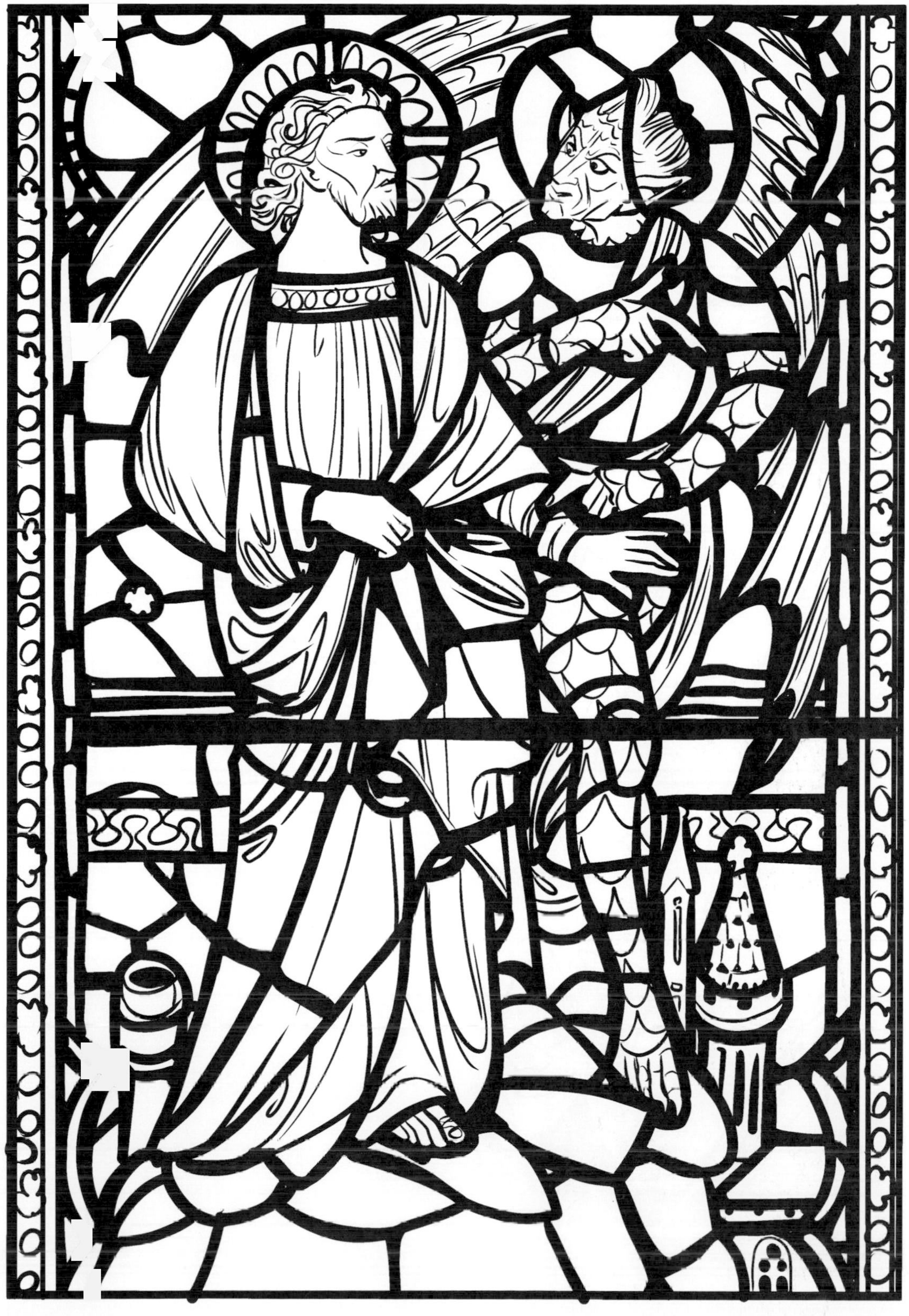

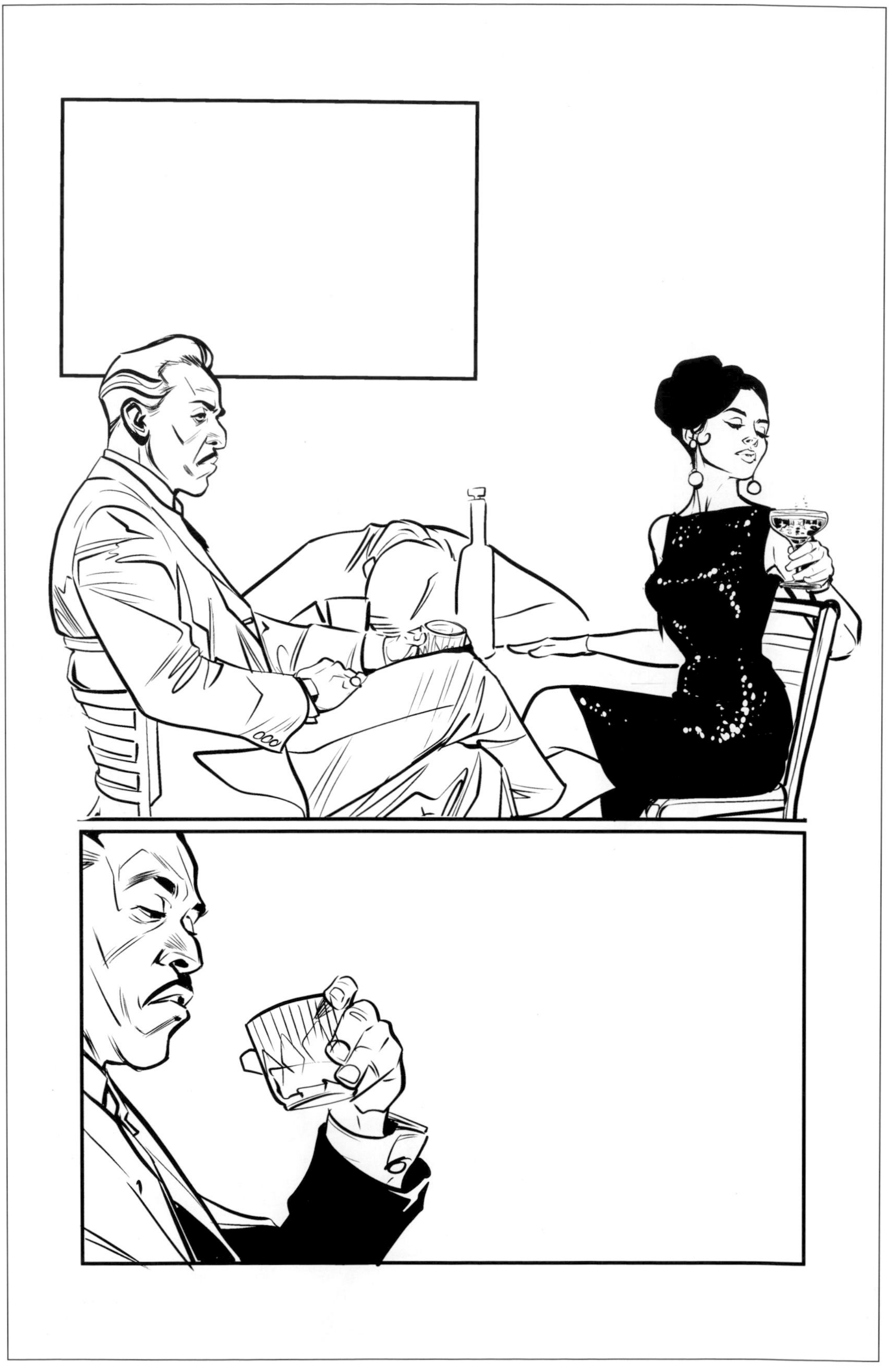

A scene of Josie meeting with a client in Chapter 4, cut for space.

FACING: Colors by Michelle Madsen.

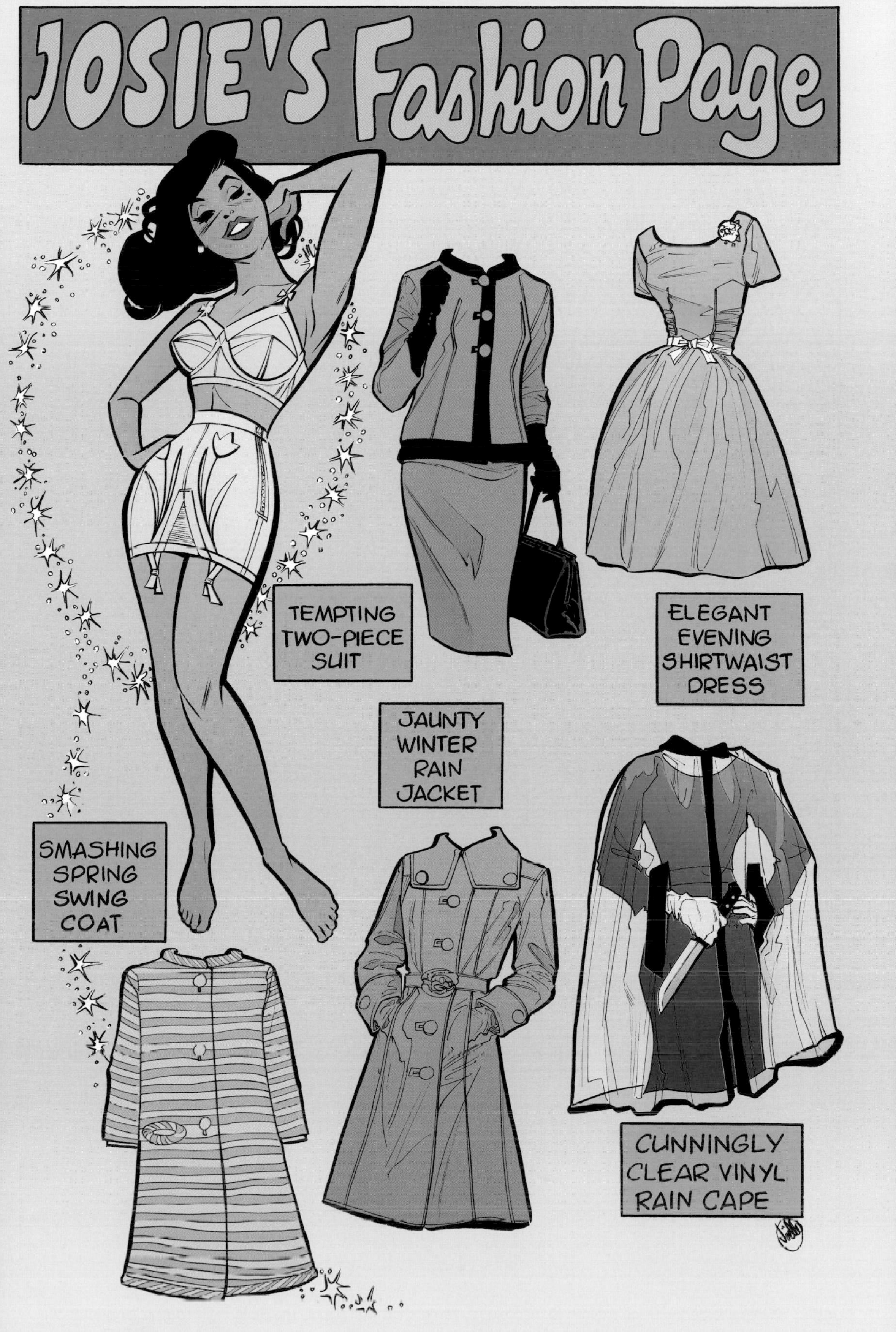
JOSIE'S Fashion Page
TEMPTING TWO-PIECE SUIT
ELEGANT EVENING SHIRTWAIST DRESS
JAUNTY WINTER RAIN JACKET
SMASHING SPRING SWING COAT
CUNNINGLY CLEAR VINYL RAIN CAPE

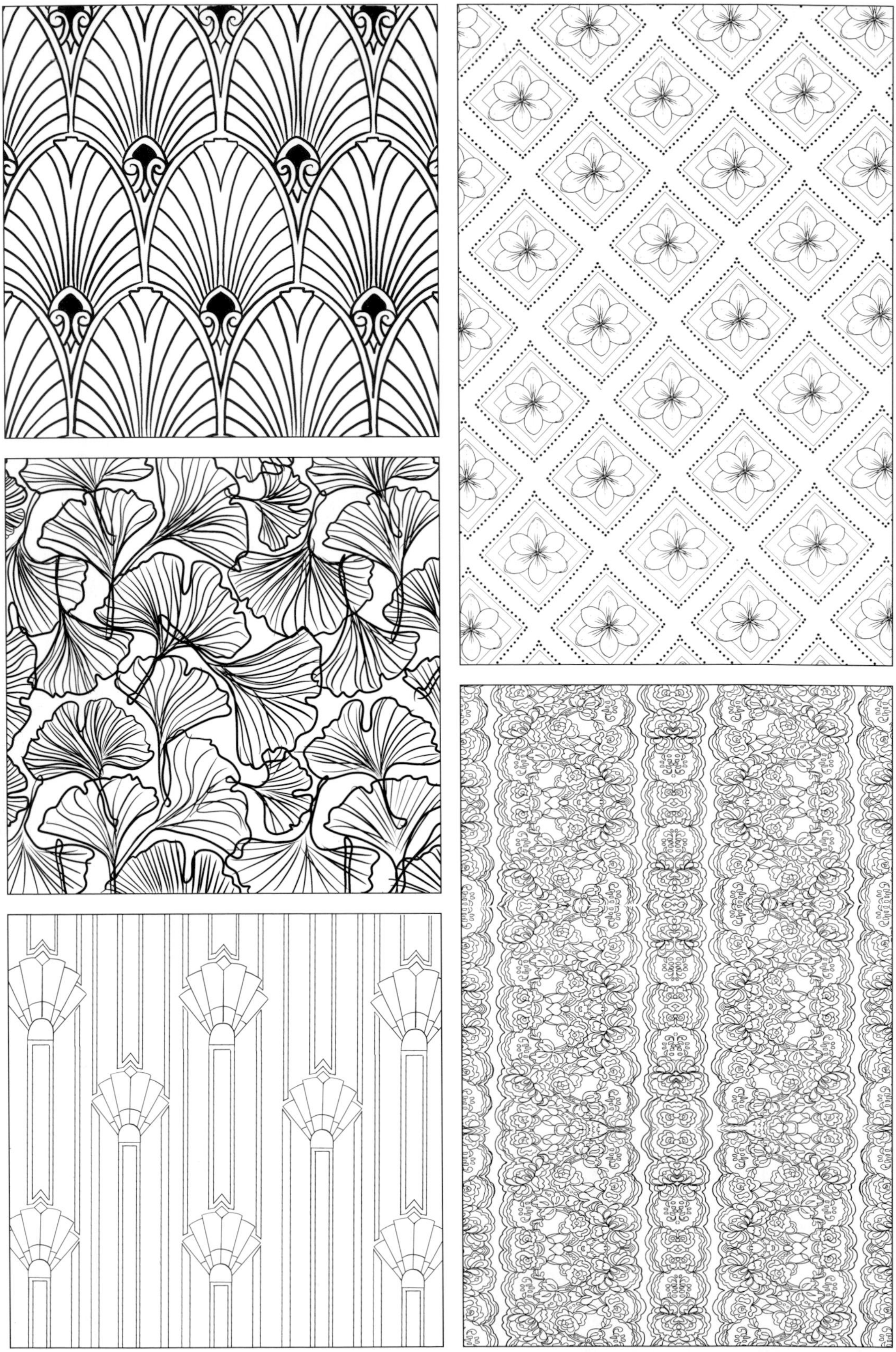

Joelle's attention to period detail extends to meticulously researched wall paper. The patterns in *Lady Killer* are usually hand drawn on the original art, although sometimes she'll create pieces by hand that can be dropped in digitally.

MORE BY JOËLLE JONES

LADY KILLER VOLUME 1
Written by Joëlle Jones and Jamie S. Rich
Art by Joëlle Jones
ISBN 978-1-61655-757-7 | $17.99

LADY KILLER VOLUME 2
Written by Joëlle Jones
Art by Joëlle Jones
ISBN 978-1-50670-029-8 | $17.99

HOUSE OF NIGHT
Written by P. C. Cast, Kristin Cast, and Kent Dalian
Art by Joëlle Jones, Jonathan Case, and others
ISBN 978-1-59582-962-7 | $14.99

TROUBLEMAKER
Written by Janet Evanovich and Alex Evanovich
Art by Joëlle Jones
VOLUME 1
ISBN 978-1-59582-488-2 | $17.99
VOLUME 2
ISBN 978-1-59582-573-5 | $17.99

DR. HORRIBLE AND OTHER HORRIBLE STORIES
Written by Zack Whedon
Art by Joëlle Jones, Eric Canete, Farel Dalrymple, Scott Hepburn, and Jim Rugg
ISBN 978-1-59582-577-3 | $9.99

BAIT: OFF-COLOR STORIES FOR YOU TO COLOR
Written by Chuck Palahniuk
Art by Joëlle Jones, Duncan Fegredo, Steve Morris, Tony Puryear, and others
ISBN 978-1-50670-311-4 | $19.99

"I can't wait to see more of Jones's art." —Comic Bastards

AVAILABLE AT YOUR LOCAL COMICS SHOP OR BOOKSTORE

Lady Killer
JOËLLE JONES & JAMIE S. RICH

HOUSE of NIGHT

#1 NEW YORK TIMES BEST-SELLING AUTHOR
JANET EVANOVICH
ALEX EVANOVICH
ART BY JOËLLE JONES
TROUBLE MAKER
BOOK ONE A BARNABY AND HOOKER GRAPHIC NOVEL

DR. HORRIBLE
E.L.E.
AND OTHER HORRIBLE STORIES BY ZACK WHEDON

TO FIND A COMICS SHOP IN YOUR AREA, CALL 1-888-266-4226

DARKHORSE.COM
FOR MORE INFORMATION OR TO ORDER DIRECT:
ON THE WEB: DarkHorse.com E-MAIL: mailorder@darkhorse.com PHONE: 1-800-862-0052 Mon.-Fri. 9 AM to 5 PM Pacific Time.

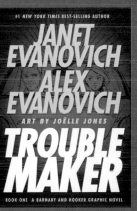

RECOMMENDED READING